International Science and Technology Education

Education in science, technology, engineering and mathematics (STEM) is crucial for taking advantage of the prospects of new scientific discoveries initiating or promoting technological changes, and managing opportunities and risks associated with innovations. This book explores the emerging perspectives and methodologies of STEM education and its relationship to the cultural understanding of science and technology in an international context.

The authors provide a unique perspective on the subject, presenting materials and experiences from non-European industrialized as well as industrializing countries, including China, Japan, South Korea, India, Egypt, Brazil and the USA. The chapters offer a wide scope of interpretations and comparative reviews of STEM education by including narrative elements about cultural developments, considering the influence of culture and social perceptions on technological and social change, and applying innovative tools of qualitative social research.

The book represents a comprehensive and multidisciplinary review of the current status and future challenges facing STEM education across the world, including issues such as globalization, interdependencies of norms and values, effects on equity and social justice as well as resilience. Overall the volume provides valuable insights for a broad and comprehensive international comparison of STEM philosophies, approaches and experiences.

Ortwin Renn is Professor and Chair of Environmental Sociology and Technology Assessment at Stuttgart University, Germany, member of the Berlin-Brandenburg Academy of Sciences and Humanities, and was Spokesperson of the Interdisciplinary Research Group TECHcultures until December 2014.

Nicole C. Karafyllis is Professor of Philosophy of Science and Technology at the Technische Universität Braunschweig, Germany, and was Deputy Spokesperson of the Interdisciplinary Research Group TECHcultures at the Berlin-Brandenburg Academy of Sciences and Humanities until December 2014.

Andreas Hohlt was Coordinator of the Interdisciplinary Research Group TECHcultures at the Berlin-Brandenburg Academy of Sciences and Humanities, Germany until December 2014.

Dorothea Taube was research associate to the Interdisciplinary Research Group TECHcultures at the Berlin-Brandenburg Academy of Sciences and Humanities, Germany until December 2014.

Science in Society Series
Series Editor: Steve Rayner
Institute for Science, Innovation and Society, University of Oxford

Editorial Board: Jason Blackstock, Bjorn Ola Linner, Susan Owens, Timothy O'Riordan, Arthur Peterson, Nick Pidgeon, Dan Sarewitz, Andy Sterling, Chris Tyler, Andrew Webster, Steve Yearley

The Earthscan Science in Society Series aims to publish new high-quality research, teaching, practical and policy-related books on topics that address the complex and vitally important interface between science and society.

International Science and Technology Education

Exploring culture, economy and social perceptions

Edited by Ortwin Renn, Nicole C. Karafyllis, Andreas Hohlt and Dorothea Taube

berlin-brandenburgische
AKADEMIE DER WISSENSCHAFTEN

earthscan
from Routledge

Routledge
Taylor & Francis Group

LONDON AND NEW YORK

First published 2015
by Routledge
2 Park Square, Milton Park, Abingdon, Oxon OX14 4RN

and by Routledge
711 Third Avenue, New York, NY 10017

First issued in paperback 2017

Routledge is an imprint of the Taylor & Francis Group, an informa business

This publication is the result of the deliberations of the
Interdisciplinary Research Group "TECHcultures" (Intercultural
Comparison of the Understanding of Science and Technology
in Selected Countries) at the Berlin-Brandenburg Academy of
Sciences and Humanities (Forschungsberichte der interdisziplinären
Arbeitsgruppen, vol. 33).

This publication has been funded by the Senatsverwaltung für
Wirtschaft, Technologie und Forschung des Landes Berlin, Germany,
and the Ministerium für Wissenschaft, Forschung und Kultur des
Landes Brandenburg.

British Library Cataloguing-in-Publication Data
A catalogue record for this book is available from the British Library

Library of Congress Cataloging in Publication Data
International science and technology education : exploring culture,
economy and social perceptions / edited by Ortwin Renn, Nicole C.
Karafyllis, Andreas Hohlt and Dorothea Taube.
pages cm. — (Science in society series)
Includes bibliographical references and index.
1. Science—Study and teaching—Cross-cultural studies.
2. Technology—Study and teaching—Cross-cultural studies.
3. Engineering—Study and teaching—Cross-cultural studies.
4. Mathematics—Study and teaching—Cross-cultural studies. I. Renn,
Ortwin, editor of compilation.
Q181.I65575 2015
507.1—dc23
2014048372

ISBN 13: 978-1-138-50681-7 (pbk)
ISBN 13: 978-1-138-88737-4 (hbk)

Typeset in Goudy
by Swales & Willis Ltd, Exeter, Devon, UK

Contents

Illustrations

Contributors

Mohan V. Avvari is an Associate Professor of Strategic Management at the Nottingham University Business School (NUBS) in the University of Nottingham—Malaysia Campus (UNMC). After receiving his doctorate in Innovation Management from the Indian Institute of Science, he visited South Korea on a Research Fellowship at the Korea Advanced Institute of Science and Technology (KAIST). His teaching and research interests are in the area of strategy and innovation, with special interests in sustainability oriented strategies (Triple bottom/CSR).

Elizabeth Balbachevsky is Associate Professor at the Department of Political Science at the University of São Paulo, Brazil. She collaborates with the University of Campinas' Strategic Thinking Forum, and is an Erasmus Mundus Scholar at the MARIHE—European Master Program in Research and Innovation in Higher Education. Her teaching and research interests include science, technology and environmental politics, technology assessment and public policy.

Ilan Chabay is Professor and Senior Fellow, Institute for Advanced Sustainability Studies (IASS), Potsdam, Germany and Chair of the international alliance on 'Knowledge, Learning, and Societal Change' (www.KLSCproject.org). He is particularly interested in models as analytical sources for decision-making on complex systems and narratives as affective forms of communication and expressions of future visions. At IASS, he co-leads the transdisciplinary research project on Sustainable Modes of Arctic Resource-driven Transformations (SMART).

Nagalakshmi Chelluri is an Assistant Professor of Sociology at University of Hyderabad (UoH). After receiving her doctorate in Sociology of Work and Work Culture in IT Organizations, from University of Hyderabad, she did her post-doctoral in a European Commission project—SET DEV—and worked at the Centre for Innovations in Public Systems (CIPS) in Administrative Staff College of India (ASCI), Hyderabad. Her teaching and research interests are in the areas of sociology of organizations, sociology of work, and science, technology and society studies.

Edilene Cruz is Doctoral Candidate at USP's Doctoral Program on Latin American Integration Studies (PROLAM-USP) and UNICAMP's Political Science. She was coordinator of CAPES-UMFT Program Initiation to Teaching in Social Sciences between 2010-2013 and is currently Assistant Professor at the Department of Sociology and Political Science, Federal University of Mato Grosso, Brazil.

Heinz Duddeck is Emeritus Professor at the Institute of Statics of Structures at the Technische Universität Braunschweig. From 1979 to 1990 he was appointed the chair member of a university study reform commission for civil engineering. Heinz Duddeck is a member of Academia Europaea, UK, AcaTech and BBAW since its refoundation in 1993.

Arthur Eisenkraft is the Distinguished Professor of Science Education, Professor of Physics and Director of the Center of Science and Math in Context (COSMIC) at the University of Massachusetts, Boston. He is past president of the National Science Teachers Association, helped write the National Science Education Standards and the Frameworks for K-12 Science Education of the National Research Council, and has served on other NRC committees. His current research projects include investigating the efficacy of a second-generation model of distance learning for professional development and a study of professional development choices that teachers make when facing a large-scale curriculum change.

Ghada K. Gholam is a senior education specialist and officer in charge at the UNESCO Cairo office. She is responsible for all educational programmes in Egypt, Sudan and Libya and works as regional advisor for science education in the Arab Region. Her contribution mainly aims at improving education reform and the situation of women in the Arab world through promoting girls' education and eradicating illiteracy. She is the author of many publications in education and in particular in science education.

Jung-Ok Ha is a Senior Researcher of the Institute for Gender Research at Seoul National University in South Korea. Her research interests include the global/local and gender politics of technology, women's health and bioethics, and feminist STS. She is currently working on a gender and solidarity project, especially the international biopolitics of assisted reproductive technologies.

Andreas Hohlt is scientific coordinator of the IAG TECHcultures at the Berlin-Brandenburg Academy of Sciences and Humanities, and a political consultant. He is a political and social scientist at Sciences-Po Paris, focusing on risk governance and communication, education policy and participation.

Nicole C. Karafyllis is a Full Professor of Philosophy of Science and Technology. She also has been a full Professor of Philosophy at the United Arab Emirates University in Abu Dhabi. Her research interests include among others epistemology, anthropology and ontology of life sciences and technology, the philosophy of nature, culture and technology, and Arab philosophy. She is co-chair of the Research Group TECHcultures at the Berlin-Brandenburg Academy of Sciences and Humanities.

Nasser Mansour is a Senior Lecturer in Education at the Graduate School of Education and co-ordinator of the STEM Research Centre at the University of Exeter in the UK. Research interests include aspects of teaching and learning in science, such as cooperative learning, STS (science, technology and society education), and the relationship between religion and science education and multi-cultural studies in science education.

Randolf Menzel is Professor for Neurobiology at Freie Universität Berlin, Germany and member of the German National Academy of Sciences, Leopoldina. His expertise extends also to behavioural biology and zoology. The focus of his current research is the behaviour of the honeybee from a neurobiological perspective.

Takuji Okamoto is currently working as an Associate Professor at the Department of History and Philosophy of Science at the Graduate School of Arts and Science at the University of Tokyo. His research interests contain various aspects of (Japanese) history of science in political, historical and epistemological perspective.

Ortwin Renn is Full Professor and Chair of Environmental Sociology and Technology Assessment at Stuttgart University (Germany) and holds affiliate professorships at Stavanger University, Norway and Beijing Normal University, China. He directs the Stuttgart Research Center for Interdisciplinary Risk and Innovation Studies (ZIRIUS) at Stuttgart University and the non-profit research institute DIALOGIK. His main fields of expertise are risk governance, political participation and technology assessment. Ortwin Renn is a member of the Berlin Brandenburg Academy of Sciences and Humanities and chairs the IAG TECHcultures.

Sundar Sarukkai is the Director of the Manipal Centre for Philosophy and Humanities (MCPH), Manipal University, India. He is the author of the following books: *Translating the World: Science and Language*, *Philosophy of Symmetry*, *Indian Philosophy and Philosophy of Science*, *What is Science?* and *The Cracked Mirror: An Indian Debate on Experience and Theory* (co-authored with Gopal Guru), as well as co-editor of three volumes on logic. He is an Editorial Advisory Board member of the Leonardo Book Series on science and art, which is published by MIT Press, and the Series Editor for Science and Technology Studies, Routledge.

Simon Schwartzman is a member of the Brazilian Academy of Science and Senior Researcher at the Instituto de Estudos do Trabalho e Sociedade in Rio de Janeiro, Brazil. He is a former President of the Brazilian Institute for Geography and Statistics and was chairperson of the Research Group on the Sociology of Science and Technology of the International Sociological Association. His earlier work dealt with questions of political change in a historical and comparative perspective in Brazil. More recently, he has worked on the sociological and political dimensions of the production of knowledge in science, technology and education.

Yvonne M. Spicer is currently Vice President of Advocacy & Educational Partnership at the Museum of Science in Boston. She received a BS in Industrial Arts and Technology and an MS in Technology Education from State University of New York-Oswego. Spicer was instrumental in establishing the 2001 Massachusetts technology/engineering curriculum framework and most recently served in the design team of technology and engineering for the National Research Council (NRC) 'Next Generation' Framework for Science Education approved in 2011.

Dorothea Taube was research associate for the Interdisciplinary Research Group TECHcultures at the Berlin-Brandenburg Academy of Sciences and Humanities, Germany until December 2014. She is a trained ethnologist and cultural scientist and works as an educator in the field of global learning and education for sustainable development.

Cosima Wagner studied Japanese Studies and History in Marburg, Berlin and Kyôto. She was lecturer and research fellow at the Japanese Studies department of Goethe-University in Frankfurt and is currently Scientific Coordinator of the Cluster East Asia at the University Library Project '24 in 1' and research fellow at the Japanese Studies Institute of Freie Universität Berlin. Her research and teaching activities focus on a cultural sciences approach to the analysis of the development and use of technology in Japan, with a special focus on 'social' robots and on the discourse of the global boom of Japanese popular culture.

Introduction

Andreas Hohlt, Nicole C. Karafyllis,
Ortwin Renn and Dorothea Taube

International STEM education—rising in importance and significance

Whether digitalization, nanotechnology, renewable energies or wireless communication–science and technology are the key factors in global change. Education in STEM (science, technology, engineering and mathematics) is thus a main source of technological development, promising to enhance national wealth and social welfare.

The Western world has long been seen as the cradle of modern approaches to science education and served as a model for STEM education worldwide, somehow justified by what is referred to as 'scientific progress' and 'modernity.' However, the last decades have also seen a strong rise in scientific output by non-Western societies, often followed by new political priority-setting and alternative methods of scientific investigation and inquiry. STEM education as a tool of technologization and social advancement has thus led to new variations on the Western model and innovative, culture-based forms of STEM education in Asia, South America and the Arab countries. In addition, the United States and European countries face their own challenges in the field of STEM education, such as motivational problems leading to inadequate student recruitment, underrepresentation of women and minorities or drawbacks from adapting to a widely internationalized working space—problems that seem partially resolved or do not even necessarily exist in some non-western nations. Given these new developments, the learning experience is starting to become mutual rather than one-sided; and countries from all parts of the world can benefit from a direct exchange of approaches and experiences.

The debate on STEM education as a subject of international comparison and cross-cultural analysis started in the second half of the twentieth century and was an integral part of the overall pursuit of scientific achievement during the Cold War. One of the first international studies on educational research to take into account STEM education was known as the 'Pilot Twelve-Country Study' and was conducted in the USA, several European countries and Israel (Foshay et al. 1962). Since then, more and more countries have been included and a vast amount of literature has been produced based on projects such as the First International Mathematics Study (FIMS), Second International Science Study

(SISS), Relevance of Science Education (ROSE) or Trends in International Mathematics and Science Study (TIMSS) and PISA (see e.g. Husén 1967, Eckstein 1982, Rosier and Keeves 1991, Sjøberg and Schreiner 2010, Martin *et al.* 2012, OECD 2014).[1] Research in this area (OECD 2014) was also fostered by the anticipation of the various challenges STEM education would have to meet in a globalizing world, and this led to further studies and considerations. The most important of these challenges as identified by this publication are as follows:

Globalization: How can STEM education prepare young professionals to respond to the far-reaching globalized challenges of our time? In a world of interdependency, acceleration and the far-reaching and often-irreversible consequences of human interventions, as in the example of climate change research and policy, STEM and STEM education have to meet new demands with respect to problem grasping and problem solving.

Interdependency: How can science, technology and society better interact and mutually inspire each other's development? In the editors' view, STEM education should lead to a more technologically literate civil society and to an improved capacity building in interdisciplinary education and science communication. There is still no clear recipe for how scientific and technological literacy can be linked to cultural and social self-images of different societies and how this interaction can be made productive for economic as well as cultural objectives.

Norms/Values: How can STEM education include insights from ethics, risk assessment and the histories of science and technology? Science and technology are not goals in themselves; they are developed to serve human needs, to improve our knowledge about the impacts of human actions on nature and society and to meet moral objectives and principles.

Motivation: How can young people be motivated to study STEM and to pursue a professional career in the STEM field? Which types of motivation exist, and how should young people be addressed accordingly to their type of motivation?

Employability: How can job opportunities be assured and—in particular for less industrialized countries—how can trust in home-grown graduates be strengthened?

Equity/Equality: How can we reach a more balanced proportion of women and other underrepresented social groups among STEM students, graduates and professionals?

Flexibility/Resilience: How can educational systems be flexible enough to adopt new teaching methods and develop the role of the teacher?

This book is an attempt to address these issues from a comparative but qualitative international perspective. To our knowledge, there is no other study available that addresses STEM education and its main challenges in such a broad international and extra-European perspective. Usually, particular issues within the overall field of STEM education are analysed in studies focusing on one country exclusively, or from a comparative perspective focusing on a larger regional context or a selection of a limited number of countries (e.g., Bauer, Shukla and Allum 2011, or the project EQUALPRIME[2], research undertaken by the Centre for Research in Education in Science, Technology, Engineering and Mathematics at King's College in London[3] or the International Centre for

Classroom Research[4]). Rarely is STEM education, its characteristics and its challenges discussed comparatively within a broader framework, and when it is, the comparison is often triggered by economic criteria, such as the countries of the OECD and with a primary focus on quantitative data. Of course, all these approaches provide valuable information. However, they tend to leave the readers and decision-makers with a bare-bones approach to educational data that does not produce a wider meaning for interpretation or comparative review. In contrast, this book includes narrative elements, descriptions of country situations from different scientific disciplinary backgrounds, the influence of 'soft factors' such as culture and social perceptions, and innovative tools of qualitative social research such as the Delphi study.

The present study is a first step in expanding the international view on STEM by collecting materials and experiences from non-European industrialized as well as industrializing countries. Therefore, it by no means represents a complete and finalized picture of STEM in the world, but rather provides useful components and insights for a broad and comprehensive international comparison of STEM philosophies, approaches and experiences.

International spotlights in a comparative perspective: this volume's approach

This book explores new and unusual perspectives and methodologies of STEM education based on special investigations into STEM structures in the Arab GCC-countries, Brazil, Egypt, India, Japan, South Korea and the United States of America. China was one of the study's countries of focus from the beginning, but although we included it in all expert talks, workshops and in the Delphi study (see Chapter 14), we were regretfully unable to include an expert chapter on the STEM-education situation of China in the present publication for reasons beyond our control.

The seven countries and regions were identified for reasons of—extra-European—geographic representation, but also for reasons of specific relevance as global players with recent STEM education reforms or as quickly industrializing countries with a lot of interest in STEM advancements. The book unites a multitude of interdisciplinary perspectives on STEM education in the different countries and regions, bringing together internal perspectives of authors who are citizens of or working in the respective countries, as well as external evaluations and perspectives of international external experts.

Understanding and comparing different national approaches to STEM education quickly raises the question of the relationship between the universality of science and cultural or national differences, which is discussed in the first part of the book: STEM *education between universalism and cultural relativism*. From two different perspectives, Randolf Menzel, Heinz Duddeck and Nicole C. Karafyllis explore the question of to what degree science education is characterized by the culturally invariant laws of nature and/or complemented by cultural discursivity, e.g. cultural specifications, social validations of knowledge and traditions of teaching.

The text by Randolf Menzel and Heinz Duddeck on *Universals in STEM education* (Chapter 2) is structured as an interview and discusses aspects that have universal relevance within the overall field of STEM education. For instance, there is a broad consensus that scientific method cannot be determined by national cultures or preferences. The core standards of experimental research as a necessary prerequisite of reproducibility of results do not vary between, for example, Brazil, Egypt and the United States. Additionally, the acceptance of international assessment projects such as PISA, which provide comparative data on young people's skills and competences in different countries, points to the importance of a universal quality of STEM education.

Still, there might be important differences in the structure and process of how discourses on knowledge are organized and shaped by national patterns and cultural worldviews. What is socially accepted as a valid stock of knowledge may differ culturally, as may the ways scientific knowledge co-exists with other knowledge forms, such as religion.

In her article on *Why 'technology' is not universal—philosophical remarks on the language and culture issue of STEM education* (Chapter 1), Nicole C. Karafyllis explores the different meanings surrounding the concept of technology, using the example of the Arab world. In contrast to highly industrialized countries, the culture of technology in the Arab world is not driven primarily by functionality, but by beauty or public utility. In this context, artefacts from the West are not simply imported as given objects, but are adjusted to the different cultural context. Furthermore, the author illustrates how concepts of technology that strongly relate to arts and craftsmanship leave traces in the language, leading back to cultural traditions and norms that have historically accompanied the making and usage of technology in specific regions.

In view of the importance of the specific cultural and national context, it becomes clear that even though STEM is rooted in modelled universalities and in internationalized scientific methodology and language, STEM education always has a social dimension. It is embedded in regional cultures and influenced by social representations, by a given political and economic structure, and by narratives woven through a cultural fabric that might or might not interconnect people's views on STEM across national borders.

The second part of the book, *STEM education worldwide: perspectives on situations in six countries*, provides background material for how STEM education is organized and structured in six countries (Japan, South Korea, India, Egypt and Gulf region, Brazil and the USA), explains the cultural background of these approaches and reports on the experiences and outcomes that each national approach has produced. Articles in this section provide a comprehensive study on each country written by an expert from the specific country followed by a shorter contribution that sheds light on a particular aspect in the field of STEM education of the country.

Japan, which is the first country discussed, faces similar challenges to several Western societies when it comes to insufficient recruitment of young STEM professionals, especially women. In his article *The shift in public perception of science and science education in post-war Japan* (Chapter 3), Takuji Okamoto focuses on how, historically, Japanese science has developed a self-image. From this angle, he establishes links to the contemporary situation of STEM education. He shows that culturally and historically rooted changes in social perceptions of science and in human relationships to nature can correlate with changes in the perception of STEM and in whether young people choose to invest in it.

In her article *Gunpla robot toys and the popularization of robotics in Japan* (Chapter 4), Cosima Wagner offers a closer look at the specific role of robotics in Japan. The author shows that robot figures are deeply embedded in popular culture in Japan and have been used to trigger interest and positive attitudes towards science and technology in the Japanese population. These insights highlight the importance of specific historically and culturally based priorities and developments and their role in the field of STEM education.

Jung-Ok Ha also applies a historical approach in her article *From national mission to what? Shifts in the implication of science and technology in South Korea* (Chapter 5). Using the example of the Korean Advanced Institute of Science and Technology (KAIST), the author discusses the historical development of science and technology in South Korean society. She characterizes the current status of science and technology in South Korea as 'transitional,' since past images of science and scientists have lost their significance and popularity and no replacement of these is in sight. A nation that has emerged as a major player in science and technology (e.g. through Samsung) has become insecure about its own role in the STEM fields—a situation that might yet, nevertheless, provide ample room for new innovations and approaches in STEM practice and education.

Particularly in emerging countries such as India, Brazil and Egypt, the field of science and technology has been influenced by historical developments resulting from colonialism and external domination. In his contribution on *Challenges for STEM education in India* (Chapter 6), Sundar Sarukkai uses a multifaceted approach to provide general information on the current status and attitude towards science and technology, but also provides a historic overview of the development of Indian science, partially in contrast to and partially in cooperation with Western influences. He traces the cultural roots of modern scientific tradition and describes how it has been strongly associated with a purely Western enterprise in the past, thereby rejecting traditional Indian knowledge systems and promoting the very idea of rationality, progress and societal change. Later on, these ideas on modern science became a fundamental pillar of India after independence and, since then, have led to the country's intensive and impressive development as a global player, particularly in the field of information technology and space research. However, the author reflects critically on the multicultural facets of modern science, and demands a stronger appreciation and remembrance of great scientific contributions by Indian scientists as a source for alternative reflections on the value and importance of science and technology for the development of the India of today.

Against the backdrop of this comprehensive picture of the development of the field of science and technology, Nagalakshmi Chelluri and Mohan Avvari—in their contribution on *Corporate social responsibility programmes for STEM education: Cases from the Indian technology cluster city of Hyderabad* (Chapter 7)—address the impact of the private sector on STEM education. Using examples of corporate social responsibility strategies of a technology cluster in Hyderabad, they argue that public education in India needs to be supplemented by private initiatives if the country should manage to become a successful innovator in the future.

Valuable insights into the meaning and role of Islamic religious beliefs as a framework that informs both Egyptian culture and its educational system are given by Ghada K. Gholam and Nasser Mansour in their study *Highlights of STEM education in Egypt* (Chapter 8). The authors shed light on the different characteristics of the Egyptian education system, including the role and relationship of culture and religion, gender differences and the pervasive role and implications of the overall examination system. They make clear that the debate between proponents of Western secularization and the Egyptian Islamic culture will strongly influence future development of science and technology education. Reflecting on current developments and outlining future prospects in light of the changes brought about since the Arab Spring, they conclude that current initiatives need the strong support of government authorities in order to foster scientific innovation and, through this, the overall development of the country.

In a complementary and comparative manner, Nicole C. Karafyllis (who has worked as a professor in the United Arab Emirates (UAE)) extends the focus from Egypt to the Arab Gulf region in her article *Tertiary education in the GCC countries (UAE, Qatar, Saudi Arabia): How economy, gender and culture affect the field of STEM* (Chapter 9). She demonstrates that states such as the UAE and Qatar serve as role models for the biggest player in the region, Saudi Arabia, and that—despite the fact that these countries still face serious challenges in the field of STEM—they are driving forces for education programmes and implementation, especially in the research fields of renewable energy, environmental management and sustainability and genetics. Karafyllis addresses the latest changes in STEM curriculum development, language and gender issues and the role of culture and religion.

Similar to GCC states that are characterized by very low levels of respect for teachers, Brazil also faces serious challenges regarding the status and quality of the teaching profession as a whole. This is a particular issue in STEM education. Simon Schwartzman explains, in his contribution on *Science culture in Brazilian society* (Chapter 10), the historical factors that affect the current educational system in Brazil, and points out the various challenges Brazil is currently facing with regard to the quality of its public education. He illustrates that the country is currently in a state of major changes in making science and technology more popular among the young generation and in working to provide economic incentives—as well as a non-material incentive system—to improve the attractiveness of scientific and technological careers.

Elizabeth Balbachevsky and Edilene Cruz, in their contribution on *Policy controversies in science education in Brazil* (Chapter 11), provide an analysis of curricula content and learning strategies for STEM fields in higher education and its discussion as part of a broader policy controversy in Brazil. They reflect on current developments, particularly on the pressure for change that the major universities' entrance examination (ENEM—National Exam of the Secondary Education) poses for the curricula of STEM education at the higher education level in Brazil.

At the end of the country-specific discussions, in her contribution on *Closing the achievement gap and building the pipeline through STEM education: A US perspective* (Chapter 12), Yvonne Spicer provides a comprehensive picture of the current situation in the United States, particularly focusing on specific problems faced by different social groups. She addresses the issues of scientific literacy and early childhood attraction to science and explores potential solutions of how to diminish the gaps by reframing (self-) identification in relation to STEM science.

This general insight is complemented by a more practical approach given by Arthur Eisenkraft in his contribution on *The NRC Framework and the Next Generation Science Standards: An opportunity to improve science education in the USA* (Chapter 13). The author presents the two latest national initiatives; the Framework for K-12 Science Education, released by the National Academy of Science, and the Next Generation Science Standard, both of which aim at improving science instructions in the USA. He demonstrates application of the standards, developing a lesson plan in science education on the investigation and understanding of the phenomenon of shadows. It becomes clear that these standards offer possibilities to improve science lessons and to enable teachers to more strongly include preferred engineering principles into lessons on a very practical basis.

Based on these country-specific discussions, the following two chapters take a qualitative and hermeneutic approach when analysing and interpreting cross-cultural and transdisciplinary patterns of STEM education. They explore the ways and intensities in which four framing systems of a given country form and influence the country-specific situation of STEM education. These four framing systems, based on structural-functional analysis in sociology, are: (1) the political structure, (2) the macroeconomic situation, (3) the epistemologically and educationally relevant traits of culture, and (4) the social understanding and perception of science and technology.

The third part of the book, *STEM education from a comparative transnational perspective,* describes and evaluates the results from a Delphi study, which was conducted by the research group in 2013. The Delphi method is a communication technique based on the judgement of a group of experts, and in this case was used to identify commonalities and idiosyncrasies among the different countries in the field of STEM and STEM education. It was designed to clarify the differences between the countries and explain them in accordance with cultural and historical developments. The participants were also asked to identify transnational or even universal aspects that had the potential to be applied to countries not their own. All in all, the Delphi process involved around sixty experts from different disciplinary backgrounds and countries, including all the authors who contributed to this publication. Among others, one central topic of the Delphi study was the motivation of young people to engage in STEM fields. During the workshop it became clear that, especially in Asian countries, most young people are motivated by pragmatic (extrinsic) reasons such as secure job prospects, adequate pay and the prestige offered by the STEM field. In contrast, more individualistic reasons such as fascination and individual interest in science and technology are more important motivations in Europe and the USA. Furthermore, for emerging countries such as Egypt, Brazil and India, working in STEM fields offers great potential for social mobility, particularly for young, socially deprived people, who can achieve more prestigious and better-paid positions in society through STEM education.

Other issues that were discussed in the context of the Delphi study included the important role of teachers, teacher education and teaching methods, in particular the positive effects of inquiry-based learning methods. Furthermore, the role of culture was stressed to be a central factor for influencing the prestige, but also the goals and objectives, of STEM education. Crucial aspects here included the role of science and technology for economic but also social development, the status and prestige of people working and doing research in science and technology, the need for interdisciplinary research on STEM education including the humanities, and the chances for social mobility in STEM-related professions. The detailed procedure, methodology and the results of the Delphi are reported in this third part of the book.

The third part of the book also includes the editors' summary on *Lessons learned: Towards unity in diversity* (Chapter 15) and a look towards the future, entitled *Responding to challenges of rapid global change by strengthening local STEM education* (Chapter 16), by Ilan Chabay. The concluding text on the lessons learned points to synthesizing the main results from the various country reports and the Delphi process. What can we learn from the comparative review and what insights could be transferred from one country to other countries or STEM education contexts? Results are presented based on the five main questions that guided the whole research process and that have been defined as the most crucial:

1   What are public attitudes toward STEM subjects in the country being presented?
2   How attractive are STEM careers and STEM education in this country? How many students succeed in completing their education in STEM education?
3   What are the key programmes that promote STEM subjects?
4   Which cultural roots affect the current state of STEM subjects?
5   What are current tendencies or trends in the STEM field/with regard to STEM subjects? Where will these developments take STEM?

In his essay on the outlook for the field, Ilan Chabay outlines current trends in STEM education, such as increasing internationalization and interdisciplinary problem solving, and makes a plea for urgent reform, which seems to hold the most promise for addressing and solving some of the major problems found in field of STEM education worldwide.

Acknowledgments

This publication is a product of the Interdisciplinary Research Group (IAG) TECHcultures (Intercultural Comparison of the Understanding of Science and Technology in Selected Countries) of the German Berlin-Brandenburg Academy of Sciences and Humanities, (BBAW) and comprises investigations and discussions undertaken from 2011 to 2014. The empirical studies were based on commissioned country reports, interviews with experts, two workshops, a Delphi process and discussions among the various bodies of the Academy.

The research group was composed of the following members: Gunnar Berg (Martin-Luther-Universität, Halle-Wittenberg), Volker M. Brennecke (The Association of German Engineers), Heinz Duddeck (Technische Universität Braunschweig), Nicole C. Karafyllis (Technische Universität Braunschweig), Irmela Hijiya-Kirschnereit (Freie Universität Berlin), Eberhard Knobloch (Technische Universität Berlin), Eva-Maria Jakobs (RWTH Aachen University, Melanie Mengel ('Little Scientists' House' Berlin), Randolf Menzel (Freie Universität Berlin), Uwe Pfenning (German Aerospace Centre), Ortwin Renn (Universität Stuttgart), Michael Schanz (Association for Electrical, Electronic & Information Technologies) and Rudolf G. Wagner (Universität Heidelberg). The group consisted of members of the Berlin-Brandenburg Academy of Sciences and Humanities from various disciplines, in addition to external experts and stakeholders working in the field of STEM education. The research group was moderated by Ortwin Renn (chair) and Nicole C. Karafyllis (co-chair) and supported by a scientific team of young researchers, Dorothea Taube and Andreas Hohlt.

The editors would like to thank the contributors to this book, all team members who helped to finalize this book, organize the workshops and the many group meetings, and in particular the directors and administrators of the BBAW for their continuous and enthusiastic support. Very special thanks is due to the team of administrators, directed by Ute Tintemann from the BBAW who supported the academic work and assisted the members of the group with their expertise. We would also like to thank the following individuals for their contribution and participation in the overall research process: Andrea Bréard (Universität Heidelberg), Marc de Vries (Delft University of Technology), Cheng Donghong (Chinese Association for Science and Technology), Mamdouh Eldamaty (Cultural Counsellor from the Egyptian Embassy in Germany), Jochen Litterst (Technische Universität Braunschweig), Katarzyna Jez (Centre for Interdisciplinary Polish Studies), Bruce Lewenstein (Cornell University), Mara Mills (New York University), Anni Sappinen (Berlin Social Science Center), Yoshinori Shimizu (University of Tsukuba), Svein Sjøberg (University of Oslo), Eva Sternfeld (Technische Universität Berlin), Jan Peter Wogart (Bremen University of Applied Sciences), Yang Yuankui (China Association for Science and Technology), Ibrahim Zeid (Monoufia University).

Notes

1 For a brief historical overview of the development of the field of international educational research, see the following article: Brief History of IEA: 55 Years of Educational Research (International Association for the Evaluation of Educational Achievement 2011).
2 The project EQUALIPRIME—Exploring quality primary education in different cultures: a cross-national study of teaching and learning focuses on teaching and learning in the science classroom and uses a qualitative study based on video data. The project compares teaching and learning practices in science classrooms in Australia, Germany

and Taiwan. For further information see the homepage http://communities.deakin.edu.au/equalprime/node/2 [Accessed 22 August 2014].

3 The Centre for Research in Education in Science, Technology, Engineering & Mathematics (CRESTEM) at the Kings College in London is also doing research from an international comparative perspective e.g. 'Towards universal participation in post-16 mathematics: lessons from high-performing countries' (Hodgen *et al.* 2013). For more information see a list of current research projects on the website available from http://www.kcl.ac.uk/sspp/departments/education/research/crestem/Research/Current-Projects/Current-Projects.aspx [Accessed 22 August 2014].

4 The International Centre for Classroom Research (ICCR) supports collection, storage and analysis of data (particularly video data) related to the study of learning and teaching in classrooms and is affiliated with several international comparative projects such as 'The Learner's Perspective Study.' This study explores patterns of participation in mathematics classrooms, from a comparative perspective, in sixteen countries. For further information on the project see the website http://www.lps.iccr.edu.au/, [Accessed 22 August 2014] or their latest publication *Student Voice in Mathematics Classrooms around the World* (Kaur *et al.* 2013).

Bibliography

Bauer, Martin, Rajesh Shukla and Nick Allum (2011): *The Culture of Science. How the Public Relates to Science Across the Globe.* Routledge, New York.

Eckstein, Max A. (1982): *A Comparative Review of Curriculum: Mathematics and International Studies in the Secondary Schools of Five Countries.* National Commission on Excellence in Education (ED), Washington DC.

Foshay, Arthur W. *et al.* (1962): *Educational Achievements of Thirteen-year-olds in Twelve Countries.* UNESCO Institute for Education, Hamburg.

Hodgen, Jeremy, Rachel Marks and David Pepper (2013): *Towards Universal Participation in Post-16 Mathematics: Lessons from High-performing Countries.* Nuffield Foundation, London.

Husén, Torsten (1967): *International Study of Achievement in Mathematics: A Comparison of Twelve Countries (Vols. 1-2).* Almqvist & Wiksell, Stockholm.

International Association for the Evaluation of Educational Achievement (2011): 'Brief History of IEA: 55 Years of Educational Research.' Available from http://www.iea.nl/brief_history.html [Accessed 22 September 2014].

Kaur, Berinderjeet *et al.* (2013): *Student Voice in Mathematics Classrooms around the World.* Sense Publishers, Rotterdam.

Martin, Michael O. *et al.* (2012): *TIMMS 2011 International Results in Science.* TIMSS & PIRLS International Study Center, Lynch School of Education, Boston College, Chestnut Hill (MA).

OECD (2014): *PISA 2012 Results: What Students Know and Can Do: Student Performance in Mathematics, Reading and Science (Volume I, Revised edition).* OECD Publishing, Paris.

Rosier, Malcom J. and John P. Keeves (1991): *The IEA Study of Science I: Science Education and Curricula in Twenty-three Countries.* Pergamon Press, Oxford.

Sjøberg, Svein and Camilla Schreiner (2010): *The ROSE project. An Overview and Key Findings.* University of Oslo, Oslo.

Part I

STEM education between universalism and cultural relativism

Part 1

1 Why 'technology' is not universal

Philosophical remarks on the language and culture issue of STEM education

Nicole C. Karafyllis

The culturalistic approach to giving science and technology meaning

In the following, I will outline why, for STEM-educators particularly in non-Western countries, it is a challenge *how* to adequately address 'technology' and 'technics,' i.e. with regard to a specific *technological culture* and language of instruction. My focus will highlight the Arab world, which lacks the specific Western concept of 'technology.'[1] However, most of the arguments involved have a general scope, given that the word 'technology' already has different meanings in the various Western languages.

Some philosophical remarks are necessary, as it still is a common misunderstanding of (mostly) Western scientists, engineers and politicians that technologies and their related objects encompass, generally speaking, *universal* functions and hence also have universal meanings. This science-driven opinion is inspired firstly by *mathematics* and general *laws* of physics, which are undoubtedly valid everywhere on the earth, and, secondly, by the debatable idea that technology is merely *applied science* and has no distinct theoretical standing of its own (as if, e.g., mechanics results from physics and geometry with an almost natural causality).[2] In this reductionist sense, 'technology' would be merely a 'practical implementation of intelligence' (Ferré 1988: 26), whereas 'theoretical intelligence,' framed in the modes of scientific investigation, would count as higher knowledge and understanding (Ferré 1988: 33)—thereby compromising the ancient concept of (Greek) *lógos* that is central to the modern term 'technology' (but not to 'craftsmanship'). Thirdly, the concepts of 'information' and 'cognition'—frequently fused into a reduced version of 'intelligence'—are mistaken for the philosophical ideas of 'knowledge' (German: *Erkenntnis*), 'comprehension' and 'judgement' (German: *Urteilskraft*). Furthermore, the learning individual is seen as isolated from their sociological and historical context. Last but not least, this view depends on the naturalistic assumption that 'the earth' or 'the universe' can be equated with the metaphysical concept of 'the world'; and that humans all over the planet have (and have always had) the same needs, desires and visions about the making of their specific *world*.

However, the problems to be solved by and the satisfaction to be reached with technology have historically been different from one region to another,[3] and the building and using of artefacts and natural objects resemble these cultural, climatic, topographic and other socio-geographic differences.[4] Furthermore, the main Christian narratives of a) technics, hereditary sin and work/labour (see Stöcklein 1969), and b) technics as a means for emancipation from nature's restraints, are not understood easily by cultures with other religious and historical traditions. Thus it is a common insight among researchers engaged in STS that the content of 'technology' and 'technics' cannot be grasped without the related idea of socio-technical systems (Ropohl 2009), which vary from culture to culture and are intertwined with political systems and moral norms. In these socio-technical systems, a specific *type of the interconnections between knowledge, perception, inquiry and practice* (a so-called 'technological culture') is constructed, in which technology actually makes sense (or doesn't).[5]

Almost the same is true for science. It is very well researched with regard to systems building in science that, for example, the biological systematic which Swedish botanist Carl Linnaeus developed in the early eighteenth century—and that has become universal in biology—is by far not the only one in existence. Ethnobotanical studies have shown that even today, many indigenous cultures still categorize the plants of their world in categories that resemble general useful-ness and useful plant materials (e.g. fibres and oil). The terms that identify the different plants and their relations are modelled (Balick and Cox 1996) according to their uses. These folk-botanical plant systems most often relate to the spheres of agriculture and sustainable ecosystem management. Therefore, from the very beginning, the mode of inquiry is *technical* and at the same time *ecological*. By the same token, indigenous cultures' knowledge and their systems inspire current biological research at universities, e.g. with regard to science on ecological *resilience*. (Resilience management is also a major topic in current engineering research.)

In contrast, Linnaeus' *Systema naturae* (1735) was built on the universal biologi-cal criteria of 'reproduction' and 'nutrition,' by which life—seen from an abstract point of view—sustains itself. However, the different life forms explained in the system were examined in the form of collections of mostly *dead* entities. As the *International Society of Ethnobiology* (founded in 1988) emphasizes, the predomi-nant 'Western' way of systemizing biological entities is intertwined with the current standardization of different bio-ecological worlds *and* languages. These standardizations, triggered by scientific universalism and model organisms (such as, e.g., *Arabidopsis thaliana* as the universal plant model used in modern genetics), happen in the light of economic globalization: 'We are concerned by the loss of traditional, local and indigenous knowledge, and the effects of that loss on biologi-cal, cultural and linguistic diversity' (International Society of Ethnobiology 2014).

The whole educational idea of 'inquiry-based learning' is challenged by the fact that one first has to have an idea of what is worth inquiring for. Therefore, we can also speak of a specific 'mindset' or 'mentality,' in which a so-called 'spirit of craftsmanship' (Sennett 2008) can develop. In the Arab world, this spirit is man-ifested differently. It has a strong alliance with the Latin medieval tradition that aligned *technics* with *art*, but due to the tradition of Bedouin culture it shows a particular dislike of 'manual work' needed for construction, as I will demonstrate in due course. According to sociologist Sennett, the spirit of craftsmanship is currently lacking in many areas of the Western world—an observation that matches, for example, the results from surveys on the challenges of STEM-education in present-day Europe (Pfenning and Renn 2012).

In the highly industrialized Western countries of today, the predominant type of technological culture is driven by *functionality*, whereas in other parts of the world *beauty* or *public utility* might be stronger uniting forces. So, if we further analyse what 'technology' can mean from an intercultural perspective, we might address three core concepts as the theoretical 'universals' of the concept of technology (as a Western concept): a) *artificiality*, b) *utility* and c) *functionality*. All three can be related to *means* and *ends* in different manners that are framed by the ranked qualities of a 'system.' When philosophers of technology Christoph Hubig and Hans Poser recently warned that a 'homogenization of world culture' is already dawning on the horizon (Hubig and Poser 2007: preface: 6) by means of technology transfer from the West, this underestimated how often imported artefacts as means are adjusted by other cultures to their own ends. Most recently, this has been shown by the Arab Spring Revolutions of 2011 and the different ways of using networked ICT, both by users and governments (see Karafyllis 2013 and contribution by Gholam and Mansour in this book).

However, Hubig and Poser have a point in stressing that the worldview of functionality, which is structurally woven throughout the whole of the imported system, might generate a homogenous mindset in which nothing other than functionality seems to matter. On the other hand, empirical modelling of technology transfer has shown that in Arab cultures, traditional beliefs form a solid resistance against the import of whole 'systems' (Straub, Loch and Hill 2003). On other grounds, political scientist Bassam Tibi (2005) has termed the desire to import artefacts rather than rationality systems depending on Western values the 'semi-modernity' of Arabic-Islamic cultures. Apart from criticizing this situation from the standpoint of 'enlightenment' (which bears specific problems), the findings concerning the Arab world may also be a chance for Western STEM-educators to reconsider teaching the almost forgotten relationship between technology and (public and moral) norms in North America and Europe (and not only its relation to economic benefit).

The dominance of *functionality*—here meaning a direct and causal relation of material means (tools) and objectified ends (artefacts) with specific purposes that relate to norms—in Western technological culture is based on a worldview that ontologically cherishes objects (objectification). This worldview queries perceived 'objects' (in both the hemispheres of nature and technics) on the instrumental use of their properties and for the purpose of production. The present concept of utility is in line with that. Whereas historically, 'utility' was seen as a measure for a people's happiness (Bentham 1789), present economic theory reduces it to the measure of preferences for decisions, usually taken by prospective customers. Utilities that do not relate to decisions measurable in monetary form and that cannot be interpreted according to materialized functions normally escape the mindset of Western technological culture and its gatekeepers: the engineers. In Arab culture, which on the Arab peninsula is still highly inspired by Bedouin culture, *objects* are in general a burden, whereas knowledge is easy to transport and therefore more admirable. Above all, these different understandings of the relationship between artificiality, functionality and utility matter for the sacral and magic aspects of technics, which in other cultures relate to the search for truth and therefore to the core of science.[6]

Example: the Emirates Telescope Project (2006)

Let me give you an example. In 2006, the government of Dubai launched the Emirates Institution for Advanced Science and Technology (EIAST) as a strategic initiative to build and implement technical innovations in the Gulf Region. ('Innovation,' however, has negative connotations on the Arabian Peninsula, meaning the reformation of Islam in the light of Western-influenced modernization). With their initiative, the UAE understands itself to be a 'hub among advanced nations' and EIAST encompassed three research programmes: 'the space, energy and astronomy programmes.'[7] The idea of a public-oriented astronomy programme, one that included the Emirates Telescope project, surprised Western observers. Whereas the space programme deals with satellite navigation and earth observation and has the potential for both military, agricultural (e.g. monitoring of desertification) and civil applications (control of national ICTs and their users), and the energy programme aims for sustainable water and energy supplies, the astronomy programme does not seem to foster industrial productivity or even appease consumer preferences. Instead, it serves educational purposes on national grounds. With the Emirates Telescope project, the government of Dubai challenged the public interest for technology's sake itself and has chosen a masterpiece of engineering culture that relates back to both the cultural identity and (almost forgotten) narratives of science and technology in the region. As a consequence, the project 'is aimed at improving science and astronomical infrastructure, scientific knowledge transfer to UAE nationals and raises public awareness and enthusiasm for astronomy.'[8]

Those native to the Arab world regard early versions of the telescope and the related scientific knowledge of astronomy as *their* 'technology,' dating back to the optical calculations and lens-modelling of mathematician Ibn al-Haitham (in Latin: *Alhazen* or *Alhazan*), who died around AD1040. From there, it is an easy geographical and historical step to the ancient 'Greeks' Euclid and Ptolemaios who lived in Alexandria. Furthermore, the Islamic calendar is a lunar calendar, contrasting with the Gregorian solar calendar of Christian cultures. Not only holy days, but also the entire history of Islamic-Arabic civilization depends on this time calculation and the question: who is authorized to observe the sky by which technical means? However, the Islamic way of time calculation and calendar construction has been under threat by globalization, particularly from the needs of international commerce, and by imported technology (mobile phones sold in the UAE and other Arab countries have an applet for the lunar calendar). The initiation of an education-oriented telescope project therefore *means* something else in the Islamic-Arabic world, compared to the Western world of the North Americas and Europe. The artefact of the telescope does not merely have to function for scientific purposes, but instead has to tell the story of a *deeper* meaning rooted in culture and the narratives of Muslim civilization: observing the sky for both acquiring truth and knowledge about navigation. The project also addresses the national awareness of the need to build its own technologies. Thus, it was also an easy step from the Emirates Telescope Project to the Khalifa Sat project, through which the Emiratis expect the first satellite being built *inside* the country to be in orbit by 2017 (EIAST 2014). Both a student research centre and a school visit programme are part of the Space Programme of EIAST. In tandem with this programme, the creation of a virtual atlas highlights that the UAE has been measured and photographed by its own satellite (and not a foreign one) for the first time, and also stresses the beauty of the country unveiled by this new technology.

It is still a thorn in the side of most technology-interested Arabs and other Muslims that historically, as far as we know, many mathematical and scientific technological advancements had already been set in motion within the cultural sphere of the Arabs' empire, but the actual *making use* of these scientific insights surrounding artefacts (including the construction of the telescope, as such) pre-dominantly occurred and still occurs in 'Western' regions dominated by Christian thinking. Rather than accepting the feeling of national inferiority, when it comes to technology issues, we could ask *why* the creation of objects was not seen as necessary as it was in the West. Throughout the history of technology, this question remains unanswered, and I can just paint a broad picture of how to further investigate it here. After all, this matters for engineering education and its relation to science education.

In ancient Greek culture (in contrast to Roman culture), the idea that science and technology are means for contemplation and acquiring truth rather than for production and domination was also particularly strong. Additionally, it is important to note that neither productivity nor creativity is addressed by the term technology itself today, though they are a component of the metaphysical background. Therefore, the idea of production (and educational claims for increasing a country's economic productivity by means of innovative engineering) is not a necessary precondition for understanding 'technology.' To sum up: from a cultur-alistic view, technology as a human means of 'world-making' can be seen as a pluralist concept that varies between cultures. However, this neither outweighs 'laws of nature' nor mathematical calculus. Rather it asks for the different ways of *understanding* them and how they matter in the actual life of people.

The challenge for STEM-educators and scholars

Nevertheless, voting for universal meanings of technology results in a radical forgetting of the *history* of science and technology, including the constant aspiration of humans to make their techniques, artefacts and technologies 'better' for the sake of *their* world and life. If so, knowledge about historical shifts and developments regarding techniques, inventions and the trade of artefacts around the globe would fall into darkness. This obscurity not only contradicts the idea of technological progress, but also fails to get students interested in technology-related subjects. As the Spanish philosopher José Ortega y Gasset (1883–1955) pointed out in a university lecture given to engineering students in 1932,[9] the 'engineering culture' of the West, being ignorant of its own historical develop-ment, thereby risks its motivating fundament: because it treats technology as something eternal, i.e. as if technology is always already *there* and at the same time *ready-at-hand* for the user. By forgetting the difficult tasks that the ancestors of present-day engineers once had to tackle, a mindset is created which cannot connect to the soul's creativity anymore and, in the long run, will fail to sustain the technological level a culture has reached. In order to describe the devel-oping of this mindset accompanying the invention of artefacts and techniques, Ortega (and Spanish-Mexican scholar José Gaos, 1900–1969) used the Spanish term *'tecnificación,'* which corresponds to the German *'Technisierung'* but lacks an English equivalent that would, at the same time, denote a history of ideas perspective surrounding 'technics' from a philosophy-of-history (of technology) point of view (see also Blumenberg 2009).

Perhaps we do not need to address the cultural figure of degeneration and decadence in order to make the argument clear: that 'technology' and 'technics' have different meanings when its ways of world-making, including objects, are seen as embedded in different cultures. With Ortega we can summarize that by means of technology, not only things but also *mindsets* are produced that inter-change, but are not identical with scientific worldviews. Because technology addresses *utility*, the related mindset-production is achieved in a more persuasive way than that achieved through science, which creates world images (German: *Weltbilder*) and worldviews based on theories, principles and measurement and is striving for truth. The challenge for STEM-educators is to first deconstruct the mindset of (Western) 'engineering culture' against the background of their own technological culture in order to make scholars *understand* it, and then eventu-ally build on it through further exploration. Textbooks used for teaching STEM have to support this culture-embedded method of making 'technology' explicit, including remarks on historical developments and so-called *leading images* of the genesis of different technics (e.g. the invention of the typewriter which was genu-inely modelled according to the piano). These kinds of textbooks that would increase inquiry-based learning and enhance creative thinking in engineering and design still have to be developed in the Arab world and beyond.

Instead of looking into a country's history books which, regarding technology, frequently tell the chronological stories of single national achievements, past 'golden ages,' winners of the Nobel Prize in science fields, or even simultaneously make technic-critical remarks on colonialization by means of Western technol-ogy (e.g. the Suez Canal),[10] one might turn to *language*. As I will argue in the following section, 'technology' and related terms have a different meaning on the conceptual level that shows in culture-sensitive terms related to the specific language used. They are not 100% translatable into an English, French or German term, but rather they have to be explained. Concepts of technology leave traces in the language, leading back to cultural traditions and norms that have histori-cally accompanied the making and use of technology in specific regions.[11]

Therefore, when educational programmes for enhancing the 'technological literacy' (VDI and acatech 2009) of a country are fostered, the specific under-standing of 'technology' or even a lack thereof has to be taken into account. On the whole, two reasons recommend this culturalistic approach: a) educa-tors might have better chances of attracting scholars to STEM subjects when connecting the content to be learned to the *intrinsic* motivation of the scholars, i.e. the wish for learning about technology in order to understand and design 'their own world' (and not just for getting a job in a global-networked company with standardized Western technology); b) as educational issues are intertwined with national goals that touch upon cultural identity and, at the same time, the challenge of modernization, a culture-sensitive STEM education might be able to overcome the known resistance in developing countries towards an assumed 'Westernization' by means of imported technology and the related norms (see the contribution of Gholam and Mansour in this book).

For STEM educators, the culturalist approach also matters regarding the language of instruction and asks for alternatives to English as *the* language of teaching about technology. I will outline this challenge with the example of technology-related terms in the Arabic language spoken by more than half a billion people worldwide and intertwined with the various cultures from the Maghreb in the Western hemisphere to Malaysia in the East—a loose connection broadly termed 'the Arab world.' The region is linked by Arabic as the language of the Holy Quran, and Islam as the dominant religion that informs culture and identity building.

Last but not least, the culture-sensitivity of technology matters for Western countries, which still predominantly design and export technologies. As sociologist and philosopher Helmuth Plessner (1892–1985) pointed out: 'whereas the usage of apparatuses and machines is connected to the understanding of theory, it is not connected to the humanist ethos of the theory. [. . .] Europism is conquering the world only by paying the price of its mechanization and instrumentalization. This transferability on non-European cultures will generate the fate of Europism itself' (Plessner 1974: 24, Orig. in German, my translation). Looking at other cultures always implies a critical look at the limits of one's own culture and the norms and values it has set as standards.

'Technics' in the context of Western languages compared to Arabic

The existing, but not ordinary English language term *technic* or *technics* (derived from the German *Technik* and also to be found in the Spanish *técnica*), relating back to the ancient Greek *téchne* (e.g. occurring in Aristotle's *Physics*), does not exist in Arabic. *Technics* can denote both an artefact and a specific mode of human creation, the latter similar to the sense of 'method.' It matters for the following, if 'method' merely relates to a rule-following *skill* (as in the case of craftsmanship and art) or a *technique* that is led by scientific principles. In today's Arabic language, there is not much of a distinction. The Arabic Wikipedia (Accessed 13 June 2011) listed the newly Arabized *taqnía* or *tiqnía* (تقنيه), whose root consonants (t-q-n) address a verb meaning 'bringing to perfection; to master.' But is the model for perfection found inside nature or in the human genus, i.e. are the ends of perfection given intrinsically or extrinsically with relation to the existing world? However, the Arabic Wikipedia did not use *taqnía* as equivalent to *technics*, but as translation of the English *technology*, i.e. it implicitly stressed the systematically ordered knowledge fundament when applying a set of different techniques from various disciplines, foremost in relation to artefacts (tools and machines).[12] The ends of perfection, it seems, are also to be found within the realm of knowledge and are therefore accessible by science.[13]

The creators of the Arabic Wikipedia entry on 'technology' have also tried to grasp the meaning of 'technologies of the self,' an expression coined by philosopher Michel Foucault (1926–1984) to describe the hidden power-relations that standards seem to recommend for the self-designing of people's lives, including psychology-driven techniques of enhancement (related to Foucault's concept of governmentality). However, the English expression used is already a misleading translation of the French original (Foucault used the French Plural *techniques de soi*, not *technologie*) that highlighted the character of a structural assembly of norms, techniques and discourses resulting in an unseen power of standardization, and did not insinuate a systematic, knowledge-based frame for it. This difference matters, above all, politically.

Here, we face a problem already present in the languages of the 'West.' The English-speaking countries tend to subordinate all *technics*-related aspects under the term 'technology,' whereas the German, Spanish and French languages differentiate between the knowledge system around the creation and usage of artefacts (French *technologie* or Spanish *tecnología*), and the artefact itself, including the instrumental action of creating it, and sometimes also the reasons why it was created. However, the latter use of (German) *Technik*, (French) *technique* and (Spanish) *técnica* as a ratioinstrumental set of actions does not necessarily have to relate to an artefact, but can also address different actions that have a rational core and serve distinct functions: for example, praying, breathing and learning techniques. Technics here is not just a means to reach a proposed end, i.e. it is (in terms of science) not bound to the relationship of cause and effect, but also implies the deeper *fulfilment* of a human action that is led by norms and values.

Other than the Arabic Wikipedia entry of June 2011, the Arabic-English standard dictionary of Hans Wehr and J. Milton Cowan (1979: 115f) lists the newly Arabized *taqnia* for the English 'technique' (i.e. the modes of mastering something according to a method) and offers different writing variations of the separately Arabized 'technology.'[14] It even introduces the new word 'technocrat' in Arabic. Time will tell what these words will actually mean for speakers of Arabic, so far still living in very different political systems to those of the West. It is noteworthy that the semantic field around *technics* in all mentioned languages today is not primarily related to the narrower fields of engineering and artefacts, but to broader concepts of instrumentality, rational knowledge and dominance.

Philosopher Hans-Martin Sass (1978: VII) who, in his introduction to Ernst Kapp's *Grundlinien einer Philosophie der Technik* (1877),[15] suggested an ordering system of the different meanings of 'Technik,'[16] would include Foucault's term of 'self-techniques' (or wrongly, though commonly, 'technologies of the self') in the classes of the 'techniques of individual self-sustenance' (German: *Techniken der individuellen Selbstbehauptung*) and 'human-techniques' (German: *Humantechniken*). This subject-related understanding of *technics* is foreign to the thinkers of the Muslim world, because the Arabic word for 'self' (*dhāt*) cannot be understood in the Western introspective and self-reflective meaning, as if a dual subject can view and master itself interiorly.[17] Rather in Arabic it means 'essence' or 'being,' striving for the wholeness of identity that is externally limited by the norms of the community and internally limited by the soul's potential. In Arabic-Islamic philosophy and psychology, where body and soul are not completely separated entities, the Self is, on the one hand, given in its dynamics by the divine anthem (*ruh*) at the beginning of its life; on the other hand, the Self has to struggle hard to sustain itself (*jihad*) by leading a virtuous life in accordance with community norms. Classic Arabic-Islamic ethics are designed around this basic construction (see Fakhry 1994). As a consequence, all the semantic fields of Western modernity that anthropologically relate *technics* to individual self-creation and self-invention (e.g. also in the Menschenbild of the *homo faber*; Karafyllis 2009) are absent in the Arabic context. The individual is not a technician or designer of himself. Therefore he or she does not necessarily have to fight against the modern rebound effect of losing 'authenticity' (though in present times, where Arab culture in the metropolitan regions of, for example, Dubai and Cairo has been affected by Western lifestyles, this might have changed).[18]

For the STEM-field, the difference can be seen in the unexpected applications of neuro-technologies and techniques for visualizing the brain (such as fMRI—functional magneto resonance imaging) since the 1990s. Not only in the Middle East, but in the Far East, too, fMRI is used for finding the mental representations of nothingness and the emergence of soul potential (the fMRI-technique is prominently endorsed by the Dalai Lama), whereas Western discourses on the nature of 'free will' and the connection between first- and third-person-status are minor matters of interest. Thus, it is not simply the case that cultural perceptions shape technology, but also that technology redefines cultural perceptions (including those associated with religion).

In Arabic, there is a strong tradition of seeing technics as *art*, for example as mechanical or rhetoric art for which the general Arabic term *fann* applies (Aristotle also used the Greek *téchne* in relation to rhetoric as an art, and for the professional activities of the craftsman, the cook and the farmer). It means both: a specialized action (or a discipline) and the specific way of doing it. It is accompanied by a good public reputation and today encompasses the visual arts. The *fannān* is an artisan first, and then a craftsman. However, the resulting work or craft as an object is less important than the accompanying skilled action.

In modern-day ordinary Arabic language, the service-oriented technician (e.g. the electrician), the sportsperson and the musician have been included in this semantic field related to art (as special skill).

Craftsmanship in the (in Arabic slightly pejorative) sense of 'manufacture,' relating to a workshop, is named, like the capital of Yemen, *san'ā'* (صنعاء); the three root consonants of the related verb belong to the semantic fields of 'making, constructing, designing' and at the same time: 'doing trade and commerce.' A *sani'* is a manually skilled *maker* without higher artistic capacities. He is a craftsman who usually works with less valuable material (e.g. a blacksmith) and is in direct physical contact with the material to be formed. The expression can be combined with many different representations, in the sense of 'the one who makes xy' (also as matchmaker who arranges marriages). Again, the resulting thing or craft is not as important as the related actions that result from modelling this thing with the aim to sell it, i.e. *utility* and *functionality* build the semantic core of the term *san'ā'*. The intension of the verb can also relate to the imitation of the (natural) original, even in a pejorative sense that highlights the imitating fake (as in the case of prostheses).

Craftspeople in Arabic culture do not belong to the most privileged groups, and in rural areas their position can relate to kinship and tribal structures, i.e. craftsmanship is often hereditary. However, they have traditionally had a good reputation for guaranteeing *maintenance*, with particular responsibility for maintaining the productivity of local agriculture (e.g. the carpenter was responsible for maintaining the water wheel). This changed with urbanization and industrialization (since the water wheel was replaced by the water pump).

Another important Arabic term for craftsmanship (*hirfā*) is highly regarded in the normative sense. It relates to the actions of calligraphic writing and cutting, stressing the *professional* action involved in creating something *artificial*. Etymologically, *hirfā* is related to the Arabic word for the single letter and for the 'cutting edge' (both: *harf*). They are united by a cultural practice specific to Semitic cultures: the cutting and sharpening of the reed cane once used for writing (in German: *Schreibrohr*).[19] The Hebrew (*charf*) led to the German *scharf* (dating back to the eighth century AD) and most probably the English *sharp*. This calligraphy-inspired term for craftsmanship also etymologically connects with the Arabic term for 'customer.' The *hirafī* is a craftsman with gifted talents, in the sense of an artisan who creates a valuable piece of work for someone else and still understands his work as *service*—to both God and the public. A member of a guild is likewise named *hirafī*. Both Arabic words used for the translation of 'craftsmanship'—*fann* and *hirfā*—also exist in combination in order to enhance the professionalism of the work: *fannan al hirafi* means a masterly skilled, i.e. experienced and rule-based working artisan/craftsman, compared to a simple tinkerer or freely experimenting (fine) artist.

In the above-mentioned Arabic term for 'craftsmanship' the semantic term 'hand' (Arabic: *yadd*) does not occur, compared to the term *manufacture* (from Latin *manus* for 'hand'), the English *handcraft* or the German *Handwerk*. The common Western concept of technics as organ projection, derived from thinkers of idealism (G. W. F. Hegel, Ernst Kapp) and meaning that technics is an extension and projection of human organs (foremost of the hand), is foreign to Arabic culture. From a perspective of historical anthropology, the hand in Arabic culture occurs in four semantic fields vaguely related to technics: a) the healing hand of the medical doctor, b) the gifted hand of the musician who is able to create harmony by means of a musical instrument, c) the hand of the Muslim who washes himself before praying and d) the hand of the trader who deals with money and credit, and signs contracts associated with property.

Only in the last years has the word 'hand' been used as an addition to demarcate the high quality of manual work compared to the standardized products of industrial production (an analogy to the West). Of course, there are Arabic words for the different types of craftsmen (carpenter, etc.), but the general term *craftsman* (or German: *Handwerker*) that in early modern times of the West separated manually made crafts for sustaining everyday life from the singularity and luxury of artistic work (once united in the Latin term *artifex*) does not exist as such. On the contrary, with *hirfā* the Arabic language stresses the double meaning of *technics* that Western cultures originally found in ancient Greek and Roman times: craftsman and artist as one person who creates something artificial which is *both* beautiful and useful for public purposes, and sometimes even strives for higher purposes (as, e.g., in building a dome in the medieval times of Europe, or in transcribing the holy words of the Quran in a calligraphic manner).

The aforementioned observations influence interior relations between science and technology because in Arabic, the craftsman is not strictly separated from the engineer, the *mohándis*. The word derives from *hándasa*, meaning: geometry. This implies that in the Arabic understanding the engineer is not someone who has a God-given inspiration (In Latin: *ingenium*), but rather someone who makes practical use of a world that is already understood as ordered according to measure and number. The academically institutionalized engineering sciences are named *hándasa tadhbiqíya* تطبيقيةهندسة , which literally means 'practical geometry.' In this understanding, it is easy to cross the line towards teaching *projective geometry* (non-Euclidean geometry), which has revolutionized engineering education in the West since the late nineteenth century and has also been inspired by art (and vice versa).

One thing remains very obvious: the Arabic word for 'creativity' (*mubdiā*) has no etymological relation to the semantic fields of crafting, making or engineering. Its lingual root relates to God as the *originator* (of the heavens and the earth, see Quran 6:101). To conclude, all forms of crafting and engineering in the Arabic cultural sense follow a *mimetic* concept of human creations, not an *innovative* concept related to genius thinking by a person ('engineer') other than God.

Conclusion

The teaching of technology-related subjects should respect the technological culture of a region and therefore has to adjust to mentalities and language. In particular, STEM-education has to make use of what Immanuel Kant once called the 'intelligible intuition.' By itself it is non-empirical and a predecessor for 'understanding.' For the cultures of the Arab world, it makes sense to address the goal of bringing *beautiful utility* to the world rather than industrialization, innovation and production. This would also make sense in the light of global discussions on the future of STEM, where the idea that the label 'STEM' also touches on culture and design questions and therefore engaged researchers and teachers might want to include the *arts* and humanities (transforming STEM into 'STEAM'), has already cropped up.[20]

In the Arab world, the prospect of working manually and for the sake of improving overall 'functionality' will not persuade students to engage in technical subjects (as is obviously also the case in Western countries); and materially working with 'the hand' is still seen as something for the lower classes to do by the male elite (similar to the mentality of the elite in ancient Greece). *Music, medicine, nature* and *trade* are main areas to now focus on—and culture-sensitive STEM-education can make use of these fields, e.g., physics and engineering explaining their laws and principles with the example of the musical instrument and the different materials involved. Other STEM-topics that make both economic and cultural sense for students in the region of the Arab peninsula are: solar energy, civil engineering and water-related technologies, including those working towards sustainable agriculture and environmental protection.[21] In addition, in recent years, students, particularly female students, have already shown significant interest in computer science (especially cryptography) and medicine (Karafyllis 2013), the latter subject advancing the extensive insights of Arab-Persian medicine that until early modern times was highly respected and adopted by Europe (foremost the writings of Avicenna/Ibn Sina). Focussing on medicine training might also transform the antipathy towards 'manual culture,' as well as fulfil the countries' needs for better healthcare. In order to further enhance the technological literacy of the region, it is recommended that school and student projects focussing on observation and navigation technologies are also encouraged, as these relate back to Bedouin culture. For the Mediterranean Arab cultures,[22] the teaching and learning situation is different and can more easily adjust to the cultural traditions of southern Europe.

In addition, public media are of crucial importance for STEM-education. In recent years, the Gulf states (the so-called 'GCC countries') have increasingly shown science documentaries on TV. Particularly popular in the Arab world, the 2009 BBC production *Science and Islam* starred the renowned British-Iraqi physicist Jim Al Khalili. He was officially invited to talk about science at the *Emirates Airline Festival of Literature* (4–8 March 2014), where the ruler of Dubai, Sheikh Mohammed bin Rashid al Maktoum, was reading his poetry. Asked about his vision by journalists from monthly periodical *What's On Dubai*, Khalili said: 'I want to inspire people with the beauty of science and a rational view of the world.'[23] Again, culturally, beauty matters with regard as to how rational knowledge is acquired and accepted *as* rational.

The problem of language of instruction, however, remains the same across today's Arab world. Local teachers, having to use English as the language of instruction, need to be trained in how to *suitably* translate the scientific terms, thereby moving towards inquiry-based learning. Merely adopting English terms is counterproductive to the scientific aim of inquiry, which in the Arab region is itself a challenge (see, for example, Richardson 2004). There are great ambitions for intelligent teacher training, which up until now has not been able to avoid using resources from the Western world, including text books, for most subjects. Scientific publishing houses with rigorous editorial standards and peer review are still rare in the Arab world. In the future, there should be the goal of building interdisciplinary teams of scientists and engineers who will work together with philosophers[24] and historians of science and technology, in order to create learning materials that—if used by curious students—actually *make sense*.

Notes

1 I thank my Palestinian philosophy colleague Dr. Raja Bahlul (teaching in the UAE and Qatar) for helpful comments on the language situation regarding the concept of 'technology' in the Arab world.

2 On some of the structural differences between science and technology, see Poser (1998). It is almost a consensus among current researchers in STS (Science and Technology Studies) that in the light of experimental cultures, being dependent on apparatuses and measurement techniques, science can be seen as 'applied technology,' rather than vice versa. Hubig, Huning and Ropohl (2013) give an excellent overview of the various positions regarding what 'technics' and 'technology' can mean, also in relation to science.

3 The locus classicus of this view is Bloch (1935), focussing on the various transformations of the water wheel and related mill-systems.

4 For clarifying the intercultural state of the problem of a 'technogenetic theory of culture' (Kapp 1877) one would first need to analyse the specific validity of the norms implemented in genesis and design of both technology and culture. However, this has not yet been feasible. Many works in the history and sociology of technology have shown that technological developments in Europe and North America incorporated normative contingencies, a phenomenon which John Law (1989) described as 'heterogeneous engineering.'

5 This view contrasts, as historian Akos Paulinyi (1999) has highlighted, with the idea of 'revolutions' in the history of technology. See also Engel und Karafyllis (2004).

6 When I address science, I still focus on what in STS is called 'mode 1 science,' i.e. a concept of science that is driven by searching for truth rather than commercial applications of the related knowledge.

7 The three programmes were on the website of the EIAST from 2006 to 2012 (quotations given here relate to that period, see the links in Karafyllis 2013). Since then, and since the launch of the two national satellites (Dubai Sat-1, in the orbit since 2009, followed by Dubai Sat-2), the space programme remains the dominant initiative, according to the EIAST-website: http://www.eiast.ae [Accessed 5 October 2014].

8 See Karafyllis (2013) for the now outdated Internet references from December 2011.

9 Spain at that time was not regarded as a highly industrialized country.

10 See e.g. Fieldhouse (2006) on this crucial aspect for the self-understanding of the modern Middle East.

11 For the building of concepts in science, there exists extensive literature on the ways that metaphors have shaped scientific inquiry and discipline-formation (see, for example, the writings of US-American historian of biology Evelyn Fox Keller).

In her renowned work *Membranes*, Laura Otis (1999) has shown how the image of the cell in relation to political concepts of invasion and nation state became a leading metaphor for nineteenth century physiology, furthermore influenced by literature.

12   In the meantime, the aforementioned Wikipedia-translation of 'technology' with *taqnía* from 13 June 2011 has been erased.

13   In oral form (and also printed in newspapers) the phonetic assimilation of the English 'technology' has recently become common in Arabic (تكنولوجيا; pronounced: tiqnulúgia), similar to the Arabized words of the English 'telephone,' 'television,' 'telescope' and 'cinema.' Most often, the newly Arabized word for 'technology' denotes electronics and digitalization (understood in a broad sense) in ordinary spoken language.

14   The Arabic Wikipedia (Accessed 1 June 2014) shows *taqāna* for the English 'technology' and the German 'Technologie.' In the Pakistani language Urdu, similar to both Arabic and Persian, 'technology' is translated as *tarzyāt*, related to the Italian *intarsia* (same in English; German: *Intarsie*), i.e. the systematic way of creating a mosaic or wood inlaying. See the Wikipedia-Website of 'technology' in Urdu: http://ur.wikipedia.org/wiki/%D8%B7%D8%B1%D8%B2%DB%8C%D8%A7%D8%AA.

15   In Europe, Kapp's book is regarded as the founding document of modern philosophy of technology.

16   Sass lists five concepts of technics as an agglomeration of tools, from which the first three have been taken from Schelsky (1961): 1. 'techniques of production' (related to the machine), 2. 'techniques of organization' (incl. administration), 2. 'Human-techniques' (incl. psychology). Sass (1978: VII) adds 4. 'techniques of individual self-sustenance' and 5. 'techniques for orientation,' which include religious and metaphysical forms of orientation in alliance with science ('scientific worldview').

17   As the Arabic language has no neutrum, the Freudian distinction between 'I' and 'It' is difficult to bring into appearance. French philosopher Paul Ricœur (1996), dwelling upon the Latin semantic difference of idem and ipse (both for 'self'), showed that the so-called idem-identity guarantees a person being the same in space and time, i.e. the person understands itself as the same throughout its life (similar to the Arabic word *dhāt*). On the contrary, the ipse-identity of a person questions this sameness in a hermeneutic and intentional way, i.e. it helps to envision oneself as another, and thereby envisions the possibility of a future-oriented self-creation. This ontological construction of the modern Self is crucial for the Western, primarily Protestant ethics, as both the concepts of 'responsibility' and 'conscience' operate with this Self-construction. In STEM-education, these differences show with regard to programmes for ethics of technology and technology assessment not only in the Middle East (see Karafyllis 2013), but also in the cultures of the Far East.

18   See Al-Issa (2010) on this topic.

19   See Mitterauer (2006) for the intercultural knowledge exchanges accompanying the artefact 'Schreibrohr.'

20   See the initiative 'STEM to STEAM,' championed by the Rhode Island School of Design (RISD) at http://stemtosteam.org [Accessed 5 October 2014].

21   Gari (2002) showed that Arab cultures have a long history of implementing principles for environmental protection. In Karafyllis (2013), I further develop how the UAE's people became interested in solar energy techniques in recent years.

22   One might remember that the city of Cairo was the first in the world to host a hospital (the Qasr el-Aini).

23   *What's On Dubai*, 3/2014 (March): 48. Khalili staged and designed the BBC4 production *Science and Islam*. (2009). Episode 1: The Language of Science, Episode 2: The Empire of Reason, Episode 3: The Power of Doubt. See http://www.bbc.co.uk/programmes/b00gq6h7 [Accessed 4 September 2014].

24   I have written on the challenges in teaching philosophy in the UAE, in Karafyllis (2014).

Bibliography

Al-Issa, Ihsan (ed.) (2010): *Al-Junun: Mental Illness in the Islamic World*. International Universities Press, Madison.

Bentham, Jeremy (1789): *An Introduction to the Principles of Morals and Legislation*. Clarendon Press, Oxford.

Balick, Michael J. and Paul Alan Cox (1996): *Plants, People, and Culture: The Science of Ethnobotany*. W. H. Freeman & Co, New York.

Bloch, Marc Léopold Benjamin (1935): Avènement et conquêtes du moulin à eau, *Annales d'histoire èconomique et sociale* 7. Pp. 538–563.

Blumenberg, Hans (2009): *Geistesgeschichte der Technik. Texte aus dem Nachlass*. Suhrkamp, Frankfurt am Main.

EIAST (Emirates Institution for Advanced Science and Technology) (2014): Khalifa Sat Project Expected into Earth's Orbit by 2017, available from http://eiast.ae/en/news/khalifa-sat-project-expected-into-earths-orbit-by-2017 [Accessed 13 October 2014].

Engel, Gisela and Nicole C. Karafyllis (2004): Technik und Moderne. In: *Technik in der Frühen Neuzeit – Schrittmacher der europäischen Moderne*, edited by Gisela Engel and Nicole C. Karafyllis. Vittorio Klostermann, Frankfurt (Main). Pp. 237–244.

Fakhry, Majid (1994): *Ethical Theories in Islam*. Brill, Leiden.

Ferré, Frederick (1988): *Philosophy of Technology*. University of Georgia Press, Englewood Cliffs (NJ).

Fieldhouse, David K. (2006): *Western Imperialism in the Middle East 1914–1958*. Oxford University Press, Oxford.

Gari, Lutfallah (2002): Arabic Treatises on Environmental Pollution up to the End of the Thirteenth Century, *Environment and History* 8 (4). Pp. 475–488.

Hubig, Christoph and Hans Poser (eds) (2007): *Technik und Interkulturalität*. VDI-Report 36. VDI-Verlag, Düsseldorf.

Hubig, Christoph, Alois Huning and Günter Ropohl (eds) (2013): *Nachdenken über Technik. Die Klassiker der Technikphilosophie und neuere Entwicklungen*. Edition Sigma, Berlin.

International Society of Ethnobiology (2014): Who We Are, available from http://ethnobiology.net/about/ [Accessed 10 October 2014].

Kapp, Ernst (1877): *Grundlinien einer Philosophie der Technik: Zur Entstehungsgeschichte der Cultur aus Neuen Gesichtspunkten*. Verlag Georg Westermann, Braunschweig.

Karafyllis, Nicole C. (2009): Homo faber/Technik. In: *Handbuch Anthropologie: Der Mensch zwischen Natur, Kultur und Technik*, edited by Eike Bohlken and Christian Thies. Verlag J.B. Metzler, Stuttgart and Weimar. Pp. 340–344.

Karafyllis, Nicole C. (2013): Zum Verhältnis von Ethik und Technik in internationaler Perspektive: das Beispiel arabische Golfstaaten. In: *Ethisierung der Technik – Technologien der Ethik*, edited by Alexander Bogner. Nomos, Baden-Baden. pp. 117–143.

Karafyllis, Nicole C. (2014): Brief aus Abu Dhabi. Section: Briefe über Philosophie weltweit, *Deutsche Zeitschrift für Philosophie* 61 (4). pp. 750–764.

Law, John (1989): Technology and Heterogeneous Engineering: The Case of Portuguese Expansion. In: *The Social Construction of Technological Systems: New Directions in the Sociology and History of Technology*, edited by Wiebe E. Bijker, Thomas P. Hughes and Trevor Pinch. MIT Press, Cambridge (MA). Pp. 111–134.

Mitterauer, Michael (2006): Schreibrohr und Druckerpresse. Transferprobleme einer Kommunikationstechnologie zwischen Europa und dem islamischen Raum. Presentation held at the Kurie Wissenschaft des Österreichischen Ehrenzeichens für Wissenschaft und Kunst.

Ortega y Gasset, José (Orig. 1932/1939): Meditación de la técnica. In: *Obras completas (1946–1983)*, tome IV, Espasa-Calpe, Madrid. Pp. 551–607. (In German) Ortega y Gasset, José (1978): Betrachtungen über die Technik. In: *Gesammelte Werke, Bd. 4*. Transl. Else Görner et al. Deutsche Verlags-Anstalt, Stuttgart. Pp. 7–69).

Otis, Laura (1999): *Membranes. Metaphors of Invasion in Nineteenth-Century Literature, Science and Politics*. The Johns Hopkins University Press, Baltimore and London.

Paulinyi, Akos (1999): Revolution und Technik. In: *Gibt es Revolutionen in der Geschichte der Technik? / Tagungsband*, edited by Siegfried Buchhaupt. Präsident der Technischen Universität Darmstadt, Darmstadt.

Pfenning, Uwe and Ortwin Renn (eds) (2012): *Wissenschafts- und Technikbildung auf dem Prüfstand. Zum Fachkräftemangel und zur Attraktivität der MINT-Bildung und Berufe im europäischen Vergleich*. Nomos, Baden Baden.

Plessner, Helmuth (1974): *Die verspätete Nation*. Suhrkamp, Frankfurt am Main.

Poser, Hans (1998): On Structural Differences between Science and Engineering, *Philosophy and Technology 4 (2)*. Pp. 81–93.

Richardson, Patricia M. (2004): Possible Influences of Arabic-Islamic Culture on the Reflective Practices Proposed for an Education Degree at the Higher Colleges of Technology in the United Arab Emirates, *International Journal of Educational Development 24 (4)*. Pp. 429–436.

Ricœur, Paul (1996): *Das Selbst als ein Anderer*. Wilhelm Fink Verlag, Paderborn and München.

Ropohl, Günter (2009): *Allgemeine Technologie: Eine Systemtheorie der Technik*. Universitätsverlag Karlsruhe, Karlsruhe.

Sass, Hans-Martin (1978): Einführung in die Technik-Philosophie. In: *Grundlinien einer Philosophie der Technik*, by Ernst Knapp. Stern Verlag, Düsseldorf. Pp. V–XXXVIII.

Schelsky, Helmut (1961): *Der Mensch in der technischen Zivilisation*. Westdeutscher Verlag, Köln and Opladen.

Sennett, Richard (2008): *The Craftsman*. Yale University Press, New Haven (CT).

Stöcklein, Ansgar (1969): *Leitbilder der Technik: Biblische Tradition und technischer Fortschritt*. Moos, München.

Straub, Detmar W., Karen D. Loch and Carole E. Hill (2003): Transfer of Information Technology to the Arab World: A Test of Cultural Influence Modeling. In: *Advanced Topics of Global Information Management*, edited by Felix Tan. Idea Group Publishing, Hershey (PA). Pp. 141–172.

Tibi, Bassam (2005): *Islam Between Culture and Politics*. Palgrave Macmillan, Houndmills.

VDI (Verein Deutscher Ingenieure) and acatech (2009): Nachwuchsbarometer Technikwissenschaften. Düsseldorf. Available from http://www.acatech.de/fileadmin/user_upload/Baumstruktur_nach_Website/Acatech/root/de/Publikationen/Sonderpublikationen/NaBaTech_Bericht_Final_210709_einzel.pdf [Accessed 7 October 2014].

Wehr, Hans and J. Milton Cowan (1979): *A Dictionary of Modern Written Arabic*. (Arabic/English). Wiesbaden.

2 Universals in STEM education

Interview with Heinz Duddeck (engineer) and Randolf Menzel (biologist)

Mr. Duddeck and Mr. Menzel: What do 'universals' in STEM education mean to you?

Duddeck: The concept of 'universals' can be characterized, in the tradition of philosophy, as talking about the general in the multiplicity of phenomena (e.g. the tree in technical terms or love by categories). It is philosophically shaped through scholasticism's problem of universals, which disputed whether universals were merely Platonic ideas or realistic generic notions, or merely linguistic nominalist designations. Edmund Husserl defines such concepts phenomenologically as empirical universalities that are also subject to disconfirmation procedures. When it comes to universals in the sciences, general, non-subjective validity is something that can only be aimed for. The same applies for the linguistic termini in the sciences. As I see it, the concept of 'universals' is abundantly over-fraught, philosophically and historically. It is a concept that essentially also includes values that are culturally dependent, per se. In the context of the topic of this book, it is perhaps too broadly defined and can be misunderstood. I would therefore suggest a more modest approach to its formulation. At any rate, I recommend that we concentrate on those aspects where the cultural roots of STEM education are not at the forefront, and ask ourselves what exactly they are and what shapes them.

Menzel: Essentially, from my understanding, the concept of universals in our context is not philosophically-historically intended, but instead quite practical, with respect to the empirical sciences. We can ask ourselves which cognitive processes and which forms of conveyance of said thought processes are valid for all people within the constraints of empirical experience, regardless of their cultural and historical involvement. Let us, for a start, talk about everyday life, our daily life as scientists and educators. When I take part in a conference in China, Japan, Australia, Brazil or South Korea, we not only speak one language (a sort of international English), but we also make use of the same modes of thought such that we can communicate to each other measurement results, their mathematical process and their integration into hypotheses and conclusions. We do this because the rules of empirically proven thought are independent of the actual cultural sphere in which these thoughts are being examined. When I plan an experiment in cooperation with a colleague in China, it is entirely irrelevant whether the experiment is conducted in China or Germany and whether the experimenter is informed by a Western or Eastern cultural sphere. Even the apparatuses that we use and that have a critical impact on our way of thinking function in the same way all over the world; and when they are repaired or developed further, it does not matter if the mechanics or engineers do it in one country or another.

The situation is also no different when it comes to the communication of empirical evidence. If I want to convey what we currently know about the workings of the human and animal nervous systems to either Australian, Japanese, Brazilian or German pupils and students, then I present the very same empirical findings, use the same formal descriptions and use the exact same rules of logical deduction. The didactic and pedagogic methods used to convey such empirical findings also do not differ between cultural circles.

The universals that come into play here are firstly shaped by the fact that the physical, chemical and biological principles of nature are independent of their geographic location. The laws of nature apply all over our globe (whether this is true above and beyond our globe is not something we wish to discuss here, as we are not familiar with any cultural sphere other than our globe). Secondly, there are cognitive universals at work that are related to our nature as human beings. Charles Darwin informed us that there is a historical continuum in the evolutionary development of living things. Acting organisms, animals including humans, have evolutionarily adapted their guiding behavioural apparatus, their nervous system and brain, to perceive the world such that events are not merely recognized, but also interpreted within their cause and effect framework. Because ultimately, with all this behaviour and action, what it comes down to is predicting the future from the past as reliably as possible. Our roots in the evolution of animals equip us with an exceedingly comprehensive behavioural apparatus, whereby the guiding principles differ only marginally between animal and human. All cultural evolution is embedded in biological evolution. Nothing can be subject to a cultural evolution without having first gone through the filter of the biological apparatus.

Duddeck: On that note, I agree with you. Cultural groups have certainly made various contributions to the knowledge of natural laws: astronomy in Babylon, mathematics and geometry in Greece, medicine and algebra in Arabia, magnetism in China, experimental methods of natural inquiry in Europe. However, through trade routes and, today, globalization, they have become the property of all peoples. Not just the results of the natural sciences, but also the paths to knowledge acquisition, and the methods and logical ways of thinking, are, due to their effectiveness, common knowledge and therefore independent of culture. There is no 'Chinese' or 'German' physics, but simply the physics of Newton and Einstein. And only these can be taught.

Insights from the natural sciences are not, however, universal truths, but simply empirical truths. They must simply satisfy the condition of providing the same answers to experimental inquiries anywhere in the world. Today, all participating nations are contributing to this culturally independent knowledge. The field of the natural science interpretation of the world is expanding internationally at an ever-accelerating pace (e.g. Cosmos, gene biology).

Strongly influenced by cultures, however, are the shrinking reserves, where nature and the world are explained through religious miracles, spirits and meta-physical powers, areas that we here, with a view to STEM education, are excluding.

Added to this are further arguments. Since the time of Galileo's mathemati-zation of physics, science and technology have developed their own languages, which are superior to spoken language in terms of precision and unambiguousness (i.e. as in the humanities). These include, among others, differential equations, chemical formulas, computer programmes and pictorial representations. If the meaning of the symbols has been precisely defined, then these languages are understood internationally. And thus, the associated unifying thought structures of science and technology are also incorporated into all cultures. For only in this way can one grasp the general laws and processes described by formulas. Anglicisms, for example, with their restrictive meaning, allow for a specification and precision that is not attainable in the native languages. Because of these specialized science languages, for the purposes of teaching (education), it does not matter whether one is explaining the benzene ring, Maxwell's equations or tensorial Riemann's geometry in Chinese or Arabic or Portuguese. The situa-tion is somewhat different when it comes to engineering: when you cross over into technical/engineering actions where society comes into effect, then verbal language is absolutely indispensable. That being said, cultural influences impact technology in more ways than simply from a language standpoint. I will discuss this further below.

Why then are the models of thought used by the natural sciences to try to explain the world the same in all cultures?

Menzel: Cognitive psychology and neuroscience can shed enlightening insights on this subject. Neuroscience draws its insights from comparative studies of many different animal species, which in this biological sense also includes humans. This approach is not a reflection of the downgrading of humans, but rather places them in the historical course of events of biological evolution. For the line of reasoning in neuroscience, it is important that the molecular, cellular and the network of nerve cell-determined processes in animal and human brains do not differ significantly. Animals, like humans, must perceive the world in such a way that they adapt their behaviour as best possible (in an evolutionary sense) to the structure and characteristics of this world. Even animals learn, form long-term memories and direct their attention to external and internal conditions. Many animal species anticipate outcomes and plan their behaviour on the basis of multiple learning processes. They experience positive (happy) and negative (unpleasant) conditions and adjust their behaviour accordingly. They communi-cate with one another in multiple ways and take into account their individual experiences with the environment and those in a social context. Although they do not possess language in a human sense, their forms of communication are extensive and adaptable. The evaluation of whether there are animal species where individuals in the social community teach each other and learn from one another is dependent upon an understanding of such 'teaching methods,' and need not be further discussed here. Regardless, following the cognitive turning point in behavioural and neurosciences, there is no question that many animal species possess mental states that comprise essential elements that correspond to our own introspective and subjective experiences.

The evolutionary continuity of mental process in animals and humans tells us that the way of perceiving the world and the knowledge of its rules is not arbitrary, but rather an expression for the brain's adaptation to the world in which it operates. Although in humans these basal processes can, in fact, lead to the limits of their worldly experience and to constructs that lack empirical reference, these are beyond the scope of the natural sciences and need not concern us further here. A feature of the empirical sciences is the fact that they make the most concerted efforts to extend the limits of world experience through the use of devices and mathematical formalisms and then test the derived expectations (hypotheses). No cultural tradition based on a limited or contradictory world experience will be able to resist this need for explanation in the long run, because the need rests upon the control of the world itself. A bacterial infection can be cured by an appropriate antibiotic and not by a ritual ceremony; a bridge will be able to withstand the load of a heavy freight train when all calculations have been done correctly and not when it has been inaugurated.

Knowledge is stored and retrievable memory. 'The power of memory is great, very great, my God, a temple, of vast and infinite profundity [. . .] This power is that of my mind and is a natural endowment.' (Aurelius Augustinus, *Confessions*). This temple is the brain, *the* part of our body that makes us what we are, that allows the future to come from the past, and that, despite its intellect-enabling characteristics, represents a living organ, so is subject to the laws of biology (and thus also the laws of physics). Because the contents of memory are widely dispersed and interconnected in the brain, the act of remembering is a constructive process and indeed one of discovery (Baddeley 1986). The fact that this constructive remembering activates the reward system explains why knowledge is, in itself, already an exhilarating experience, and even more so when the application of knowledge brings about a confirmation of expectations and new insights.

Is there a biology of learning and teaching, i.e. universals of learning and didactics that can be traced back to a biologically explained set of rules?

Menzel: The biology of learning and teaching is still in its infancy, despite the intensive and in many areas successful work of cognitive neuroscience. We understand a lot on a molecular and small neuronal network level, but understanding the biological rationale for particularly effective learning is still some way off (see also Menzel 2012). All the same, cognitive neuroscience can confirm and provide some explanation for rules that were already part of the Roman School of Rhetoric 2,000 years ago. The last great rhetorician Quintilian (AD35–96) formulated such rules in his most important work 'Institutio oratoria', and in it references Cicero, whose rules he expanded upon and condensed into practical recommendations. For him, the focus is on the 'learning man,' his interests and his active concern.

The following eight rules cover a good portion of his message: 1. Arouse attention, 2. Stimulate curiosity, 3. Tie into what is familiar, 4. Involve as many sensory experiences as possible, 5. Repetition is the mother of wisdom, 6. Do as much as possible yourself ('grasp'), 7. Do not learn too much at once and spread out your practice, 8. Make the settings for learning and recall as similar as possible. These rules have been valid for 2,000 years (and had their application even before), and although they were developed in ancient Roman society, they are still valid today in all parts of the world. It also does not matter what content is being learned and taught. Even animals learn according to such rules, and cognitive neuroscience can offer some good rationale for the validity of the rules, even if it can not necessarily explain it yet in a mechanistic sense. Such universals of knowledge acquisition and knowledge transfer are based on the functioning of our brain (and that of animals). Further rules will be added, such as the importance of a good diet, the need for a stimulating environment and the role that sleep plays in consolidating memory. Specifically human forms of verbally and mathematically conveyed knowledge acquisition allow for the assigning of capacities and failure to certain areas of the brain, an opportunity to make use of early, compensatory training strategies. Although the bridge between neuroscience and pedagogy is still weak, preliminary fruitful approaches demonstrate just how strong they will become in the future.

Is technology education less international than science education?

Duddeck: The answer to this is a discriminating yes/no. The societal environment, particularly the economy of a country, can determine specific preferences for the technologies that are taught at universities. The technological level of development may also be reflected in this. Once one has decided upon the choice of subjects, though, the contents and the teaching and learning methods of technical curricula are largely the same, so are international.

Bridge engineering is an exemplary demonstration of this: the Chinese Ministry of Transport decides to build a suspension bridge over the Hwangho (Yellow River). The engineers investigate the building site, gather all possible local information that currently exists about floods, hurricanes and earthquakes, plus all information available internationally regarding experiences, collapses, damage and developmental trends. The various possible design variants of the bridge are evaluated in static calculation models for maximal impact scenarios of the stresses of typhoon, earthquake, traffic prognoses, etc. During the iteration process, the optimal form and construction of the bridge and its phases of construction are determined. Now, they can be designed in detail for construction, which will possibly be carried out by an international building consortium.

The detailed drawings are internationally readable. These processes of designing and constructing technical artefacts are structured in the same way in all technologies. Even the making of related models is independent of culture. And, as such, technology education is no different in Stanford than it is in Cairo.

Menzel: PISA (Programme for International Student Assessment) and TIMSS (Trends in International Mathematics and Science Study) can be implemented in all countries and are recognized by all countries as benchmarks of STEM education. This is, perhaps, a particularly convincing argument for the importance of universals in STEM education. It is not the cultural traditions of the respective countries that matter, but rather the knowledge and ability levels of the pupils and students. This is not to say, however, that such test programmes and their subsequent conclusions are acknowledged equally in all cultures. Of course they are not, since attitudes towards records of achievement, competition and testing are largely contingent upon the economic situation of both the individual and of the entire country, as well as on familial, religious and cultural traditions.

Some cultures are well over 1,000 years old. Does this not influence their science and technology?

Duddeck: The difference to the humanities is great. Philosophers immediately think back to Plato. Historians ask what the Athenian democracy can teach us in the present day. Cicero provides a model for language education. Engineers, on the other hand—and even most natural scientists—are rather ahistorical. They do not have to refer back to the evolution of their discipline in order to understand or explain their insights. Application requires only the most recent state of knowledge. The present-day BMW engine, for example, captures virtually the entire course of engine development, even though this development is not made explicit. If other technologies are acquired (for example, from China), the most recent developmental step is introduced, regardless of how it came about. No loss of technical and economic profit is involved. The acquisition process is subject to virtually no cultural restrictions. So it is of little importance how old the country's culture is.

Menzel: Human cultures have (only) developed over the last 20,000 years—a very short time when one considers the more than 5 million years of the development of the human being and the biological evolution of animals that has been taking place over many hundreds of million years. Science and technology is a specialized form of the empirical experience of the world. The specialization does not decouple them from the biological evolution of man and renders them only marginally dependent upon cultural evolution.

But are there not major differences in the assessment of technology in the different countries on this earth?

Duddeck: Yes. Because inherent in the assessment are values of what should be. Here the cultural influence is strong. Science and technology alter the living environment greatly. Therefore, a societal dispute of, for example, which technologies should be promoted and to what intensity is inevitable. Values, as a general rule, are not constants (perhaps with the exception of religiously laid-out ones, an area we will not get into here). They often transmit the entire history of a country. Moreover, in the richness and complexity of a society, they are mostly pluralistic, and therefore compete with one another. Questionnaires show—for obvious reasons—that worldwide, the advanced nations are rather sceptical of an excess of technology, whereas the developing countries are rather in favour. A shift in values often then comes about when a learning process (for example, China's environmental problems) compels other priorities.

Consequently, the content and methods of Science and Technology are largely culturally independent, but not so their implementation in society. With a strong influence on values, this may strongly shape STEM-education.

Menzel: The significant correlation between the results of standardized performance criteria for the level of training in STEM subjects and the GDP of the respective country has led to the implication that there is a causal relationship between scientific and technical education and a country's industrial performance capacity (Hanushek and Woessmann 2008). However, this conclusion must take into account that only the immediate effects on the GDP are factored in, and that long-term effects are not captured. As such, for a country's long term productivity and prosperity, it will be crucial for ecological perspectives to be of equal importance to economic perspectives, as only a sound environment contributes to the well-being of the population (Donovan *et al.* 2014) and will therefore influence society's stance on technical products. The question of how sensitively the population reacts to these relationships is certainly dependent upon political factors and cultural traditions. In the global context, it will be important to agree upon intercultural standards, and thus compensate for the potentially one-sided focus on economic objectives.

Bibliography

Baddeley, Alan D. (1986): *Working Memory*. Clarendon Press, Oxford.

Donovan, Brian M. *et al.* (2014): Revising the Economic Imperative for US STEM Education, *PLOS Biology* 12 (1). Pp. 1–5.

Hanushek, Eric A. and Ludger Woessmann (2008): The Role of Cognitive Skills in Economic Development, *Journal of Economic Literature* 46 (3). Pp. 607–668.

Menzel, Randolf (2012): Zweitausend Jahre Regeln des Wissenserwerbs im Licht der Neurowissenshaft. In: *Wissenschafts- und Technikbildung auf dem Prüfstand. Zum Fachkräftemangel und zur Attraktivität der MINT-Bildung und -Berufe im europäischen Vergleich*, edited by Uwe Pfenning and Ortwin Renn. Nomos, Baden-Baden. Pp. 61–72.

Part II

STEM education worldwide

Perspectives on situations
in six countries

3   The shift in public perception of science and science education in post-war Japan

Takuji Okamoto

Introduction

In 1868, right after the Meiji Restoration, Japan started to incorporate modern science in its education and culture on a much larger scale than before. By the end of World War II, this country had reached what can be called 'maturity' in scientific culture in its own way, though its perspectives were restricted by the rise of militarism, overemphasis of its monarchical, political and religious culture, and its varying sense of rivalry against Western civilization (Okamoto 2006). Partly by boosting this pre-war achievement in the effort to democratize and rebuild the country, which had been heavily damaged during World War II, the nation achieved economic growth between 1954 and 1973. In the following, I will discuss the shift in public perception of science and science education after this period.

Science and technology becoming unpopular in higher education

For the nation struggling to recover from defeat in World War II, science and technology was one of the country's most pressing concerns: politicians often admitted that Japan had lost the 'science war' represented by the atomic bomb; the Nobel Prize awarded to the particle physicist Yukawa in 1949 caused a boom for science; and cooperation of personnel from science, industry, government and military during the war resulted in the birth of new types of industrial technology in the post-war years. After the post-war economic growth, Japan suffered from the two so-called 'Oil Crises' in the 1970s; and yet, the number of young students who chose to major in engineering steadily increased during the 1980s as the national economy recovered from the damages that these caused. Though the proportion of students who applied for engineering departments slightly decreased between 1975 and 1981 (from 13 per cent to 11 per cent), it increased continuously between 1981 and 1986 (from 11 per cent to 17 per cent) (Agency of Science and Technology 1994a: Figure 1-1-3).

During the economic boom of the late 1980s, however, Japan saw the number of applicants for engineering departments at universities and colleges start to decrease. In 1989, 800,000 students applied for engineering, while in 2008, the number decreased to 530,000 (Agency of Science and Technology 1994a; MEXT 2010a: 65).

Engineering as a profession seemed to cease being attractive. For example, in the five years after 1989, the number of graduates from the Faculties of Science, Engineering and Agronomy at the University of Tokyo who chose to work in the financial industry increased rapidly; and, 37 per cent of those who graduated in 1992 found their jobs outside the manufacturing industry (Mainichi Shinbun Kagakukankyobu 2007: 108–109). Mitsutoshi Nishikawa pointed to future decreases in the number of science and/or engineering majors: the number was 360,000 (20 per cent of college or university students) in academic year 2000; 300,000 (15 per cent) in 2010; which would make it 250,000 (10 per cent) in 2018 (Hayashi 2010: 34).

Compared with other Western countries, Japan has a smaller number of doctoral degree holders per 1,000 people, especially in natural science and engineering (MEXT 2011a: 57). Despite the government's effort to encourage college graduates to study further for doctoral degrees in engineering and natural science, the number of students admitted to doctoral courses stopped increasing in 2001 (MEXT 2011a: 59). Since many doctoral degree holders in natural science look for jobs in academia, the proportion of PhD holders working for private corporations remains low (around 4 per cent).

The 'New Growth Strategy' (Cabinet Decision 2009) issued by the Democratic Party's cabinet in June 2010 pointed to the importance of human resources in science and technology as one of two platforms for the country's growth (the other being information technology). However, it admitted that the nation's expectations and esteem for science and technology waned as its growth proceeded, though Japan had achieved high growth by utilizing its scientific and technological capabilities. Based on this observation, the cabinet adopted policies to improve education in science and mathematics.

Personnel with scientific or engineering training

Several statistical surveys have revealed that those with scientific or engineering educational backgrounds are apparently rewarded unfairly when it comes to

Table 3.1 Numbers of doctoral degree holders in natural science per million people in selected countries (2005)

	A	B
Japan	109	56
United States	98	74
Germany	228	124
France	96	91
United Kingdom	188	144
South Korea	120	79

A: *The numbers of doctoral degree holders in medical, physical and agricultural sciences, engineering and technology.*
B: *The numbers of doctoral degree holders in physical and agricultural sciences, engineering and technology.*
Source: Adapted from MEXT 2011a: 58

promotion and income, when compared with those trained in human or social science, such as law, economics or literature. In 2001, a committee of the Liberal Democratic Party presented some quantitative evidence (Mainichi Shimbun Kagakukankyobu 2006: 29): out of 18 ministers in the cabinet, 14 (78 per cent) were from humanities or social sciences, while only 2 were from scientific or engineering fields; and among 31 secretary generals (heads of ministries) in the government, 27 (87 per cent) were from humanities or social science (mostly from law). Among the presidents of the top 2,143 private companies, 25 per cent were from economics, 21 per cent from law, 26 per cent from other branches of social science and only 28 per cent from science or engineering. Meanwhile, out of 22 presidents of the top companies in the United Kingdom, 54 per cent were from science or engineering; in Germany, 54 per cent; and in France, 55 per cent (Mainichi Shimbun Kagakukankyobu 2006: 31).

The first two prime ministers from the Democratic Party were trained in science and engineering: Yukio Hatoyama majored in engineering at the University of Tokyo and earned his PhD from Stanford University; and Naoto Kan studied applied physics at the Tokyo Institute of Technology. However, their careers as politicians or in the party had very little to do with their education: Hatoyama is from a famous family with a strongly political background, while Kan was known as an activist in civic movements (Hayashi 2010: 42).

In recent years, Kazuo Nishimura at Kyoto University has published different types of results from those mentioned above (Urasaka *et al.* 2010, 2011). He showed that the average annual income of graduates from scientific or engineering departments was 6,244,000 yen, while that of graduates from departments of human or social science 4,887,000 yen. The samples of his survey were 13,059 college graduates (aged 24 to 74 years). He also showed that among 3,790 graduates from scientific or engineering departments, those who favoured physics had higher incomes (6,609,000 yen) than those who preferred biology (5,766,000 yen) or chemistry (5,899,000 yen). Among the graduates in human or social science, those who had taken at least one maths exam at college entrance examinations (3,977) had higher annual incomes (5,430,000 yen on average) than those who had not (3,795 samples, 4,430,000 yen on average). Since his survey focuses on the samples' educational background regardless of their current occupation, its results may show the increasing variety of job opportunities for personnel trained in science or engineering. New job markets, such as the ones related to financial engineering or computational finance, may have newly opened for those with scientific educational backgrounds.

Public perception of science and technology

The relatively unfavourable situation in society for personnel with scientific or engineering backgrounds may be one of the reasons that science and technology have become unpopular in Japan. As shown in the following, the general trend of people continuing to lose interest in and enthusiasm over science and technology may be another significant cause.

Throughout the 1980s, people in their twenties continued to lose interest in news and topics related to science and technology, while those in their thirties, forties and sixties kept their interest in this field to almost the same precise degree. Surprisingly, those in their fifties showed an increased interest in science and technology during the same period: while in December 1981, 50 per cent of people in this age category said that they were interested in news and topics of science and technology, by November 1991, the number had risen to 65 per cent (Agency of Science and Technology 1994b: Figure 1-1-1).

The results of the nationwide statistical surveys on the national character of the Japanese, conducted over several years between 1953 and 2008, also show the shift in the social perception of science and technology (Nakamura *et al.* 2011). The general trends are:

1   An increasing number of people feel the need to preserve nature for the happiness of the human race, while fewer and fewer people prefer to 'conquer' it (Table 3.2);
2   More and more people believe that neither science nor religion can save human beings (Table 3.2). On the other hand, many still find science useful and are confident in Japan's presence in the field of science and technology;
3   Eighty to ninety per cent of people continue to find science useful in their daily life, at least to some extent (Table 3.4);
4   More than eighty per cent of people acknowledge that the level of science and technology in Japan is high or rather high (Table 3.5).

Japan experienced severe environmental pollution from the mid-1950s until the 1980s (George 2001). As people's concern about environmental issues grew, they

Table 3.2 People's perception of nature: the distribution of people's answers to the question, 'What must we do for human beings' happiness?' (%)

Year	Obey Nature	Utilize Nature	Conquer Nature	Other	Don't know
1953	26	41	23	1	8
1958	20	37	28	1	13
1963	19	40	30	1	10
1968	19	40	34	1	7
1973	31	45	17	1	7
1978	33	44	16	1	6
1983	36	47	11	1	1
1988	42	44	9	1	4
1993	48	38	7	0	7
1998	49	39	6	1	5
2003	45	43	5	2	6
2008	51	38	5	1	5

Source: Adapted from Nakamura et al. 2011: 53[1]

Table 3.3 The relation between religion and science: the distribution of people's answers to the question, 'Which can save human beings, science or religion?' (%)

	1953	1983	2008
Religion cannot save human beings. Only the progress of science can save human beings.	10	7	9
To save human beings, cooperation of religion and science is necessary.	63	54	49
The progress of science cannot save human beings. Only the power of religion can save human beings.	9	4	2
Neither science nor religion can save human beings.	8	27	32
Other	0	1	1
Don't know	9	7	8

Source: Adapted from Nakamura et al. 2011: 81

Table 3.4 Usefulness of science: the distribution of people's answers to the question, 'How useful are scientific discoveries and their applications in improving your daily life?' (%)

Year	Useful	To Some Extent	Not Useful	Other	Don't Know
1983	39	48	7	1	4
1993	47	41	6	0	6
1998	40	44	8	0	7
2003	38	44	9	0	8
2008	39	47	8	0	5

Source: Adapted from Nakamura et al. 2011: 133

Table 3.5 Level of science and technology in Japan: the distribution of people's answers to the question, 'How do you evaluate the current level of science and technology in Japan?' (%)

Year	Very Good	Somewhat Good	Somewhat Bad	Very Bad	Other	Don't Know
1973	33	49	6	2	0	10
1978	37	48	5	1	1	9
1988	43	45	4	1	0	7
1993	46	43	4	0	0	7
1998	24	57	10	1	0	8
2003	28	54	7	0	0	10
2008	35	51	6	1	0	6

Source: Adapted from Nakamura et al. 2011: 147

started to value the prospect of living in harmony with nature over conquering or utilizing it. Although they appreciate Japan's international presence in the field of science and technology, they seem to regard it as someone else's business.

Changes after March 11, 2011

The explosions of nuclear reactors in Fukushima and the behaviours and attitudes of some scientists and engineers in responsible positions after the great earthquake on March 11, 2011 damaged people's trust in science and technology immensely. The level of trust had not returned to what it was before the earthquake, by February 2012 (Table 3.6). Only 45 per cent believe that experts should lead research and development in science and technology (Table 3.7), while 39.4 per cent admit that human beings cannot control science and technology (Table 3.8). People seem to have ceased to believe that science and technology have the potential to solve current social or environmental problems (Table 3.9).

Nevertheless, although the proportion of people who answered 'Somewhat yes' to the question 'Do you find scientists' statements trustworthy?' was as low as 37.7 per cent in April 2011, within just a few months it rose to 60 per cent (May to June 2011) and remained so afterwards, while only 2.9 to 6.2 per cent answered 'Yes' to the same question during the same period. People seem to have reluctantly admitted that they have no choice but to accept scientists' statements as 'somewhat trustworthy.' By 2011, the nation had experienced events that represented various aspects of science and technology: antipathy towards nuclear weapons became apparent after 1954; serious health problems caused by pollution had brought about several famous lawsuit cases since the 1950s; Japan's strength in science and technology was understood to be one of the main thrusts in the economic growth it had experienced since the 1950s; and the number of Japanese Nobel Laureates steadily increased, particularly after 2000. Though the

Table 3.6 The Japanese public's trust in scientists: the distribution of people's answers to the question, 'Do you find scientists' statements trustworthy?' (%)

	Yes	Somewhat yes	Don't know	Somewhat no	No
Jan. to Feb. 2012	6.0	60.5	15.7	14.4	3.5
Oct. to Nov. 2011	6.2	58.0	20.7	13.0	2.2
May to Jun. 2011	5.8	60.5	17.1	12.3	4.4
Apr. 2011	2.9	37.7	31.2	22.6	5.6
Oct to Nov. 2010	15.9	68.6	10.4	4.3	0.9
May to Jun. 2010	11.5	46.4	13.2	7.9	3.1

Source: Adapted from MEXT 2013: 53, Section 2

Table 3.7 Can experts direct R&D and S&T? The distribution of people's answers to the question, 'Is it better for trained and experienced experts to determine the direction of research and development in science and technology?' (%)

	Agree	Somewhat agree	Can't say	Don't know	Somewhat disagree	Disagree
Dec. 2011	19.5	25.5	29.6	3.2	11.7	10.6
Nov. 2009	59.1	19.7	17.7	-	2.5	1.0

Source: Adapted from MEXT 2013: 54, Section 2

Table 3.8 Control of science and technology: the distribution of people's answers to the question, 'Do you agree that human beings cannot control science and technology?' (%)

	Agree	Somewhat agree	Can't say	Don't know	Somewhat disagree	Disagree
Dec. 2011	19.5	19.9	24.9	3.2	14.2	18.3
Nov. 2009	13.1	5.1	20.6	-	19.9	41.3

Source: Adapted from MEXT 2013: 59, Section 2

Table 3.9 The Japanese public's expectation toward science and technology: the distribution of people's answers to the question, 'Do you agree that further development in science and technology will solve emerging social problems such as resource/energy problems, environmental problems, water/food problems and infectious disease problems?' (%)

	Agree	Somewhat agree	Can't say	Don't know	Somewhat disagree	Disagree
Dec. 2011	20.2	42.2	-	7.0	23.4	7.1
Jan. 2010	36.5	38.6	-	6.0	14.1	4.7
Dec. 2007	28.6	33.5	7.7	4.5	17.3	8.3

Source: Adapted from MEXT 2013: 70, Section 2

accident at the reactors in Fukushima and some scientists and engineers' apparently irresponsible behaviour shook people's trust in science for a few months and made them somewhat more sceptical than before, this did not lead to judgement that the community of scientists and engineers as a whole would not live up to their current or future expectations.

Science at school

The statistical surveys conducted in the late 1980s and early 1990s show that the number of pupils who like to study science or find science interesting decreases as their grade advances (Agency of Science and Technology 1994c). Since the curriculum at elementary school emphasizes the importance of observation and experiment, the subject 'science' attracts pupils' interest. However, as the knowledge and skills of mathematics become more essential in studying science at junior high school and high school, pupils tend to avoid science. Or, around the ages when they have to choose their careers, pupils start to think of their future in the fields more closely related to humanities or social science, rather than those related to science or engineering.

In FY (fiscal year) 2012, MEXT (Ministry of Education, Culture, Sports, Science and Technology) started to include issues in science education in the nationwide surveys on the academic performance and learning situation (MEXT 2012; JST 2013a). Japanese pupils' perception of science as an academic subject as shown by these surveys is as follows (Tables 3.10 and 3.11): though Japanese pupils like to study science, they rate its importance and usefulness as lower than Japanese or mathematics; more pupils start to find it hard to understand science lessons at junior high school than Japanese or maths lessons. Roughly half of junior high school pupils answered in the negative to the question, 'Will studying science lead you to your preferred job?' (Table 3.12). This inclination does not appear all that different from that seen in other Western countries, as shown by Svein Sjøberg and Camilla Schreiner in 2007 and 2008 (Schreiner and Sjøberg 2007; Sjøberg and Schreiner 2008).

Table 3.10 Pupils' perception of the importance of subjects

	Elementary School			Junior High School		
	Science	Japanese	Maths	Science	Japanese	Maths
I like to study this subject.	82%	63%	65%	62%	58%	53%
It is important to study this subject.	86%	93%	93%	69%	90%	82%
What I learn at school in this subject will be useful when I start to work in society.	73%	89%	90%	53%	83%	71%

Source: Adapted from MEXT 2012: 2

Table 3.11 The percentage of pupils who replied 'Yes' to the question, 'Do you understand the lessons of Science/Japanese/maths?'

	Elementary	Junior High	Difference
Science	86%	65%	21%
Japanese	83%	72%	11%
Maths	79%	66%	13%

Source: Adapted from MEXT 2012: 2

Table 3.12 Will studying science lead you to your preferred job? (Study conducted Feb–Mar 2013 on 13,000 middle high school pupils)

Yes	Somewhat yes	Somewhat no	No	Don't know
11.0%	17.0%	22.8%	25.5%	23.2%

Source: Adapted from JST 2013a: 105

The responses of scientists and business leaders

For a few years after the economic boom abruptly ended in 1991, the younger generation returned to science and technology for their education and careers (MEXT 2010a: 65). As a result, fears of so-called 'Science and Technology Phobia' (Agency of Science and Technology 1994d) were slowly seen to be groundless, at least temporarily. However, the increasing attention paid to science phobia ignited a debate over another aspect of the same phenomenon: scientists and science teachers began expressing their concerns with the quality, not the quantity, of science and engineering majors at universities. They pointed to the lack of creativity, or the lack of ability to ask original questions (not simply finding the right answers to given problems), among students (Iwata 1999). In 1994, the Agency of Science and Technology also published a statistical survey revealing that the younger generation was enthusiastic about the use of the technological applications of scientific research but uninterested in their scientific principles or mechanisms (Agency of Science and Technology 1994e). In 1993 and 1994, academic societies such as the Science Council of Japan and the Physical Society of Japan publicly stated their concerns over the need to attract more students to science and technology and to reform science education at elementary and secondary levels (Iwata 1999: 592).

Meanwhile, as Japan's international competitiveness in the international market grew in the 1980s, Japanese leaders of business and industry suffered criticism by their counterparts in the United States and Western Europe for 'free riding' on intellectual properties created by other countries. In 1993 and 1994, the Japan Association of Corporate Executives and the Tokyo Chambers of Commerce and Industry publicly reported their analysis and worries over the current state of science and technology personnel (Iwata 1999: 592). MEXT's statistical survey, conducted in 2002, revealed that private companies demanded that colleges and graduate schools put more emphasis on cultivating students' ability to think than on increasing their mere knowledge, and called for them to change the system of entrance examinations accordingly (MEXT 2003).

The government's response

Lawmakers responded to scientists' concerns by passing 1995's Science and Technology Basic Law which enabled the cabinet to create a Science and Technology Basic Plan every five years (the first plan appeared in 1996). Although policies concerning science education were part of the main issues in each plan, a larger social and historical context influenced the actual reform.

In 1989, the Ministry of Education, Culture and Sports (to be enlarged and renamed MEXT in 2001) revised the Government Curriculum Guidelines, which considerably reduced the number of hours in elementary and secondary education (Table 3.13). The leading principle of this reform was 'cram-free education', which first appeared in the Curriculum Guidelines announced in 1977 and was emphasized more strongly when the guidelines were revised in 1998. The revision in 1989 also underlined the importance of 'the new concept of scholastic ability' based on 'respect for individual differences' (Yamaki 2011: 214–215).

The traumatic experiences and memories of highly competitive entrance examinations for high schools and colleges, largely shared by the generations of those who were students in the 1970s, furthered the case for 'cram-free education' policies in the 1980s. The introduction of the five-day workweek system to public schools that began in 1992 was also a thrust.

The revision in 1989 aimed at nurturing 'creativity' as well and thus seemingly tried to respond to scientists' and business leaders' worries concerning the change in students' ability, something that would become more evident around 1993. However, what the ministry actually did was not what they expected: for example, science in the first two grades at elementary school was abolished and replaced by 'living environment studies,' which caused the reduction of a total 138 hours of science at elementary school (Yamaki 2011: 223). With the revision in 1998, the number of hours in elementary and middle high schools was reduced further, taking the figure to just 61 per cent of that in the Guidelines in 1968 (Table 3.13). As the number of hours in science decreased, in some cases students had no chance to learn concepts such as 'ions' or 'evolution' at any stage of their years at elementary, junior high or high school (Yamaki 2011: 224).

Scientists and sociologists started to lead the criticism of the ministry's 'reform' by pointing to the deterioration of students' performance (Nishimura 2001). Leaders in politics, business and industry followed them. As early as December 2003, MEXT decided to revise guidelines that had only been enforced for one year. At the end of 2004, when the results of the Programme for International Student Assessment (PISA) was published, the outcome of the reform became clearer: the rank of Japanese pupils in mathematics literacy and reading literacy were still high, but slightly lower in the year 2003 (Table 3.14). The results of the survey of Trends in International Mathematics and Science Study (TIMSS), conducted by the International Association for the Evaluation of Educational Achievement (IEA), also showed a similar short-term trend (Table 3.15). Though the difference compared to previous results seems small, these statistical surveys were often referred to as the index of decline in pupils' academic performance (MEXT 2011a: 80).

The decline in student performance resulted partly from another social phenomenon that had just begun to be problematic: as public education tended

Table 3.13 The number of hours of science and mathematics per year in the government curriculum guidelines

Academic Year of Announcement	1968	1977	1989	1998	2008
Academic Year of Enforcement	1971	1980	1992	2002	2011
Science at Elementary School	628	558	420	350	405
Science at Junior High School	420	350	315–350	290	385
Sum	1,048	908	735–770	640	790
Mathematics at Elementary School	1,047	1,011	1,011	869	1,011
Mathematics at Junior High School	420	385	385	315	385
Sum	1,467	1,395	1,395	1,184	1,361

Source: Adapted from Yamaki 2011: 222, Table 4

Table 3.14 The rank of Japan in the Programme for International Student Assessment (PISA), 2000–2009

Year	2000	2003	2006	2009
Mathematics Literacy	1/32	6/41	10/57	9/65
Science Literacy	2/32	2/41	6/57	5/65
Reading Literacy	8/32	14/41	15/57	8/65

Source: Adapted from National Institute for Educational Policy Research 2009: 18–22

Table 3.15 The rank of Japan in the Trends in International Mathematics and Science Study (TIMSS), 1995–2011

Year		1995	1999	2003	2007	2011
Elementary School, 4th Grade	Maths	3/26	Not conducted	3/25	4/36	5/50
	Science	2/26	Not Conducted	3/25	4/36	4/50
Junior High School, 2nd Grade	Maths	3/41	5/38	5/46	5/49	5/42
	Science	3/41	4/38	6/46	3/49	4/42

Source: Adapted from MEXT 2011b: 1

to minimize its requirements, those who could afford to do so became eager to be exposed to more demanding education and tried to enter more competitive schools and colleges. In 2009, MEXT admitted the existence of the disparity in children's educational opportunities caused by the gaps between their families' financial situations (MEXT 2010b: Chapter 1).

The change in educational policy

In 2005, MEXT started to consider further revision of the curriculum guidelines. New guidelines that aimed to restore the decreased hours and contents were announced in 2008. This revision reflected the social concern about science and mathematics literacy: the hours in science in elementary school increased by 15.7 per cent (from 350 to 405 hours) and those in mathematics by 16.3 per cent (from 869 to 1011). While they did not increase as much as foreign languages, for which the number of hours increased by 33.3 per cent, the importance of science and mathematics were also recognized in the guidelines for junior high school (science gained 32.8 per cent, from 290 to 385, while maths jumped 22.2 per cent, from 315 to 385) (Yamaki 2011: 221). This revision, however, was actually only a return to the levels of 1989, when the cram-free policy first started to be effective.

Meanwhile, scientists voluntarily started their own activities to encourage young students to choose careers in science and technology. One programmatic way of motivation lies within the various 'Olympiad' contests that were held for pupils in natural science disciplines and mathematics. To support their effort, the Japan Science Olympiad Committee[2] was established in 2007 with its chair being the Nobel Laureate, Leo Esaki, and its office located at the Japan Science Foundation (JSF). JSF had also been instrumental in holding the Youngster's Science Festival since 1992, an event where local science teachers voluntarily presented attractive scientific demonstrations. In 2011, 118 festivals (117 local and one nationwide) took place with more than 360,000 participants (Momoi, Ikeda and Tanabashi 2011).

MEXT was not indifferent to activities to promote science education at schools. In 2002, through the Japan Science and Technology Agency (JST), it inaugurated the Science Partnership Programme (renamed Science Partnership Project in 2006), which provided financial support for special courses in science education planned by schools, universities and museums (Science Partnership Programme 2013). The same year, several high schools were designated as Super Science High Schools (SSH), which were allowed to teach materials outside the Guidelines and which received financial support (25 million yen per school for the first year) and advice from JST for five years for enhancing the creativity and originality of students (Support for Super Science High Schools 2014). As of 2012, 178 schools were designated as SSH. A similar programme for elementary and junior high schools *Rika Daisuki Sukuru* (Schools Loving Science) began in 2003 and helps schools organize special educational activities in science, develop educational materials and cooperate with local specialists and science museums (MEXT undated). Though some criticize these programmes as increasing the disparity among schools and therefore students, MEXT seems to have accepted the inequality in opportunities in education and decided to make the peaks higher.

Concluding remarks

The shift in the government's policy on science education has not yet led to particularly remarkable results. Furthermore, whether and how the government's policy will influence actual education is unclear, especially when its environment is undergoing such rapid transformation as it is now. For example, as learning anything through the Internet becomes increasingly convenient, more skills and knowledge about handling information in cyberspace seems necessary, even for studying scientific subjects at elementary school, although this does not yet seem to have been fully incorporated in the current educational system.

Still, what makes the last decade different from the rest of the history of science education in Japan is that the frontier of scientific research has come to seem within reach for the large part of the nation. The steady increase in visibly prominent Japanese scientists represented by the Nobel Laureates, frequent news reports of achievements and problems caused by bio-medical technology in fields such as infertility treatment, the rise of consciousness of environmental issues, etc. help raise the younger generation's concern about science and technology as something that has direct relevance to their future and daily lives, rather than something carried out in faraway, foreign countries. Such sense of 'proximity' to science and technology may influence the nation's related activities even more critically than the formal educational system.

Table 3.16 MEXT's attempts and programmes to improve science education

---

A. Survey of the Current Situation

The nationwide survey (MEXT 2012) on the academic performance and learning situation conducted by MEXT in FY 2012 shows that pupils at elementary school and junior high school are relatively poor at organizing and analysing the results of observations or experiments.

B. Programmes for Teachers

B-1 Science Leaders Camp

This programme was started by JST in 2011 to provide science and mathematics teachers in junior high and high schools with opportunities to experience research activities in advanced fields in science and technology and to learn skills for guiding talented pupils (JST 2013b). Its aim is to encourage teachers to raise the level of their teaching abilities, as well as to offer chances for them to form networks amongst themselves for further activities and communication. The courses that last for three to four days during summer vacation are organized by universities, research institutes, museums and so on, with financial aid from JST contributing up to around 4 million yen. In August 2013, six universities in Hokkaido, Tokyo, Ishikawa, Kyoto, Ehime and Yamaguchi hosted 140 teachers.

B-2 Programme for Establishing Training Centres for Core Science Teachers

This is also a programme financed by JST for science and mathematics teachers in elementary and junior high schools (JST 2013c). In most cases, a pair comprised of a university (or a graduate school) and a local (mainly prefectural) board of education cooperated to develop and conduct a course to provide teachers from the area with opportunities for enhancing teaching skills and for constructing networks amongst themselves. Before it stopped accepting new applications in 2012, 16 such pairs completed their courses (7 in FY 2009, 5 in FY 2010, 2 in FY 2011, and 2 in FY 2012).

B-3 Science Education Assistants Allocation Programme

With this programme JST supported efforts to allocate human resources other than teachers, such as graduate students and retired teachers, as assistants to classes in science for the fifth and sixth grades in elementary schools (JST 2013d). They helped teachers with preparing and conducting experiments and developed educational materials. From FY 2007 to FY 2012 (the programme's final year), some 28,000 were allocated to some 14,200 schools (about 70 per cent of elementary schools in Japan). The total financial aid was 9.7 billion yen.

C. Programmes for pupils

C-1 *Jisedai Kagakusha Ikusei Puroguramu* (Programme for Raising Scientists of the Next Generation)

JST also offers aid for programmes organized by universities, graduate schools and research institutes in order to directly present opportunities to experience parts of advanced research activity to motivated, high-achieving pupils at elementary, junior high and high

---

(continued)

Table 3.16 (continued)

school (JST 2013e). Between FY 2008 and FY 2011, 18 universities hosted some 2,000 pupils in such courses. This programme clearly shows the government's attempt to 'make the peaks higher.'

C-2 Chukosei no Kagakubukatsudo Shinko Puroguramu (Programme to Encourage Junior High and High School Pupils' Extracurricular Activities in Science)

JST financially helps junior high and high schools with their pupils' extracurricular activities in scientific fields, such as experiments, field works, participation in academic meetings and competitions, attending scientists' lectures and so on (JST 2013f). This programme started in FY 2010 with 101 schools and still provides 100 schools with financial aid in FY 2013.

C-3 Science Partnership Programme

The Science Partnership Programme is JST's activity that supports educational attempts oriented to hands-on and problem-solving subjects (JST 2013g). In this programme, universities or science centres (such as NPOs or science museums) collaborate with local boards of education or schools to create opportunities for pupils to be exposed to observational and experimental activities guided by front-line researchers and engineers. In FY 2007, when this programme started, 33 elementary schools, 260 junior high schools and 841 high schools attended the programme, while in FY 2012, 77 elementary schools (with 10,048 pupils), 146 junior high schools (26,641 pupils), and 577 high schools (54,783 pupils) joined in.

C-4 Science Camp

Science Camp is another programme supported by JST that organizes camp-style learning courses at universities and research institutes. From the summer of 1995 when this programme started with 9 national research institutes as hosts, to the spring of 2012, 10,703 high school pupils attended its courses. Its courses are held in summer, winter and spring recesses.

Notes

1 The sum of the figures of each year does not always equal 100 because of rounding. This applies also to the tables 3.2, 3.3, 3.4, 3.5, 3.6, 3.7, 3.8, 3.9 and 3.12.
2 For further information see the official website of the Japan Science Olympiad Committee, available at http://www.jsoc-top.jp/index.html [Accessed 10 September 2014].

Bibliography

Agency of Science and Technology (1994a): *White Paper on Science and Technology 1993- Figure 1-1-3 (in Japanese)*. Agency of Science and Technology, Tokyo. Available from http://www.mext.go.jp/b_menu/hakusho/html/hpaa199301/hpaa199301_2_006.html [Accessed 19 October 2014].
Agency of Science and Technology (1994b): *White Paper on Science and Technology 1993- Figure 1-1-1*. Agency of Science and Technology, Tokyo. Available from http://www.

mext.go.jp/b_menu/hakusho/html/hpaa199301/hpaa199301_2_005.html [Accessed 10 October 2014].

Agency of Science and Technology (1994c): *White Paper on Science and Technology 1993-The Figures 1-1-12 and 1-1-13*. Agency of Science and Technology, Tokyo. Available from http://www.mext.go.jp/b_menu/hakusho/html/hpaa199301/hpaa199301_2_008.html [Accessed 10 October 2014].

Agency of Science and Technology (1994d): *White Paper on Science and Technology 1993-Chapter 1, Part 1*. Agency of Science and Technology, Tokyo. Available from http://www.mext.go.jp/b_menu/hakusho/html/hpaa199301/hpaa199301_2_004.html [Accessed 10 October 2014].

Agency of Science and Technology (1994e): *White Paper on Science and Technology 1993-Figure 1-1-9 and Table 1-1-10*. Agency of Science and Technology, Tokyo. Available from http://www.mext.go.jp/b_menu/hakusho/html/hpaa199301/hpaa199301_2_007.html [Accessed 10 October 2014].

Cabinet Decision (2009): On the New Growth Strategy (Basic Policies). Available from http://www.sg.emb-japan.go.jp/jp_new_growth_stgy.pdf [Accessed 20 October 2014].

George, Timothy S. (2001): *Minamata: Pollution and the Struggle for Democracy in Postwar Japan*. Harvard University Asia Center, Cambridge (MA).

Hayashi, Yukihide (2010): *Rikakei Reigu Shakai* (Society That Treats Scientific Personnel Unfairly). Chuokoronshinsha, Tokyo.

Iwata, Kozo (1999): Rikokei Jinzai Yosei o meguru Mondai: Rikokei Banare, Kagakugijutsu Banare, Rikabanare (Human Resource Problems in Science and Technology). In: *Tsushi Nihon no Kagakugijutsu* (A Social History of Science and Technology in Contemporary Japan) 5 (II), edited by Shigeru Nakayama, Kunio Goto and Hitoshi Yoshioka. Gakuyo Shobo, Tokyo. Pp. 586–599.

JST (Japan Science and Technology Agency) (2013a): Heisei 25 Nendo Chugakkou Rikakyoiku Jittaichosa Shukeikekka (Sokuho) (Summary of the Current Situation of Science Education at Junior High School in FY 2013, Temporary Report). JST, Tokyo. Available from http://www.jst.go.jp/cpse/risushien/secondary/cpse_report_016.pdf [Accessed 20 October 2014]

JST (2013b): Science Leaders Camp. JST, Tokyo. Available from http://www.jst.go.jp/cpse/slc/index.html [Accessed 8 September 2014].

JST (2013c): Programme for Establishing Training Centres for Core Science Teachers. JST, Tokyo. Available from http://www.jst.go.jp/cpse/cst/ [Accessed 20 October 2014]

JST (2013d): Science Education Assistants Allocation Programme. JST, Tokyo. Available from http://scot.jst.go.jp/ [Accessed 20 October 2014].

JST (2013e): Jisedai Kagakusha Ikusei Proguramu (Programme for Raising Scientists of Next Generation). JST, Tokyo. Available from http://www.jst.go.jp/cpse/fsp/ [Accessed 8 September 2014].

JST (2013f): Chukosei no Kagakubukatsudo Shinko Puroguramu (Programme to Encourage Junior High and High School Pupils' Extracurricular Activities in Science). JST, Tokyo. Available from http://www.jst.go.jp/cpse/kagakubu/ [Accessed 8 September 2014].

JST (2013g): Science Partnership Programme. JST, Tokyo. Available from http://www.jst.go.jp/cpse/spp/ [Accessed 8 September 2014].

Mainichi Shimbun Kagakukankyobu (2006): *Rikei Hakusho: Kono Kuni o Shizukani Sasaeru Hitotachi* (White Book on Scientists and Engineers: Those Who Quietly Support This Country). Kodansha, Tokyo.

Mainichi Shinbun Kagakukankyobu (2007): *'Rikei' toiu Ikikata: Rikei Hakusho 2* (Life in Science and Technology: White Paper on Personnel in Science and Technology 2). Kodansha, Tokyo.

MEXT (Ministry of Education, Culture, Sports, Science and Technology, Japan) (2003): Annual Report on the Promotion of Science and Technology 2002. MEXT, Tokyo. Available from http://www.mext.go.jp/b_menu/hakusho/html/hpbb200301/hpbb200301_2_016.html [Accessed 8 September 2014].

MEXT (2010a): Chapter 3: Searching for a New R&D System. MEXT, Tokyo. Available from http://www.mext.go.jp/component/english/__icsFiles/afieldfile/2011/02/23/1302525_006.pdf [Accessed 8 September 2014].

MEXT (2010b): Chapter 1: The Burden on Household Finances and Standards of Educational Investment. In: *White Paper on Education, Culture, Sports, Science and Technology, 2009.* MEXT, Tokyo. Available from http://www.mext.go.jp/b_menu/hakusho/html/hpab200901/detail/1305849.htm [Accessed 8 September 2014].

MEXT (2011a): Chapter 2: S&T Systems That Mobilize People and Connect Knowledge. In: *White Paper on Science and Technology 2010.* MEXT, Tokyo. Available from http://www.mext.go.jp/component/english/__icsFiles/afieldfile/2011/02/23/1302537_005.pdf [Accessed 8 September 2014].

MEXT (2011b): Kokusai Sugaku Rika Kyoiku Doko Chosa (TIMSS2011) no Pointo, (Key Issues in TIMSS 2011). MEXT, Tokyo. Available from www.mext.go.jp/b_menu/houdou/24/12/__icsFiles/afieldfile/2012/12/12/1328789_01.pdf [Accessed 8 September 2014].

MEXT (2012): Heisei 24 Nendo Zenkoku Gakuryoku Gakushu Jokyo Chosa no Kekka ni tsuite (Gaiyo) (Summary of the Nationwide Surveys on the Academic Performance and Learning Situation). MEXT, Tokyo. Available from http://www.mext.go.jp/b_menu/shingi/chousa/shotou/085/shiryo/__icsFiles/afieldfile/2012/09/03/1325111_01.pdf [Accessed 8 September 2014].

MEXT (2013): *White Paper on Science and Technology 2012. Toward a Robust and Resilient Society: Lessons from the Great East Japan Earthquake (GEJE).* MEXT, Tokyo. Available from http://www.mext.go.jp/english/whitepaper/1323541.htm [Accessed 8 September 2014].

MEXT (undated): *Kagakugijutsu Rikakyoiku Suishin Moderu Jigyo ('Rika Daisuki Sukuru' Jigyo) no Gaiyo: Outline of Model Program for the Promotion of Science Education ("Schools Loving Science" Program)* (in Japanese). MEXT, Tokyo. Available from http://www.mext.go.jp/b_menu/shingi/chukyo/chukyo3/013/siryo/04052601/014/002.pdf [Accessed 8 September 2014].

Momoi, Naomi, Yasue Ikeda and Masaomi Tanabashi (2011): Nijusshuunen o Mukaeta 'Seishonen no tame no Kagaku no Saiten' (The Twentieth Anniversary of 'Youngster's Science Festival'), *Bulletin of Science Museum* 5. pp. 1-6.

Nakamura, Takashi *et al.* (2011): A Study of the Japanese National Character: The Twelfth Nationwide Survey (2008). General Series No. 102. The Institute of Statistical Mathematics. Available from http://ismrepo.ism.ac.jp/dspace/bitstream/10787/903/1/kenripo102.pdf [Accessed 24 October 2014].

National Institute for Educational Policy Research (2009): *OECD Seito no Gakushutotatsudochosa 2009 nen Chosa Kokusai Kekka no Yoyaku* (Summary of the Survey Conducted under PISA, 2009). National Institute for Educational Policy Research, Tokyo. Available from http://www.mext.go.jp/component/a_menu/education/detail/__icsFiles/afieldfile/2010/12/07/1284443_01.pdf [Accessed 8 September 2014].

Nishimura, Kazuo (ed.) (2001): *Gakuryoku Teika ga Kuni o Horobosu* (Decline in Academic Ability Will Ruin the Country). Nihon Keizai Shinbun, Tokyo.

Okamoto, Takuji (2006): Science and Competition: The Case of Physics in Japan, 1886–1949. In: *UTCP (University of Tokyo Center for Philosophy) Bulletin* VI. Pp. 57–67.

Schreiner, Camilla and Svein Sjøberg (2007): Science Education and Youth's Identity Construction: Two Incompatible Projects? In: *The Re-emergence of Values in the Science Curriculum*, edited by Deborah Corrigan, Justin Dillon and Richard Gunstone. Sense Publishers, Rotterdam.

Science Partnership Programme (2013): The Official Website of Science Partnership Programme. Available from http://www.jst.go.jp/cpse/spp/ [Accessed 8 September 2014].

Sjøberg, Svein and Camilla Schreiner (2008): Concerns for the Environment. Data from ROSE (The Relevance of Science Education). Available from http://roseproject.no/network/countries/norway/eng/nor-sjoberg-env2008.pdf [Accessed 8 September 2014].

Support for Super Science High Schools (2014): The Official Website of Super Science High Schools. Available from http://rikai.jst.go.jp/eng/e_about/e_sshs.php [Accessed 8 September 2014].

Urasaka, Jyunko *et al.* (2010): Mathematics Education and Human Capital Accumulation: Empirical Study in Japan (in Japanese), *Journal of Quality Education* 3. Pp. 1–14.

Urasaka, Jyunko *et al.* (2011): Rikei Shusshinsha to Bunkei Shusshinsha no Nenshu Hikaku: JHPS Deta ni Motoduku Bunseki Kekka (Comparison of Annual Incomes of Those with Scientific and Humanistic Educational Backgrounds: Analysis Based on JHPS Data) (in Japanese), RIETI Discussion Paper Series 11-J-020. Available from http://www.rieti.go.jp/jp/publications/dp/11j020.pdf [Accessed 8 September 2014].

Yamaki, Toshinori (2011): 'Yutori Kyoiku' Seisaku to Rikakyoiku ('Cram-free Education' Policy and Science Education in School). In: *A Social History of Science and Technology at the Turn of the Century*, Vol. 3, edited by Hitoshi Yoshioka. Hara Shobo, Tokyo. Pp. 213–231.

4 Gunpla robot toys and the popularization of robotics in Japan

Cosima Wagner

Introduction

'Technical creativity is certainly influenced by technical preconditions, however it is not entirely determined by them. There are historical conditions, which allow the imagination to run free so that it goes beyond the conclusions related to technological possibilities, which are based on mere reason, and accepts the vision as a realistic proposal. If such notions become fixed, they can even have an effect on reality in that they offer new images of the future and thereby set a goal for further technical development or serve as a stimulus for future engineers—as in the case of Astro Boy' (Itō 2010: 372).

This summary of a study by history of science scholar Kenji Itō on robot images in post-war Japan points to the role of a popular robot character—*Astro Boy* (Japanese: *Tetsuwan Atomu*)—created by Osamu Tezuka (1928–1989) in 1951, and considered an important 'techno-imagery' and mascot for research on robots in general, and on humanoid robots in particular ever since. In 2004, *Astro Boy* was inducted into the 'Robot Hall of Fame' at Carnegie Mellon University, where robots of science are honoured alongside science fictional robots 'that excite audiences about what the future may hold and inspire roboticists to greater achievements' (Carnegie Mellon University). However, *Astro Boy* was moulded into an ambassador for technological optimism, against the will of his creator. As Tezuka himself often stated, it was never his intention to promote a positive view of a 'glorious scientific civilization' in the future where humans had robots as friends. As careful reading of his *Astro Boy* stories shows, the underlying theme of his manga work was discrimination against others, with a rather pessimistic view of science and technology, especially the (mis)use of science and technology by the human race, which was how he himself had experienced it during World War II (Tezuka Productions 1998: 84–85, reference in Schodt 2007: 121).

In an interview with the science writer and translator of Tezuka's manga into English, Frederik L. Schodt, conducted in 1986, Tezuka said that he had been forced to draw a very optimistic picture of technology (including the 100,000 horse power atomic engine within *Astro Boy*'s body symbolizing the 'peaceful use' of nuclear power) by his publishing company and readers in order to give hope to the Japanese, who in the 1950s were still suffering from the destruction of war and from an awareness of their technological inferiority to the Western winners of the war (Schodt 2007: 99, 115; see also the analysis of this point in the previous chapter written by Takuji Okamoto). As a result, Tezuka's message criticizing human behaviour was not understood. Instead, *Astro Boy* came to be a symbol of hope and a mascot for the Japanese high-tech industry during the high-growth era that lasted until the 1970s. Tezuka was even asked to plan a robot pavilion for the world Expo 1970 in Osaka and, in 1986, was invited to a discussion with robotics scientists on the subject of 'Astro Boy and his influence on Japanese robotics' (Asahi Shimbunsha/Tezuka Productions 2002: 88–91, 96) by the *Journal of the Robotics Society of Japan*. Since the 2000s *Astro Boy* has been 'revived' as a robot role model who is introducing cutting edge robotics research and new robot prototypes—especially next generation 'social' robots—to the general public.

Yet, when exploring the interface between the fictional and the scientific-technical construction of technology futures in Japan, it must be noted that *Astro Boy* is only one of many famous robot characters, from an extensive pop cultural robot fiction genre created during the 1950s, that play an important role in imparting knowledge about robot technology to the general public and who are especially important for the process of promoting 'social,' so-called 'next generation robots' (Japanese: *jisedai robotto*), as a desirable part of the future for today's Japanese society.

Examples of how popular culture is used as an interface for popularizing science, technology and engineering (STE) in Japan can be observed through exhibitions in museums like the National Museum of Emerging Science and Innovation (Japanese: *Nihon Kagaku Miraikan*)[1], where robot characters among others are used to present the latest technology projects to school children and their families[2]; through numerous publications intended for the general public with titles such as 'Do Robot Manga Become Reality? An Anthology of Famous Robot Manga and Reports from Cutting Edge Robotics' (Yonezawa 2002) or 'The Birth of Giant Robots. Latest Robotics Research Produces a Gundam Robot' (Shikano 1998); through government strategy papers published since the beginning of the 2000s citing robot characters as evidence of the easy acceptance of new 'social' robots in everyday life in Japan (CAO 2003); and last, but not least, through robot toys, which are ubiquitous not only as merchandising products, playthings and plastic model kits in children's rooms but also as programmable platforms for student robot competitions like the nationwide contest 'Robocon,' broadcast annually by national television broadcaster NHK (Nippon Hōsō Kyōkai, English title: Japan Broadcasting Corporation).[3]

A detailed analysis of fictional robot role models and the cultural background of recent robot technology development in Japan has already been presented elsewhere (see Wagner 2013), but in order to pick one example as a contribution to the TECHculture project, this short essay shines a spotlight on the giant robot genre or *mecha*-genre (mecha means mechanical) with special consideration of the series *Mobile Suits Gundam* (Japanese: *Kidō senshi Gandamu*). During the thirty-five years since its first appearance on Japanese television in the year 1979, the *Gundam* series developed into an entire science fiction universe with anime, movies, manga, video games, merchandising products and plastic model kits. As a robot toy bestseller for the entertainment company Bandai Namco, the *Gundam* character became yet another popular 'techno-imagery' who has been, like *Astro Boy*, instrumentalized for STE in the field of robotics in Japan up until the present day. After, a brief description of the *Gundam* robot fiction-toy image alliance, its 'effects on reality' and how it 'serves as a stimulus for future engineers' (Itō 2010: 372) will be illustrated. Finally, together with a look at recent robot education initiatives for primary school children in Japan, further research questions on the role of commodified robot toys in shaping worldviews and perceptions of technology during childhood will be posed.

The *Gundam* universe and robotics in Japan

The thirty-fifth anniversary of the first screening of TV anime series *Mobile Suits Gundam*—from anime creator and director Yoshiyuki Tomino (Anime Production Studio Sunrise)—was celebrated in August 2014. The robots that star in the series are actually robot suits piloted by young heroes and heroines fighting evil. An important factor in the continued popularity of the series is the close cooperation between anime production companies and toy companies, which planned the merchandising around a new robot series from the beginning (Schodt 1990: 86). *Gundam* plastic model kits known as *Gunpla* (the short from of *Gundam plastic model*) first emerged in July 1980, targeting male middle and high school kids.

Since that date, as of the end of March 2011, 406 million units had been sold in Japan, which works out at 13 million units sold per year since 1980 (Bandai Co. Ltd. 2011: 1). Overseas, *Gunpla* is currently sold in 12 countries and regions around the world, with total sales of more than 28 million units recorded between January 2000 and December 2010. According to Bandai Namco's Annual Report for FY (fiscal year) 2010/2011, sales related to the *Gundam* character in Japan amounted to 34 billion yen (as of March 2011), which equates to nearly 5 per cent of the whole toy industry market in Japan in that year, and makes *Gundam* the most profitable character product made by Bandai Namco Group (Bandai Namco Group 2011: 7).

As a cultural icon, *Gundam* has featured on stamps and has been used for PR campaigns for the Tokyo Fire Department, as well as for an announcement by the Ministry of Defence's Technical Research and Development Institute regarding the development of a new mobile suit of armour for the military in 2009 (Game News 2007). Furthermore, from July to August 2009, a 'Life Size Gundam' robot statue measuring 59 feet (18 metres) was exhibited in the newly opened Shiokaze Park on Tokyo Bay's Odaiba Island to commemorate the thirtieth anniversary of the screening of the TV anime series.[4] It drew over 52 million visitors to the site.[5] In 2012, a whole *Gundam* theme park (including the 'Life Size Gundam' statue), called 'Gundam Front Tokyo,' opened on Odaiba Island.[6]

In addition to its recent function as a tourism attraction, *Gundam*'s creative influence on the field of robotics could be observed through the construction of real robot suits by the 'Skeletonics' team for the Robocon competition 2013. Skeletonics even established a robot building company that same year, with the vision 'a world where giant robots exist' (Skeletonics Corp. 2013). Furthermore, following the publication of the aforementioned book on 'How super robots move,' the robotics scientist and editor Katsuya Kanaoka conducted a seminar on 'Delightful learning with super robots: applied mathematics, physics and automation control' in June 2014, where he promised to teach the technological basics of super robots like *Gundam* (Nikkan Kōgyō Shimbun Robonable 2014).

Summary

Due to the short character of this 'spotlight' essay, it is not possible to elaborate in more detail on *Gundam's* and other giant robots' role in the popularization of STE in Japan. However, it has been shown that popular culture robot figures like *Astro Boy* and *Gundam* are deeply engraved in the collective memory and foster a positive attitude among the general public towards the science of robotics. As fictional robots from stories materialized in robot toys and merchandising products since the 1950s, these robot characters have been important parts of the socialization process for both children and today's adults in Japan.[7] Modern Japan's perception of itself as a 'High Technology Nation' (*gijutsu rikkoku*), and the recent promotion of research and development on new 'social' robots for everyday use, raise questions about the role of commodified robot toys such as *Gunpla* in shaping worldviews and perceptions of technology during childhood. Can technical creativity be inspired by commodified and programmed robot toys? Or does the childhood dream of building a robot in the style of existing robot toys prevent critical thinking, creativity and the invention of new (robot) technologies?[8] Do robot toys strengthen gender roles by deterring girls from building and playing with robots, or can these toys be a tool for girls to become more interested and integrated in STEM subjects in school? With regard to the latter, the Robotics Society of Japan (Nihon Robotto Gakkai) proposed a 'robot fascination education' initiative (*robotto kandō kyōiku*) in 2011 in order to promote robotics-related curricula nationwide, from primary school through to university. The survey on 'Robot Education in Japan' recommended the suitability of robot education for raising interest in STEM subjects in school, stating that robots should be considered an ideal learning object for the interplay of many technologies, as well as for discussing social sciences and humanities-related questions. According to the report, school experiments in primary and secondary schools in different regions of Japan showed that both male and female children had great curiosity about building and programming robots. This curiosity and fascination should be taken as a starting point for motivating young children in general to become deeply interested in STEM subjects and in future careers as engineers (RSJ 2011: 1–2, 5–6, 9).

A more detailed analysis of robot education activities and the role of robot toys in promoting interest in the scientific field of robotics engineering in Japan is beyond the scope of this paper. However, by shining a spotlight on the cultural background—the TECHculture—of robotics in Japan, it aims to stimulate further comparative discussions on the future of STEM education in general, as well as on the integration of robots into future everyday life in different countries of the world.

Notes

1 For further information on the museum see the website, available from http://www.miraikan.jst.go.jp/en [Accessed 8 October 2014].
2 See e.g. the exhibition on 'The World of Manga Experienced Through Science' in 2012, available from http://www.miraikan.jst.go.jp/en/spexhibition/tour/kagaku-manga-ten.html [Accessed 8 October 2014].
3 See the official homepage of the robot contest 'Robocon'—available in Japanese from http://www.official-robocon.com [Accessed 8 October 2014]—and the homepage of broadcasting corporation NHK—available in Japanese (including a broadcasting timetable and videos of the participating robots)—from http://www.nhk.or.jp/robocon [Accessed 14 October 2014].
4 For a picture of the 'Life Size Gundam' see http://upload.wikimedia.org/wikipedia/ja/5/5d/Odaiba_Gundam_20090731.jpg or several pictures of plastic model action figures on the Bandai Hobby Net Homepage, available from http://bandai-hobby.net/site/gunpla_build_02a.html [Accessed 27 October 2014].
5 The official homepage has been closed, but is available from web.archives http://web.archive.org/web/20090418054803/http://www.greentokyo-gundam.jp.
6 For further information see the official homepage available from http://gundamfront-tokyo.com/en/welcome [Accessed 8 October 2014].
7 Valid data on the distribution of robot toys per household, year and gender in Japan is not yet available. However, the ubiquity of *Gundam*-related toys and merchandising alone is proven by the number—406 million *Gunpla* units—sold since 1980, by continuously high sales figures that peaked at 65.2 billion yen in FY 2013 (Bandai Namco Group 2013: 07), and by an estimated 80.2 billion yen sales for FY 2014 (Business Journal 17.06.2014).
8 These concerns have already been raised in a special issue of the *Journal of the Robotics Society of Japan* on 'Toys and Robotics' in 2000 (Ichikawa 2000: 161).

Bibliography

Asahi Shimbunsha, Tezuka Productions (ed.) (2002): *Atomu no kisekiten. Kūsō kagaku kara robotto bunka e. 1900–200X* [Exhibition in the Footsteps of Astro Boy. From Science Fiction to a Robot Culture 1900–200X]. Asahi Shimbunsha, Tōkyō.

Bandai Co. Ltd. (ed.) (2011): The Gunpla Builders World Cup 2011 Begins this July! Press release on 20.7.2011. Available from http://www.bandainamco.co.jp/files/Gunpla20builders20world20cup20201120HP.pdf [Accessed 8 October 2014].

Bandai Namco Group (ed.) (2011): Bandai Namco Group annyuaru repōto 2011 [Bandai Namco Group Annual Report 2011]. Available from http://www.bandainamco.co.jp/ir/annual/pdf_bnh/j_2011_3.pdf [Accessed 8 October 2014].

Bandai Namco Group (ed.) (2013): Annual Report 2013. Available from http://www.bandainamco.co.jp/ir/annual/pdf_bnh/en_2013_9.pdf [Accessed 8 October 2014].

Business Journal (2014): Nenkan uriage 802 oku en. Gundamu bijinesu wa ikani shite seichō? Seme no senryaku tsuzuketa 35nen [Annual Sales of 80.2 billion Yen. How is the Gundam Business Ever Expanding? A 35-year Long Offensive Strategy], June 17. Available from http://biz-journal.jp/2014/06/post_5139.html.

CAO (Cabinet Office of the Japanese Government, jap. Naikakufu) (ed.) (2003): Dai 24-kai Sōgō Kagaku Gijutsu Kaigi giji yōshi [Minutes of the 24th convention of the Council for Science and Technology Policy]. Available from http://www8.cao.go.jp/cstp/siryo/giji/giji-si24.html.

Carnegie Mellon University: About the Robot Hall of Fame. Available from http://www.robothalloffame.org/about.html [Accessed 8 October 2014].

Game News (2007): Bōeishō gijutsu kenkyū honbu rikujō sobi toshite 'Gandamu' no jitsugen o mosaku. [The Technical Research and Development Institute of the Ministry of Defense Plans the Realization of Gundam Fighting Suits for the Ground Forces]. Available from http://www.gamenews.ne.jp/archives/2007/10/post_2793.html.

Ichikawa, Makoto (2000): Gangu to Robotics [official English translation of the title: Plaything and Robotics], *Journal of the Robotics Society of Japan* 18 (2). Pp. 160–161.

Itō, Kenji (2010): Vor Astro Boy. Roboterbilder im Nachkriegsjapan [Before Astro Boy. Robot images in Postwar Japan], Technikgeschichte 77 No. 4. Pp. 353–372.

Nikkan Kōgyō Shimbun Robonable (2014): 6 gatsu 6 nichi ni suparobo de sūgaku, butsurigaku seigyō kōgaku o kaisetsu suru seminā [On June 6 a Seminar on Super Robots and Mathematics, Physics and Automation Control will be Held]. 21 April. Available from http://www.robonable.jp/news/2014/05/super-robot-0410.html [Accessed 8 October 2014].

RSJ (The Robotics Society of Japan) (ed.) (2011): Robotto kyōiku kenkyū senmon iinkai hōkokusho [Report of the Robot Education Research Expert Committee]. Available from http://www.rsj.or.jp/databox/committees/00houkoku.pdf.

Schodt, Frederik L. [1988] (1990): *Inside the Robot Kingdom. Japan, Mechatronics, and the Coming Robotopia.* Kodansha International, Tōkyō/New York.

Schodt, Frederik L. (2007): *The Astro Boy Essays. Osamu Tezuka, Mighty Atom and the Manga–Anime Revolution.* Stone Bridge Press, Berkeley.

Shikano, Tsukasa (1998): *Kyodai robotto tanjō: saishin robotto kōgaku ga Gandamu o umu.* [The Birth of Giant Robots: Latest Robotics Research Produces a Gundam Robot]. Tōkyō.

Skeletonics Corp. (2013): Official homepage in Japanese available from http://skeletonics.com.

Tezuka Productions (ed.) (1998): *Tezuka Osamu zenshi: sono sugao to gyōseki* [A Complete History of Osamu Tezuka: The Real Man, and his Accomplishments]. Akita Shoten, Tōkyō.

Wagner, Cosima (2013): *Robotopia Nipponica – Recherchen zur Akzeptanz von Robotern in Japan.* Tectum Verlag, Marburg.

Yonezawa, Yoshihiro (ed.) (2002): *Robotto manga wa jitsugen suruka. Robotto manga meisaku ansorojī + robotto kaihatsu saizensen hōkoku* [Do Robot Manga Become Reality? An Anthology of Famous Robot Manga and Reports from Cutting Edge Robotics]. Jitsugyō no Nihonsha, Tōkyō.

5 From national mission to what?

Shifts in the implications of science and technology in South Korea

Jung-Ok Ha

Introduction

In early 2011, four students committed suicide at the Korean Advanced Institute of Science and Technology (KAIST), South Korea's foremost science and technology-oriented institution. KAIST has consistently ranked as high, or higher, than other South Korean ivy leagues in domestic and international university rankings. In actuality, KAIST students receive a high-quality, intensive education and, after graduation, fill key roles in universities, research institutes and industries. For example, in 2008, around 25 per cent of the development human resources of Samsung Semiconductor was reportedly made up of KAIST graduates, and its graduates also occupied 20 and 10 per cent of South Korea's science and technology (S&T) doctoral degree holders and professorships, respectively (KCUE 2008).

The KAIST suicides are clearly tragic, but they also allow insights into the particular state of S&T in South Korea. Using this incident as a reference point I would like to shed light on the specific background and situation in the field of S&T, which was largely overlooked by the media at the time. In my opinion, the situation of S&T in Korea today can be described as a state of anomie where the past value of S&T is no longer meaningful, yet no new value has been derived to replace it.

The KAIST incident was considered by many to be 'an accident' that required structural analysis, rather than as a situation where students had crumbled under the weight of intense competition. Of course these were not the first suicides at KAIST: the school had reported one or two suicides each year, as had other engineering universities. What was unprecedented in this case, however, was that four students had taken their lives in a single semester, and that these suicides occurred while drastic reforms were being instituted by former KAIST President Seo Nam-pyo.

In the aftermath of the tragedy, debates centered mainly on the pros and cons of educational reforms which KAIST had started to implement around 2000. On the one hand, people claimed that the suicides had been the result of the stern Seo-style policy leading to comprehensive changes at KAIST, including English-only courses and differentiated tuition fees based on grades. On the other hand, people who supported the reforms asserted that the intensely competitive atmosphere of the school actually serves to strengthen, not weaken, students' resolve.

Interestingly enough, the reforms were accepted, but nobody asked about their aims or even questioned their necessity. Neither side raised the question of the legitimacy of the reform. I would therefore like to address this issue and focus on both personal and structural factors influencing the field of S&T and historical developments in this realm in South Korea exemplified by the KAIST institute. These issues are also related to the current changes within the field of S&T.

What I want to make clear, referring to the context in which the KAIST suicides took place, is the fact that the current state of anomie can be traced back to a failure to propose a value for the credo of competition, not to the competition itself. The institution of KAIST has been the driving force to perform and lead a national mission in the field of S&T in the past. However, today its position is neither meaningful to the public nor is it creditable to the institution's insiders. A new position needs to be found in order to end the current state of anomie. Nevertheless, I believe that this state of anomie offers an invaluable opportunity to reflect critically on the history and situation of South Korean S&T and on the role of scientists and engineers. Within my evaluation I will also critically review developmentalism and instrumentalism, which are still the governing ideologies employed to explain S&T, and particularly scientists and engineers as instruments for economic development.

Overview of KAIST

KAIST as the role model for S&T education

KAIST has represented South Korea's science and technology human resources policy (S&T HR policy) as part of a government-funded national project since its establishment in 1971. A special law was enacted for KAIST, and South Korea's then-president headed the organizing board of directors at the Ministry of Science and Technology as the school's founder.

The school is known for producing elite scientists. Since its foundation, KAIST has attempted to secure educational quality through high academic standards and a difficult entrance exam. KAIST students are particularly proud that they have been selected to study at a university that offers more intensive and challenging courses than other universities.

Colleges in South Korea are fully aware of their role not only as educational institutions but also as S&T research institutes. They first gained social acceptance for the importance of their research role in the 1980s, and KAIST was the key driving force behind and the model for that turnaround.

As KAIST is considered the role model of S&T education in South Korea, similar institutes serving the integrated functions of colleges, graduate schools and research institutes have sprouted up all over the country, hoping to follow its lead. In 1993 and 2004, the Gwangju Institute of Science of Technology (GIST) and Daegu Gyeongbuk Institute of Science & Technology (DGIST) were founded. Furthermore, Pohang University of Science and Technology (POSTECH) and Ulsan National Institute of Science and Technology (UNIST) were established in 1986 and 2009, respectively. Although these educational institutes have different funding sources, all students receive full scholarships. They live in dormitories and major only in science and engineering-related fields. As indicated by South Korea's high college entrance rates (Figure 5.1), there are many colleges in South Korea, and these colleges are strictly ranked.

Although there are many colleges and many of their graduates major in the science and engineering fields, not all graduates are hired by companies. Only graduates of relatively high-level colleges—such as KAIST—have the freedom to be selective in terms of jobs.

Previous research on and evaluations of KAIST generally stress the fact that the foundation of KAIST has contributed tremendously to the development of the field of S&T and can be related to the country's overall economic growth. This view is applied consistently in reviews on KAIST and in evaluations of S&T policies.

In fact, many South Korean scientists and engineers miss the Park Chung-hee era (1961 to 1979), which has been credited with giving the closest attention to and most aggressive support for S&T. Moreover, those in science and engineering circles harbour great expectations for the current president, the daughter of the former president Park Chung-hee, seeing in her the possibility for a revival of the 'golden time' of science and engineering.

Evaluations of KAIST rarely raise questions about S&T being defined as an instrument for economic development or that of scientists and engineers being designated as the actors to shoulder that mission. This is very unlike other sectors, where proactive steps toward more realistic diagnoses and theoretical discussions are undertaken especially within post-developmentalism frameworks. In contrast, developmentalism still governs academic discussions on and policy decisions and evaluations of S&T in South Korea today.

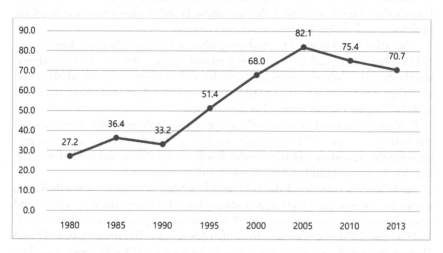

Figure 5.1 College entrance rate in South Korea (1980–2013) (Unit: % of high school graduates entering colleges)

Source: Adapted from National Statistical Office 2014

Under its framework, the actors are portrayed as either heroes of a 'success story'—i.e. those who devoted themselves to successfully carrying out the mission; or as 'losers'—i.e. those who were unable to adapt to the demands of the situation. As such, scientists and engineers are treated only as instruments for S&T development or economic growth. However, from the perspective of such actors, personal dreams and subjective perspectives coincided with the aims of the national mission and its achievement.

As I mentioned in the introduction, in KAIST's case, no new value has appeared to replace the former value in order to guide and lead the current mission. Thus, evaluations of KAIST have failed to examine what role scientists and engineers and the field of S&T in general could and should play in the new era. From the mid to late 1990s, KAIST students began to see the appeal of more stable jobs such as those found in careers as government officials or lawyers. This new preference proves that inevitable changes have occurred in the status of S&T and in the role of scientists and engineers. Nevertheless, the existing literature on KAIST cites only changing social sentiments towards S&T or shifts in the personal strategies of KAIST students as reasons for KAIST's altered position in society. None of the literature published in S&T circles or by KAIST itself points to the failure to present new values for the school in a rapidly changing environment.

Discourses on the S&T crisis

At the beginning of the twenty-first century, debates on the S&T crisis were provoked by a drop in enrollment rates at Seoul National University (SNU)'s Natural Science and Engineering colleges in 2002 (81.9 per cent for the former and 81.7 per cent for the latter, far below the school's overall average enrollment rate of 89.6 per cent). In South Korea's strict college rankings, SNU stands clearly at the top. Given this, the fact that only around 82 per cent of students were enrolled at SNU's natural science and engineering colleges actually came as a major shock.

This incident led to the diagnosis of a crisis in the field of science and engineering, and the task of coming up with alternatives and solutions has been a priority for many ever since. In a nationwide survey in 2003, 85.7 per cent of respondents indicated 'Diagnosis and resolution of crisis in science and engineering' as the best answer to the question 'What do you predict will be the main agenda of the science and engineering fields in 2004?'[1] (Oh 2004).

Many point to the low social standing and salaries of scientists and engineers as the main factors driving the avoidance of such fields. Students seem to find such majors less and less appealing because of the instability of the labour market, disadvantages in professional development and differences in wage levels compared to other professional jobs (Bak 2007).

Table 5.1 is based on the results of a survey on the public's perception of S&T conducted in 2004. The survey attempted to discern the general public's impression of the treatment of S&T human resources. The table shows that 71.6 per cent of

Table 5.1 Public awareness of social and economic compensation level of S&T human
resources (%)

	Strongly disagree	Somewhat disagree	Somewhat agree	Strongly agree	No opinion
Scientists and engineers are not sufficiently compensated for their contributions to society.					
	2.6	19.3	**50.1**	**21.5**	6.5
The fact that there are fewer science and engineering graduates among society leaders such as politicians, high-ranking officials or executives in South Korea compared to other advanced or competing countries is an obstacle to national competitiveness improvement.					
	2.3	14.0	**50.0**	**26.0**	7.6
Students avoid science and engineering majors because in both areas it is more difficult to get a job after graduation.					
	3.1	11.3	**45.8**	**37.5**	2.3
Students avoid science and engineering majors because societal position is low compared to the effort to become a scientist or engineer.					
	2.7	15.6	**44.8**	**34.6**	2.4
Students avoid science and engineering majors because there is a societal preference for professional jobs like lawyers, accountants or medical doctors.					
	2.3	8.9	**42.2**	**44.4**	2.2

Source: Adapted from Korea Science Foundation 2004

those surveyed strongly or somewhat agreed that scientists and engineers are not
sufficiently compensated for their contributions to society.

Avoidance of science and engineering is ongoing and becoming more of a
problem. According to a news report in September 2013, the percentage of South
Korean student International Science Olympiad winners who later entered science
or engineering schools at colleges dropped from 62.5 per cent in 2008 to 28.2 per
cent in 2012 (Won 2013). Many chose to enter medical schools in South Korea or
colleges in other countries. Moreover, the report stated that around 70 per cent of
students who dropped out of the top five colleges in South Korea (including SNU)
in 2011 were science or engineering majors, four times more than in other fields.

Some people question the existence of this so-called crisis (Han 2004). The
most vocal proponents of the crisis are science and engineering experts who have
expressed nostalgia for the Park Chung-hee regime described above.

Even though responsible people within the field of S&T and the overall
majority of the population have acknowledged the current crisis in S&T, they
have failed to identify critical factors that have been contributing to the current situation since the establishment of the initial goals of the 1970s and 80s.
Once again, I would like to stress that the view that posits S&T as a tool for
national economic development through its actors is no longer valid in South
Korean society. The 'catch-up' model of the past is no longer rational, but the
ideological and practical bases for S&T in the post-catch-up model today are
nevertheless still insufficient. In the current situation, scientists and engineers
need to be trained to develop competency to raise and solve problems in contrast

to the mere implementation of a given mission, e.g. by the government. This includes the availability of sufficient research and development (R&D) budgets and human resources that need to be overseen to a broader extent by the government and enterprises of the country.

Theoretical background and research methods

The concept of anomie

This paper began with the diagnosis of KAIST as being in a state of anomie, a term introduced by the French sociologist Emile Durkheim to sociology to describe a condition wherein social change has eroded past norms but no new norms are available to take their place (Giddens 1971). I have defined KAIST in this way because its past role as an actor of a national mission is neither meaningful to the public today nor is it credible to the institution's insiders. Yet no new role has appeared to replace it.

The reforms of the former KAIST president Seo Nam-pyo failed because they were too harshly pursued, without the proposition of new values and exclusive of agreement from insiders. Such 'reforms,' which emphasized 'neoliberalism' and 'competition,' presented no new values for KAIST's new direction and justification in the changing environment. Of course, some may claim that the values of 'being an elite scientist' or 'a world famous scientist' remain significant, but perspectives on S&T and the status of scientists and engineers has changed since the 1970s—especially in the 1990s. The appeal of becoming an elite scientist is no longer fully shared and supported by the population. Even KAIST professors are well aware that students are no longer attracted and encouraged to enter the STEM area because of its importance for the economic growth of the country or for its potential to gain a leading position for the future of science in South Korea.[2]

Developmentalism and its application to the field of S&T in South Korea

Research in the area of developmentalism is broad in subject range and it is beyond the scope of this paper to review the entire debate. In South Korea, there is a great deal of research on the theoretical application of post-developmentalism, which often includes debates on the changing characteristics of developmentalism in the state and in civic society beginning from the economic crisis in 1997 (Cho 1998, 2002; Lee 1998). A considerable number of researchers have published papers and reviews on the developmental state model and on the exceptional growth of Asia's so-called 'four dragons': South Korea, Taiwan, Hong Kong and Singapore (Evans 1997; Wade 1996). However, when the financial crisis hit Asian countries in 1997, critical debates on negative aspects, including the 'contradiction and internal crisis generated by exceptional growth' and the 'inherent contradictory structure and harmful influence' of developmentalism arose (Cho 1998: 54; Lee 1998: 252).

58   Jung-Ok Ha

Within the field of S&T, developmentalism is widely used as the dominant analytical framework. When examining the influence of South Korean developmentalism on S&T, it is useful to discuss the views of Joseph Wong, who explored the relationship between biotechnology and developmental states in East Asia (Wong 2005). Wong partly agrees with the post-developmentalists' argument that the developmental state is no longer an autonomous entity and its capacities to direct industrial change have diminished (Evans 1997; quoted from Wong 2005: 170). He still asserts, however, that the developmental state has an innovative power that encourages both cooperation between the knowledge and industrial sectors and industrial competition.

I also would like to raise the issue of inhomogeneity of post-developmentalism in East Asia. Wong describes that in the event that powerful state-initiated developmentalism loses its impact in the economic sector, strong state-driven interventions remain influential in developing 'knowledge-intensive, innovation-driven' industry (Wong 2005: 169).

Until now, governing theories on the development of S&T in South Korea have centered on state intervention and developmentalism. The example of the rapid development of S&T is usually referred to as the success story. In his developmental model 'Imitation to Innovation' (Kim 1997), Kim Linsu stresses the importance of the government, which set up the basic framework and provided the fuel for conglomerates (chaebol) to operate like economic engines (Kim 1997: 15).

Nevertheless, because South Korean S&T has always been studied in connection with state economic development, critical reviews on developmentalism itself and its relation to S&T are extremely rare.

In my paper I would like to present an alternative way of applying the concept of developmentalism. Developmentalism in this research is not a neutral concept; rather, it is itself a subject of critique since 'developmentalism has not been challenged but [has] existed under a so-called false consensus' (Cho 2002: 308). In fact, the negative effects of economic growth-oriented developmentalism are closely related to the progress of S&T policies in South Korea (i.e. the treatment of S&T and scientists and engineers as instruments for economic development). I intend to emphasize the ways developmentalism victimizes other sectors in the name of 'economic growth.' In this aspect, the developmentalism discussed in this research is one oriented towards one-way (economic) achievement, which is similar to the concept defined by Cho, who posited developmentalism as a '[. . .] growth-oriented or growth-pursuing trend, represented by terms such as industrialization, GNP or GDP, export, or trade expansion' (Cho 2002: 307).

Research methods

This study is based on an in-depth interview with a former KAIST student representative and now science-technology NGO activist and policy researcher. Within the scope of the interview, questions on the history and current state of KAIST were raised based on the interviewee's own personal experiences and career. The interview took place on April 23, 2013 and lasted for four hours. Basic ideas of this study were inspired by the interviewee's statements.[3]

Furthermore, another interview with a KAIST student who attended the school during the late 1990s took place on May 23, 2013 and lasted three hours. This interview helped in particular to further understand the changes at KAIST in the 1990s.

In addition to these in-depth interviews, both personal conversations with professors and former students of KAIST and my own lecturing experience at KAIST in 2006 served as important background sources for my research.

Of course, secondary literature, KAIST-related laws, as well as policy evaluation reports and media materials were reviewed in order to offer an accurate and comprehensive picture on KAIST.

In the following main part of the chapter I would like to take a look at the history of KAIST based on the named source. I classified the history into three stages. My discussions of each of these three stages will focus on reflections on the changes in the different time frames and their implications for KAIST as the leading institution in the field of S&T.

The history of KAIST

The start-up stage (1970s)

S&T education for developing the South Korean economy

The Korea Advanced Institute of Science (KAIS), the forerunner of KAIST, was founded in 1971 during Park Chung-hee's administration. Before its establishment, in 1969, a draft foundation plan for KAIS was submitted to USAID by Chung Kun-mo, who was a professor at the Polytechnic Institute of Brooklyn in New York at the time. The South Korean government and the Ministry of Science and Technology (MOST) developed Chung's draft into a master plan that resulted in the passing of the 'Law for the Korean Advanced Institute for Science' by the National Assembly on July 16, 1970 (Lee 2011a).

The financial support granted by USAID played a critical role in the establishment of KAIS and was based on the Terman Report, which was an investigation on the situation of S&T education in South Korea at that point in time. It stresses the weak points as follows: 'Laboratory facilities are very inadequate [. . .] Students are typically taught to memorize what is in their textbooks [. . .] In addition, many South Korean faculty members lack adequate training in modern science and engineering [. . .] These factors [. . .] have caused undergraduate education in science and engineering to lag behind the needs of the dynamic and rapidly developing South Korean industrial economy' (Terman *et al.* 1970: Chapter 1). Similar problems are also identified with regard to the graduate level, which therefore 'had little, if any, impact on the Korean economy' (Terman *et al.* 1970: Chapter 1).

To be fair, the circumstances of higher education were quite hopeless at the time of the report. For example, even Seoul National University (SNU), South Korea's top national university, which was considered to have the best conditions, had only produced 48 masters in physics by 1966. 'The fact that SNU as Korea's representative national educational institution was in such a situation during those times just verifies that graduate schools in general were nothing but nominal institutes' (Kwon, Chang and Byeon 2006: 79).

Most retrospective accounts of KAIST strongly emphasize the personal association of professor Chung Kun-mo, the de facto leader of the Terman Report, with John A. Hannah, the former head at USAID. Although such personal relationships did play a role, the final loan granted by USAID, 6 million dollars, a highly significant amount, was offered more on the basis of the US Department of State's world domination strategy and USAID's policy stance. According to Hannah, US aid to developing countries was especially focusing on investment in educational institutes (Kwon, Chang and Byeon 2006).

The aid provided was based on the application of a particularly American developmentalist framework for the Third World. That is, US foreign policy under the Cold War system focused on supporting the development of newly independent nations in order to protect them from becoming communist states. These supports coincided with the aid policy stance of the Rockefeller Foundation, a representative private foundation in the United States, as well as USAID (Cueto 1994).

Rapid establishment thanks to a number of special benefits

KAIS was quickly established owing to the USAID loan and the support and benefits from the South Korean government. The Terman Report offered exceptional treatment of students under its foreign aid policy. Besides a tuition-free education, KAIS students stayed at dormitories for free and were given living expense support. They were also exempted from military service, which was the most extraordinary benefit, especially in the light of the tensions between North and South Korea at this time. Of course, other universities complained about this special treatment, since it was something they could never offer.

KAIS professors were also given exceptional treatment relative to South Korea's then economic level and received financial aid as support for research (books, equipment, etc.). Such supports and benefits helped KAIS successfully find its place. The competition rate for college entrance was maintained at three to one, and SNU graduates made up 80 per cent of master's programme students (Lee 2011b).

Career paths of students

According to Lee Sang-su, the first president of KAIS, the demand for KAIS graduates was so high that in the early 1970s all of the graduates from a specific department were offered jobs at POSCO or Samsung Electronics (Kwon, Chang and Byeon 2006: 107). Nevertheless, many KAIS graduates chose to become professors at domestic colleges after graduation.

As my interviewee made clear, most of the PhD holders became professors at various colleges across the country in the initial stages.

The institutional enlargement stage (1980s to the mid 1990s)

Government reform instead of self-initiatives for change

When KAIS took root, there were many opinions, internally and externally, on how to expand the model. Some internal groups tried to set up undergraduate courses at KAIS, but failed. The new military regime took a more extreme approach, integrating KAIS and the Korea Institute of Science and Technology (KIST) into KAIST (its current name) in January 1981 in the name of government-oriented S&T reform. The integration was not really organizational since a kind of dual system was established, composed of a research body and a teaching body. This dual system was maintained until 1989 when a re-separation occurred (Kim 2011).

The Chun Doo-hwan administration continued with its 'S&T prodigy rearing' programme. Four science high schools were established across the nation from 1983 to 1984, followed by the establishment of the Korean Institute of Technology (KIT) in 1985 (Kim 2011). In 1989, KAIST consolidated a union with KIT for the purpose of integrating undergraduate and graduate education. KAIST held its first entrance ceremony in March 1990, after its move to the current Daedeok campus in Daejeon.

The official history shows that the integration with and separation from KIST was criticized as 'politically-motivated' or 'helter-skelter' (Kim 2011), while the integration with KIT was deemed as an opportunity for expansion and for the movement of the campus from Seoul to the larger site in Daedeok.

Altogether, the process of consolidation and separation of those organizations was smoothly carried out because they were state-oriented institutions with unilateral, top-down decision-making systems. Under these circumstances, any protest against such governmental decisions would have been very unlikely.

From high school to graduate school, the track for rearing
scientists and engineers

After much meandering, the newly established KAIST followed the typical track of science prodigy rearing, including undergraduate, graduate and doctoral courses and establishing science high schools. In other words, the KAIST model, as one for carrying out the nation's national mission, was gradually expanded to undergraduate and high school education.

First of all, to enter KAIST, a student was required to pass intensive screening at the science high school level. The first science high schools in South Korea were established between 1983 and 1984; by 2012, that number had grown to twelve. Among them, some were transformed into Korean science academies, in which students are allowed to enter after two years of middle school (normally it takes three years).

In the period between 1980 and the mid-1990s many students believed that entering KAIST after two years at a science high school was a desirable course to take. Such students usually finished their general courses in the first year of high school and began preparing for the KAIST entrance exam by concentrating on mathematics and science (particularly physics and chemistry). The KAIST entrance exam was composed of mathematics, science, and English questions and known to be quite difficult. The students who successfully passed the difficult procedure of entering KAIST were then confronted with relatively flexible yet stern undergraduate courses compared to other colleges. On the one hand, they enjoyed a kind of flexibility in academic programmes unimaginable at other colleges. On the other hand, KAIST was famous for its strict academic management system. The students' GPAs (grade point averages) had to be around 2.5 out of a perfect 4.3 under the strict criteria, and they were controlled through an academic probation system wherein a student with a GPA below 2.0 was given a warning, and after three warnings was expelled. KAIST students were proud of this differentiated academic system, calling other colleges' performances mere 'academic inflation.'

Most KAIST graduates went on to enter graduate programmes at the school up until the mid-1990s. KAIST's graduate programmes were also strict: students were required to publish at least two articles in SCI (Science Citation Index) journals in order to obtain a doctoral degree. Such requirements led to successful research performances and publications in foreign academic journals, as well as industrial property rights registrations. Upon graduation, these students were guaranteed positions at colleges, national research centres or in various industries.

All in all, nobody questioned KAIST's position as an institution charged with carrying out the national mission during this time. In reality, because the contributions of KAIST's professors and students to South Korea's S&T research environment as well as to the everyday lives of people (most importantly through Internet technology development) was so much greater than any other university, nobody could deny the benefits that derived from the KAIST system. The school had reached its so-called 'golden period.' But it couldn't last forever; and it didn't. From then on, according to my interviewee' statements, KAIST began to be swayed by challenging global and domestic circumstances, challenges that were particularly significant in the late 1990s.

The stage of confusion (late 1990s–present)

Economic crisis and the gloomy prospects of the S&T field

The crisis and confusion, characteristic of the third stage, was, to a great extent, triggered by a new government. The Kim Dae-jung administration took over in 1998 after a presidential election held in 1997. This festive event in South Korea's modern political history constituted a democratic and peaceful transfer of power. At the same time, though, it was a gloomy starting point in a neo-liberalist environment—a time when South Korea found itself under IMF supervision due to the financial crisis that swept the Asian region in late 1997. South Koreans suffered from employment instability (expressed as 'flexible employment'), forced resignation ('restructuring'), personal bankruptcy, family deterioration, etc.

The S&T field was also impacted by the economic depression. From 2002 until the present, the situation has been gradually worsening for natural sciences and engineering majors in South Korea. In the 2003 Survey on the Employment Status of 2002 Graduates from Community Colleges and Universities, natural sciences and engineering majors made up the highest number of graduates and the highest number of unemployed. While the average unemployment rate at that time was 6.8 per cent, the unemployment rates for graduates of engineering and natural sciences departments were estimated at 9.8 per cent and 8.2 per cent, respectively (Kim, Kim and Jeon 2003).

Table 5.2 shows that the number of S&T graduates in 2003 was more than quadruple that of 1981. The reason can be found not in population growth, but in the increased number of higher education institutions including universities and junior colleges. This phenomenon is closely related to the cultural and structural characteristics of South Korea. Firstly, South Korean parents are largely dedicated to their children's education. Secondly, educational backgrounds have greater influence in South Korea than individual capability when it comes to employment. Nowadays, nearly 100 per cent of middle school graduates enter high schools, and more than 70 per cent of high school graduates make their way to colleges and universities (Figure 5.1).

Natural sciences and engineering departments have seen particularly high growth in the number of students enrolled over the years due to increased government support for universities since the 1990s. The percentage of science-related majors in South Korea is reported to be 41.6 per cent, much higher than the OECD average of 25.5 per cent. The problem is that though the number of science-related majors has increased, the number of jobs in those areas has not, resulting in a high rate of unemployment.

Despite the demand for change from outside, there are no alternatives

The Kim administration was determined to adjust the roles and structures of governmental departments and pursue economic reforms. As part of such efforts, it attempted to move KAIST into the Ministry of Education (MOE) from MOST.

Table 5.2 Distribution of majors among college and university graduates (unit: person, %)

	No. of Graduates	Science & Engineering	Humanities	Social Science	Medical Science	Athletic & Artistic Field	Education
1981	55,846	40.1	10.5	18.8	6.3	7.3	17.1
1985	118,584	35.1	15.8	23.2	4.0	6.3	15.6
1990	165,916	34.7	17.2	27.2	4.1	6.9	10.0
1995	180,664	39.9	15.5	25.8	4.0	7.8	7.1
2000	214,498	39.9	15.1	26.5	4.3	8.5	5.8
2003	257,526	40.4	15.1	25.3	4.5	9.3	5.4

Source: Adapted from Lee and Chung 2005; quoted from Park et al. 2006: 37

Even though the move would have kept intact the benefits given to KAIST students, KAIST students and professors protested against the attempt.

Here was an expression of a specific kind of anxiety. The transfer from MOST to MOE would have likely meant that KAIST would no longer be considered a 'unique' institution.

In a sense, this crisis occurred as a result of KAIST's failure to cope with the new situation. When KAIST could no longer cling to its identity as an institution carrying out the national mission—with that identity being questioned in government, in society and even within its own walls—in the absence of any new identity, anomie resulted. As far as the government was concerned, KAIST was just a normal university controlled by the MOE, instead of an institution charged with a national mission. The protest against the organizational change could not, in the end, bring back the school's golden days.

This crisis gradually began to seep into KAIST's student body. The number of KAIST students who prefer to take various state exams including the patent lawyer test instead of attending graduate school at KAIST has been on the rise since the late 1990s. Many high-ranking science high school students choose to enter medical schools, not KAIST. The importance of S&T and scientists and engineers in our society has been gradually degraded. Finishing a KAIST doctoral programme no longer guarantees a professorship at a domestic university, and KAIST now faces more competition with other high-quality S&T graduate schools.

Actually, this crisis is not unique to KAIST and can be seen in other national and public research institutes that also focus on S&T. My interviewee told me that, 'Now we cannot consider it [KAIST] a national mission organization any more. [. . .] They justify themselves through more patents and commercialize them for better business performance in accordance with neo-liberalist principles. This is not an age of national missions, but an era of self-legitimacy under a neo-liberalist structure'.

So what is the solution? In the next part, I would like to discuss this question focusing on whether S&T organizations and educational institutions, including KAIST, have an answer. At the beginning I would like to refer to some of the issues that have arisen from KAIST's history.[4]

Issues arising out of the history of KAIST

KAIST has suffered many organizational reshuffles since its creation out of KAIS. As the evaluation of the history of KAIST has shown, these changes have not been carried out predominantly because of internal needs, but because of external causes, such as a change of government. Such circumstances have resulted in unnecessary shifts, under which the school has suffered. Therefore the example of KAIST demonstrates how South Korean S&T policy has been mostly set up as a kind of exhibition put on according to the political purposes of the government rather than as something consistently promoted according to its own independent vision and legitimacy.

Technology or science: contribution to industrial development or pure academics

The founding law of the Korean Advanced Institute of Science defines that KAIS 'shall educate such persons with both profound theories and practical adaptability as are required in the fields of science and technology for industrial development' (Terman *et al.* 1970: Appendix A, Law of the Korean Advanced Institute of Science: Article A).

Although the clauses of this law emphasize both 'profound theories' and 'practical adaptability,' KAIST members and government officials have focused on one or the other different historical periods.

During the initial phase of KAIST, its members were likely to stick to 'profound theories' and to stress the importance of producing Nobel Prize winners and becoming professors instead of going into industry.

On the other hand, the dominant line of thinking in charting the evolution of KAIST has been focused on 'practical adaptability.' Most policy evaluation reports on KAIST, including even its own descriptions of its history, overwhelmingly emphasize 'practical adaptability.'

The discrepancy was a thorny issue that could not be bypassed in policy evaluation reports, however uncomfortable it was to admit (Kwon, Chang and Byeon 2006). There was in fact a low demand for doctoral degree holders in South Korea's industries in the late 1970s, whereas there was high demand in college faculties because the number of colleges had continued to grow steadily from the early 1980s on.

The duplicity of special favors: freedom or fetters?

KAIST students were granted various special benefits that gave them the freedom of mind to take on challenges in their studies. In this sense, they commonly focused on carrying out their own research missions rather than on pursuing economic value. At the same time, KAIST students also carried the burden of repaying the various supports given to them. This weight had the effect of blocking, at times, their ability to soar and innovate, since they were perceived as 'intercepting mechanisms.'

KAIST students took advantage of a development track given by the state or institution. However, they were not encouraged to raise their voices. It appears that they did not even want to speak up, for they required continuous support. For example, they were less likely to take advantage of the complex master-apprentice relationship between professors and students, common in all graduate schools. Any disagreement with their professors could have potentially led to various disadvantages, which might have forced them to leave their academic circle. Additionally, KAIST students were given various social favours. Although they were expected to feel confident after benefitting from those advantages, they did not in fact do so. It was almost like they had settled for these advantages alone.

Because the students were blocked from broader, freer thought under the weight of the special treatment, they were not able to muster the internal strength needed to counter the current crisis. The era of KAIST leading the national mission is over, and transformed circumstances on a global scale and within South Korean society have complicated governmental efforts to set up a new position for the school. While ideally this new position should come from the inside, it is too difficult for an actor who has up until now only focused on S&T in response to 'favours' to find the agency to propose such a new position.

Conclusion

In this study I examined the shift in implications in S&T in South Korea from the 1970s until now through a case study on KAIST, South Korea's foremost S&T-oriented educational institution. With its high academic standards and accomplished graduates, KAIST has consistently been ranked at the top of domestic and international best university lists. Its accomplishments, however, could not keep it from suffering a major tragedy and facing a firestorm of controversy after four of its students committed suicide in a single semester in 2011.

If we look deeply into the KAIST suicides in the context of the ever-changing S&T environment, it is clear that the failure to propose a value for competition stands at the root of the problem. When KAIST could no longer cling to its identity as an institution carrying out the national mission, it ended up in a state of anomie.

The anomie of KAIST is emblematic of the current status of S&T in South Korea. And it is neither an exceptional case of just one institution nor a case limited to S&T HR policy. Since the 1970s, South Korea set up a national mission for S&T development backed by tremendous government support and a nationwide consensus on the need for economic development. This development was to be accomplished through nurturing S&T, which has been an essential factor in South Korea's economic progress. Around 2000, however, people became sceptical about the actual availability and theoretical validity of state-initiated developmentalism. Moreover, the global craze for neo-liberalism denied the exceptional privileges given to S&T, pressuring governments worldwide to withdraw such support. Scientists and engineers were suddenly forced to compete with their peers to get the funding they needed. Indeed, in this new environment, no new value has appeared to replace the former value—that is, the sense of S&T as a national mission.

I believe that the current anomie offers an invaluable opportunity to reflect critically on the history of South Korean S&T and on the role scientists and engineers played in the past and could play in the future. It also serves as a background to identify and explain the various problems currently confronting the field of science and technology.

It is clear that a set of new values has to be defined. However, it is unclear who would be capable of pushing forward a new agenda. It remains to be seen how the current situation of anomie will develop. I believe that further research can acquaint readers with the significance of the field of S&T for South Korean society in the past and future.

Notes

1 This was followed by the answers 'Improvement of national R&D budget allocation system' (36.3%), 'Change of R&D paradigm' (35.7%), 'Popularization of science and engineering and citizen participation' (31.5%), 'Ways to implement next generation growth engines' (30.4%), and 'Restructuring of science and engineering administrative system' (28.3%).
2 An interviewee who works as a professor at KAIST reported that most KAIST applicants feel as if they are 'less than' the top ranked students at science high schools who mostly enter medical schools. This is very much in contrast with KAIST applicants of the past, who were brimming with self-confidence.
3 I would like to acknowledge here the invaluable contributions this interviewee made to the study.
4 Park Geun-hye's new government inaugurated in 2013 revived S&T's former role as 'contributing to economic development' when it renamed the 'Ministry of Science' as the much grander 'Ministry of Science, ICT & Future Planning.' This is a move highly reminiscent of her father, former President Park Chung-hee. However, it is doubtful whether this harkening back to the past actually coincides with changes in the times and reflects the needs of scientists and engineers working in the field today.

Bibliography

Bak, Hee-Je (2007): Determinants of Public Preference for Science Related Occupations and the Phenomena of Avoidance of Science and Engineering Fields (in Korean), *Korean Journal of Sociology* 41 (6). Pp. 142–170.

Cho, Hee-Yeon (1998): *Korea's State, Democracy, and Political Changes: For an Open Competition among Conservatism, Liberalism, and Progressivism* (in Korean). Dangdae, Seoul.

Cho, Hee-Yeon (2002): A Study on the Change in the State, Civil Society and Social Movements in Relation to Transformation of the So-called 'Developmental State': Focused on the Change in the Characteristics of the Developmentalism and Social Movements in South Korea (in Korean), *Social Philosophy* 4. Pp. 293–351.

Cueto, Marcos (ed.) (1994): *Missionaries of Science: The Rockefeller Foundation and Latin America*. Indiana University Press, Bloomington and Indianapolis.

Evans, Peter (1997): The Eclipse of the State? Reflections on Stateness in an Era of Globalization, *World Politics* 50 (1). Pp. 62–87.

Giddens, Anthony (1971): *Capitalism and Modern Social Theory: An Analysis of the Writings of Marx, Durkheim and Max Weber*. Cambridge University Press, Cambridge.

Han, Kyong Hee (2004): Reinterpretation of the Crisis in Science-and-Technology Sector and Self-reflection of Engineers (in Korean), *Korean Journal of Sociology* 38(4). Pp. 73–99.

KCUE (Korean Council for University Education) (2008): KAIST (in Korean), *Higher Education* 153. Pp. 29–34.

Kim, Hyung-Man, Mi-Lan Kim and Jae-Sik Jeon (2003): The 2003 Survey on the Employment Status of 2002 Graduates from Community Colleges and Universities (in Korean). Korea Research Institute for Vocational Education and Training, Seoul. Available from http://www.krivet.re.kr/ku/ca/prg_kuAADvwVw.jsp?gn=E1-E120040077 [Accessed 17 September 2014].

Kim, Linsu (1997): *Imitation to Innovation: The Dynamics of Korea's Technological Learning*. Harvard Business School Press, Boston.

Kim, Seon-Reen (2011): KAIST as the Nucleus of Korea's Science Hopes (in Korean). *The KAIST Times*, March 12. Available from http://times.kaist.ac.kr/news/articleView. html?idxno=886 [Accessed 17 October 2014].

Korea Science Foundation (2004): The 2004 Survey on the Public Understanding of Science and Technology (in Korean). Seoul.

Kwon, Won-Ki, Soo-Young Chang and Myeong-Seop Byeon (2006): A Study on Effects of Industrial Development by Major Science and Technology Policy (in Korean). Ministry of Science and Technology, Seoul.

Lee, Byeong Cheon (1998): Korea's Development Capitalism and Development Dilemma. (in Korean), *Creation and Criticism* 101. Pp. 250–270.

Lee, Byung-Hee and Jaeho Chung (2005): A Study on the Labor Mobility and Skill Development (in Korean). Korea Labor Institute, Seoul. Available from http://www. kli.re.kr/kli_home/isdata/vew.home-21010?branch=1&seq=6136&listNum=6136#n one [Accessed 17 September 2014].

Lee, Min-Woo (2011a): The 'Great Birth' of Korea's First Graduate School of Science & Technology: Special Series, 'The Past Forty Years and the Future of KAIST' (in Korean). *The KAIST Times*, February 2011. Available from http://times.kaist.ac.kr/ news/articleView.html?idxno=817 [Accessed 17 October 2014].

Lee, Min-Woo (2011b): Ten Years after Establishment, KAIST Continues onwards (in Korean). *The KAIST Times*, March 2. Available from http://times.kaist.ac.kr/news/ articleView.html?idxno=858 [Accessed 15 October 2014].

National Statistical Office (2014): e-National indicators (in Korean), Available from http://www.index.go.kr/potal/stts/idxMain/selectPoSttsIdxSearch.do?idx_ cd=1520&clas_div=&idx_sys_cd=732&idx_clas_cd=1 [Accessed 17 October 2014].

Oh, Choon-Ho (2004): Avoidance of Science and Engineering, the Main Challenge of Science and Technology Fields in 2004 (in Korean). *The Korea Economic Daily*, January 6. Available from http://www.hankyung.com/news/app/newsview. php?aid=2004010594661 [Accessed 17 October 2014].

Park, Jaemin *et al.* (2006): A Study on the School-to-Work Transition and Employment Structure of S&T Graduates: Statistical Analysis and Policy Recommendation (in Korean). Science and Technology Policy Institute, Seoul. Available from http://www. stepi.re.kr/app/report/view.jsp?cmsCd=CM0012&categCd=A0201&ntNo=378 [Accessed 17 September 2014].

Terman, Frederick E *et al.* (1970): Survey Report on the Establishment of the Korea Advanced Institute of Science. Prepared for US Agency for International Development. Available from http://large.stanford.edu/history/kaist/docs/terman/ [Accessed 17 September 2014].

Wade, Robert (1996): Japan, the World Bank, and the Art of Paradigm Maintenance: The East Asian Miracle in Political Perspective, *New Left Review* 217 (May-June). Pp. 3–36.

Won, Ho-Seop (2013): International Science Olympiad Winners Do Not Choose to Enter Science or Engineering Schools in Korea (in Korean). *Maeil Business Paper*, September 25. Available from http://vip.mk.co.kr/news/view/21/20/1056920.html [Accessed 15 October 2014].

Wong, Joseph (2005): Re-Making the Developmental State in Taiwan: The Challenges of Biotechnology, *International Political Science Review* 26 (2). Pp. 169–191.

6 Challenges for STEM education in India

Sundar Sarukkai

STEM in higher education

Many complex factors have influenced STEM education in India. These factors range from unique historical influences due to colonialism, to the belief in science as the vehicle for modernity and development in independent India, as well as the difficulty in integrating this vision with traditional practices of its citizens.

This report will begin by listing some numbers related to higher education in India and will then go on to reflect on public attitudes towards STEM, attractiveness of this education in India today, and key programmes initiated by the government and the private sectors to support STEM. It will also analyse the cultural roots that play a role in understanding these practices and conclude with current trends.

The All India Survey on Higher Education (AISHE) (Department of Higher Education 2013) has generated a very useful database about higher education in India. This includes statistics not only related to students but also to teachers. It also includes important socio-economic data on the distribution of students and teachers. Most of the data cited in this contribution comes from this particular survey.

First of all, we should note that Indian universities are more generally modelled on the British system where a university has many constituent colleges. For example, Bangalore University has over 600 colleges, and Delhi University has nearly 100,000 students enrolled in all its colleges. This means that such state universities are very unwieldy, and also makes it difficult for changes to be introduced into this huge system. While one might contrast this with smaller, more autonomous, private universities, we should also remember that the public universities in India play a very important role in allowing access to education to the disadvantaged sections of society. Thus, these universities must not be evaluated only in terms of certain educational practices but should be evaluated through their contribution to social justice in India.

As AISHE points out, there are 621 universities, 32,974 colleges and 11,095 stand-alone institutions of which there are 89 technical, 34 agriculture, 25 medical, 17 law and 9 veterinary universities. The total enrolment of students is 27.5 million, out of which 15.5 million are male and 12 million are female.

Thus, the Gross Enrolment Ratio (GER) in higher education is 19.4 per cent, out of which male students constitute 20.8 per cent and female students 17.9 per cent (Department of Higher Education 2013: iiif).

Higher education starts with the undergraduate programmes. According to the All India Survey on Higher Education, the distribution of students according to disciplines is as follows:

Arts/humanities/social science is around 47 per cent of all students (Department of Higher Education 2013: iv). As we can see, the largest number of students is enrolled in these disciplines. Generally, in the Indian context, there is no specific distinction made between these terminologies at the undergraduate level. The basic degree is a BA (Bachelor of Arts), which includes subjects of both humanities and social sciences. Although there are specific fine arts courses that lead to degrees like Bachelor of Fine Arts, they are very few in number.

The next highest enrolment is in engineering and technology, which is around 16 per cent. Although there is huge state support for science, at the undergraduate level, the number of students in commerce is significant and accounts for 13 per cent of all the students. Science follows at 11 per cent enrolment (Department of Higher Education 2013: iv). In terms of numbers, BAs have 5,711,000 students. In comparison, the science degrees, which include engineering, pure sciences and medical sciences, have enrolment as follows: BE (Bachelor of Engineering) 869,761, BTech (Bachelor of Technology) 1,452,239, MBBS (Bachelor of Medicine and Bachelor of Surgery) 89,463, other medical students, such as nursing, around 376,000, and BSc (the degree in pure science) 1,741,575 students (Department of Higher Education 2013: T-29ff).

As mentioned above, engineering and technology is the second major stream having 2,139,491 undergraduate students enrolled, and it consists of 13 streams, including electronics engineering, which has the most students (around 542,000 students), computer engineering (around 47,000 students), mechanical engineering (around 356,000 students), electrical engineering (around 287,000 students), information technology (around 244,000 students) and others. The number of students in the science stream is 1,467,000 and computer science/ computer application is 401,000. Computer science is also taught as a science stream in addition to the engineering/technology stream (Department of Higher Education 2013: T-37).

The number of students going from undergraduate to postgraduate and doctoral degrees is quite small. The primary reason for this is the possibility of getting a job after an undergraduate degree. Although this tendency was more prevalent with engineering degrees and less so for the BA and BSc, we find that more students take up jobs after their undergraduate arts and science degree due to the wide variety of jobs that have been catalysed by the IT sector, including call centres and service sectors. Eighty per cent of all higher education students are in the undergraduate courses. Thus, increasing this number is a focus for the government. In India, there is a degree called an MPhil, which is like a research degree after an MA. The percentage of students in MPhil and PhD programmes is 0.5 per cent each. The overall numbers for postgraduate degrees are MSc 362,000 students and MTech has 88,064 students. In total, there are 209,000 students at the postgraduate level and 15,346 students enrolled in PhD studies. The number of postgraduates in computer science/computer applications is 166,000 and for PhD in these fields it is 1,402 students. The number of students in postgraduate studies in computer engineering is 68,467 and in information technology it is 20,012 (Department of Higher Education 2013: T38).

Postgraduate and doctoral enrolment in the sciences is better compared to its position in undergraduate education. The total number of postgraduate students in the Sciences is 303,000, out of which there are 67,317 in mathematics and 60,342 in chemistry. Physics has 28,848 and zoology 19,767. Incidentally, zoology also has the highest number of female students. For PhD programmes, the highest enrolment is in the sciences and consists of 22,717 students. Medical PhDs are 1,781.

In any analysis of education in India, we have to take into account sociological factors, particularly community representation. In the total number of students, Scheduled Caste students constitute 11.1 per cent and Scheduled Tribes students 4.4 per cent. Other Backward Classes constitute 27.6 per cent, and 3.6 per cent belong to Muslim minorities (Department of Higher Education 2013: iv).

In terms of public-private distribution, 70 per cent of colleges are run by the private sector. The total number of teachers in higher education institutions is 765,349 leading to a pupil-teacher ratio of 26.4 in universities and colleges (Department of Higher Education 2013: v). In the Indian context, distance education is an important component of higher education. A significant number of students get educated through distance education programmes. They constitute 12.1 per cent of the total enrolment in higher education, of which 40.1 per cent are female students (Department of Higher Education 2013: 21). Distance education and correspondence degrees are popular both among rural and urban students. Because of this mode, older students are more easily able to re-enter education, thus enabling them to get a degree after a few years in a job. Another great advantage is that one can pursue these degrees even while working in a regular job. There are a large number of students who take up these courses—particularly in semi-urban and rural areas—since it is much cheaper than attending college or university as they can stay at home and get a degree at the end of it. For example, one of the biggest such courses today is the Sikkim-Manipal correspondence course, offered in a wide variety of topics.[1]

Public attitudes towards STEM and STEM education

There are many reasons why STEM education is comparatively well off compared with other disciplines. First of all, there is strong public support for it, both at the family level and government level. Generally there is also strong support among teachers in schools and colleges for continuing to study STEM subjects.

But the numbers given above show a different picture: the majority of students are in the arts and humanities fields. This is paradoxical given the disproportionate support for the sciences as mentioned above. There are many reasons why so many students do a BA, including not doing well in science sub-jects and having a genuine problem with mathematical education. Moreover, there is a serious problem in the medium of instruction. In general, students who do science in a non-English medium lose out much more than those in English medium education. Compounding this problem is the lack of English proficiency of science students in rural and semi-urban areas, so even when they do science in English (which has become the de facto mode of mainstream science education), their language skills get in the way of effective learning. Thus, it is not really a surprise that more BA students come from non-urban areas and also that many of them do their undergraduate course with specialization in the many Indian languages.

From my experience of talking to students over many years, I can isolate some common pointers about science education and the expectations of family and society. As far as the family support is concerned, very often it is based on the social prestige of these fields as well as the job opportunities that follow from degrees in science education. For a very long time in India, there has been strong family pressure on many students to do either engineering or medicine. While there are variations across urban and rural families, or between the rich and the middle class as compared to the poorer sections of the society, or between males and females, it is nevertheless the case that such professional education was seen not just as a way to get jobs but was also associated with social prestige. Since these professional degrees were seen as an escape from a life of poverty, those among the poorer classes who could afford to also sent their children to these courses. Today, management studies and computer education have joined medi-cal and engineering in terms of social prestige. The appreciable number of Indian students who are working abroad in areas like computer science and software application has led to greater family pressure on students to pursue degrees in these fields.

Family and public pressure on children to get medical and engineering degrees is not new. This attitude has defined Indian education over many decades. Indian medical education is somewhat different compared to some other countries since students do not have to have any special training like pre-med education. They directly join the medical degree (MBBS) right after twelfth grade. The pressure to study medicine is often due to family pressure as well as a larger public pressure on students. The public pressure is from peers, teachers and the larger extended family and friends. There are many instances where students become traumatized by their failure to get into professional education.

The demand for medical education has also catalysed a major change in Indian education. Education in India was primarily public and driven by the government. The first private initiative in higher education was primarily driven by the lack of seats in medical education. This initiative, by Dr T. M. A. Pai, led to the creation of the first private medical school at a small place called Manipal. It was initially met with great scepticism but has now grown to become one of the premier private universities in the country. Reflecting this changing scenario, the government has approved the establishment of private universities in the country. This trend, along with a growing interest in setting up campuses of foreign universities from the US and UK, for example, will definitely impact the nature and deliverance of education in the coming decades, as discussed later (see also Chapter 7).

While the growth of medical schools has been steady but slow (perhaps because of the investment costs in setting up medical schools which need a teaching hospital attached to them), the growth of engineering colleges has been phenomenal. In the first spurt of liberalization, thousands of private engineering colleges were set up in India. They not only catered to the growing demands of engineering education, but also led to increased access and interest in it. This spurt also overlapped with the growth of the Indian IT sector. Perhaps one of the most significant influences was the global spread of Indian IT companies. Computer education initially became a synonym for foreign jobs and later on became the ideal for students to aspire to. In a direct response, not only were computer engineering courses popular, but interesting new degrees such as Bachelor of Computer Application (BCA) and Master in Computer Application (MCA) were also introduced to give degrees in these fields for students who did not manage to get into the engineering degree. The growth of these courses has been quite strong over the years.

The public attitude towards education primarily as a guarantor of jobs inspired the growth of professional education at the expense of 'basic' education like the BSc or the BA. In particular, a phenomenal growth in business administration degrees led to an increased number of students who joined the MBA bandwagon. Interestingly, many science and engineering graduates also decided to take up this degree after their science degrees. In fact, today, engineering students dominate in most of the best business schools.

However, there is an important trend today, which has implications for these courses in the coming years. Many engineering colleges and business schools are closing down (Murray 2014). Some see this as a market correction as colleges with poor infrastructure and quality are being forced to close down. However, given the complexity of governance of educational institutions in India there is little that one can predict about the future of these disciplines.

In contrast to private initiatives in education, the government's support is largely based on its belief that science education is the pathway to development and necessary for being a part of global economy. Often the government releases projections of how many engineers and doctors it needs. These numbers for engineers are often calculated with the support of private companies in these fields. In order to be competitive in the Intellectual Property (IP) regime, the government also supports science education for promoting research in science and technology.

But without much doubt, we can claim that public attitudes are responsible for the growth of certain sectors in education. Interestingly, there are strong correlations between this attitude and certain social practices. For example, even now we hear about reports that medical and engineering students get higher dowries, a practice that has been quite endemic for some time. In fact, getting suitable brides in the past was dependent on their degree. Doctors often got enormous dowries, especially in the state of Andhra Pradesh. This social practice not only continues today, but is now often seen as a way to subsidize the enormous cost of postgraduate degrees in medicine.

I recently discovered another interesting social practice that is influenced by these public attitudes. There is a community called Havyak Brahmins, found in certain parts of Karnataka. This community is facing a crisis in that the boys of marriageable age are not finding suitable partners from the same community. This is because many of these families are traditional plantation or agricultural land owners, and the girls of this generation do not want to marry these boys who live in their family houses. Instead, they want boys who live in Bangalore or elsewhere and who have a professional degree. Although this might sound like an insignificant issue, the pressure to be professionally educated in order to be successful in finding a spouse has consequences on the social structure and aspirations of the younger generation.

Attractiveness of STEM and STEM education

STEM education is attractive for many reasons. For the aspiring middle class, a bachelor's degree is a pathway to get jobs in the government sector. Some of the points about the public attitudes described above also made these degrees very attractive. The growth of skill oriented courses like bachelors in business management, in computer applications and so on, are now geared primarily to create students for the job market. In particular, the global need for those with software skills has led to growth in courses that market these skills. Basic undergraduate education is also of great use for the supportive services around software, including call centres and Business Process Outsourcing, commonly called BPOs.

In this shift to utilitarian education, the pure science subjects are not doing that well. Although the situation is slightly better on account of stronger government intervention through fellowships and starting of new quality science teaching institutions, the number of students opting for serious study of science subjects has been going down. So now we have the situation that if a student were to be interested in the pure sciences, he or she would go to one of these specialized institutions, whereas the science education in most of the thousands of colleges remains quite poor. Added to this is the sharp drop in number of students who pursue postgraduate degrees. This is particularly true of engineering and technology education, although in science courses there is a better percentage of students who go on for their master's degree. One of the major reasons for this is that engineering students get jobs immediately after their undergraduate degree.

The fact that only 0.5 per cent of students enter PhD programmes is also a great cause of worry. Nowadays, there is good incentive to get a PhD degree for all teachers, particularly those who are teaching in the universities and teaching undergraduate courses. Schoolteachers do not have this requirement or pressure to get a PhD. For the universities, this requirement by the University Grants Commission (UGC), the regulatory body for higher education in India, holds good for teachers in higher education. By making it more difficult to get promoted or get teaching jobs at a particular level without a PhD, the UGC is pushing for a greater number of PhDs as teachers. Thus, we find that a large number of teachers are registering for PhD programmes across the country.

Key programmes and initiatives in the field of STEM

There are many government-funded initiatives such as national scholarships, mentorship programmes, sponsored visits to laboratories and institutions and free tuition in almost all major science programmes. For supporting science, the government starts giving fellowships and other incentives right from school. There are also major private fellowships and scholarships to support science education.[2] The establishment of new science and technology institutes in line with the earlier Indian Institute of Technologies (IIT) has led to a growth in quality science education. The number of IITs has almost doubled, while a few institutions of science education and research (IISER) have been started over the last few years.

Historically, science education and research had become bifurcated in post-independence India. Universities were expected to take on the job of teaching science while research institutes would do the job of research. For a long time, this led to a deep fissure between teaching and doing science. The research institutions were very well funded and attracted good talent, while over the years the universities had to bear the brunt of many problems including lack of autonomy, lack of funds and explicit politicization of the university system. While institutions such as the Tata Institute of Fundamental Research, Mumbai or the Indian Institute of Science, Bangalore made a name based on the quality of their research, over the years the universities lost their standing as well as public prestige. However, without a good educational system it was not possible to generate good graduate students to support research in India. Thus, the engagement of active scientists with school and undergraduate education was absolutely necessary. Although this hierarchy of research institutes and universities continues, there has been some attempt to get research scientists to engage a little more with education at the lower levels.

A delayed recognition of this malaise caused due to an artificial segregation between teaching and research led to the creation of institutions like IISERs. Funding for research in universities has also increased over the last few years and the University Grants Commission (UGC) now places more accountability towards research publications for faculty in universities.

In this context, it is worthwhile remembering that a significant percentage of the 'good' students in postgraduate courses go abroad for their doctoral studies. There is a significant number of PhD students from India who study in the US, UK and Australia, and now increasingly in Europe. The earlier generation of students who went in the 1960s and 70s largely stayed in these countries. This trend continues even now, although there has been a marked shift in the number of people who return to India for academic and industry jobs. The question of brain drain, although repeatedly invoked, is really not a significant issue for many reasons, one of which is that there is not enough infrastructure right now to absorb all these students if they return to India, particularly in universities. Moreover, the quality of PhDs from Indian research institutions has also improved so there is more competition from within India itself.

Social and cultural dimensions of STEM and STEM education

There are many aspects that relate cultural roots and STEM education. First is the impact of colonial education policies. Modern education is often seen as a product of British rule in India. While it definitely introduced English to Indian education, it also introduced science as a way to counter the traditional knowledge systems in India. The valuing of European thought along with a rejection of the importance of Indian knowledge systems meant that education in India was based on two skewed views of what constituted valuable knowledge. The rejection of anything Indian also meant that Indian traditions could not be part of any history of science, since science was seen as a special capacity possessed only by European cultures. Association of values such as rationality and reason with science meant that such science could not have been developed by natives. This led to viewing science as a purely Western enterprise. For a historical account of the reception of non-Western science and technology, which also describes in detail the colonial discourse on Indian science and technology, see Adas (1989) or Alvares (1991).

Not only was science seen to be Western in spirit, it was also seen as the agent for change from a traditional, superstition-ridden society. Unfortunately, the founding fathers of independent India continued this story. To them, science would not only get rid of superstition and traditional practices, but it was also the only path to progress and development.

The belief in science as the path to development also meant that the Indian nation began building big science programmes like the space and atomic programmes. The scientific ambition of the young independent nation was indeed very high. In the fields of space, nuclear physics and computers, for example, India has had considerable growth and is now one of only a handful of nations that has certain high technology capabilities in these fields. Colonial education was indeed a defining moment in the establishment of modern science education in India (in this context see Kapila 2010; Kumar 1988). Sangwan points out that the British rulers first allowed the continuation of traditional education in India and later changed it on the lines of their own system (Sangwan 1990). It is also important to note, as Sangwan does, that many influential Indians wanted the British to introduce 'modern' education—with an emphasis on science education—as opposed to traditional education.

But the state of science education is not limited to the colonial influence alone. The beginning of independent India began with certain deep commitments to the value of science and science education. The first leaders of independent India believed that modern India could only be built on the basis of scientific rationality. They also identified the problems of India as a by-product of its traditional mindset. Thus, the possibility of modernity in India—at least to these leaders—was based on establishing science as the fundamental pillar of independent India.

This led to the incorporation of 'scientific temper'[3] as a fundamental duty for all Indian citizens in the Indian constitution. This drastic articulation was more a hope, for there was little that was clear about the definition of 'scientific temper.' However, the belief that scientific ways of thinking and doing would get its citizens out of their traditional beliefs and customs was one that has been re-articulated in various ways over the years since independence. In particular, scientific temper was supposedly a way to overcome the problems of superstition and blind faith, which seemingly afflicted ordinary Indian citizens. This belief and the associated rhetoric around it remain strong even today. In staking this claim, these leaders also naively opposed science and religion. Perhaps more than anything else, this problematical conflation of religion with anti-science has been the greatest obstacle to the establishment of a national scientific temper, since religious belief is deep rooted within the very cultural practices of this country.

Science was also seen, at the dawn of independent India, to be the main vehicle for development and change. Thus, the first Prime Minister of India, Jawaharlal Nehru, claimed that industries would be the temples of the new India. Similar to the Australian Council for Scientific and Industrial Research (CSIR), a new institution was formed in India. The support for the establishment of an atomic programme almost from the inception of independent India meant that the country had ambitions to leapfrog into contemporary science right from the beginning.

The atomic programme and the space programme have been two public faces of Indian science. While the atomic programme has been mired in many controversies, including questions on its value and cost, the space programme, on the other hand, has had a far more successful public presence. This is primarily because of the use of its satellites for telecommunication in India. Almost all the launches of the Indian Space Research Organization (ISRO) are covered quite extensively in the press. The latest successful Mars Mission in September 2014 (Sebastian 2014) was headline news. Both these organizations have also been at the forefront of indigenous science and technology. While this term, indigenous, may be confused with ancient technology, in this case it refers to the creation of technologies for space and atomic programmes by the community of Indian scientists with little help from the technologically advanced Western countries. Following the testing of the atomic bomb, India was placed under sanction by the US and other Western countries. This sanction forced India to become self-sufficient in technology and the success of the space programme is often attributed to the indigenization of technology.

Along with these sophisticated technologies, over the last two decades India has been at the forefront of a computer revolution. Although this revolution is largely in the software sector, it has nevertheless had a great impact on cultural engagement with science. For example, within India, it catalysed a large of number of students to study computer science and a host of related courses like computer application, courses on software, on Session Announcement Protocol (SAP) etc. Even in public services, like the booking of railway tickets, the introduction of computers has revolutionized the nature of service and, through it, brought the lure of digital technology into the cultural sphere. The IT revolution in India has also helped to change the perception of India in Europe and the Americas. Along with an increased number of computer scientists of Indian origin who are at the forefront of many technology companies across the world, the cultural questions around technology and its role in Indian society are slowly but surely changing (for a description of the interplay between technology and religion in India, see Sarukkai 2008).

However, there are still some earlier perceptions of science that have not changed much. One of these is the belief that science is predominantly 'Western' in character. Interestingly, this claim has been made repeatedly in most of the standard texts of science published around the world. In fact, when Indian mathematics and science were discovered and brought to the attention of the Western scholars, most of these scholars dismissed the claims. For example, popular books on science and mathematics are often completely silent about non-Greek, non-European contributions to early science. They also go to the extent of claiming that the scientific imagination was possible only in the Greco-European imagination.[4] This view, perhaps more than anything else, has harmed the internalization of science in India. Not only has this claim made the very idea of science alien to India (and generally to non-Western civilizations), it has also been accomplished at the expense of a rich heritage in science and technology right from ancient India.

I would argue that the difficulty in accepting science as something Indian has harmed science education in many ways. First of all, the narratives of science often begin with a history of modern science, which is situated entirely in Europe. Thus, the examples of scientists who are invoked in these texts are often European or, in later times, American. Added to this selective historical rendering of science is the almost complete absence of Nobel Prize winners working in India. Somehow this narrative of science seems to suggest to science students that not only was science absent in ancient and medieval India, but its present day scientists do not seem to have the creative capacity of successful Western scientists. One should not underestimate the importance of this worldview on how students learn and internalize science. Given this narrative, students in India tend to look at science as something alien to the intellectual practices of their society. This tends to decrease the confidence they have in their own scientific practices, since generations of students grow up with the belief that the Western mind has somehow got special capabilities to do science.

Moreover, contemporary science is taught through homogenized, universally used books. There are very few quality science books that are written by Indian scientists, compared with the enormous volume of such books from the West. This means that Indian students grow up on a diet of texts whose authors are all mostly marked as Western. Next to the missing self-confidence, this distorted perception also leads to a sense of scepticism about work done in India and by Indians; so much so that there are many cases where Indians hesitate to cite other Indians' work and instead choose to cite work from other countries instead.

In order to understand these narratives and the wrong impression they invoke, it is extremely important to take into account a historical perspective for two main reasons. Firstly, the historical account of science as if it existed primarily in the Greek tradition and not in other traditions is false. Secondly, the story about the origin of modern science in Europe has to be modified to take into account current work in multicultural histories of science, which have shown how the origin of modern science in Europe was based on the science from other cultures including the Chinese, Indians, Arabs and the Greeks (on multicultural origins of science, see Bala 2006). Rewriting world histories of science, as well as taking these into account in science texts in all cultures, is necessary not only to set the record straight but also to remove the inherent hegemony of scientific knowledge and scientific imagination as something special to a few communities in the West.

Firstly, we should note that what is called 'ancient science' flourished in India. In fact, India was the crucible of some of the most important technological inventions that influenced world technology. Foremost among them was the art of metallurgy, where the first example of steel making as well as the complex metallurgical process of zinc extraction stand as monumental achievements (see Adas 1989; Alvares 1991). Other than the great expertise in making alloys, major developments in the fields of chemistry and medicine also have to be noted. Arguably, the contribution of Indian science to medicine is perhaps one of the greatest contributions of this civilization. Ayurveda was not only seen as a medical science in the ancient period, but it is also a practice which is flourishing even today in India and also elsewhere. Interestingly, in parts of India, the allopathic system is often referred to as 'English Medicine.' Medical shops selling allopathic medicines often carry this 'title.' The Ayurvedic system of knowledge competes with the claims of modern medical science and is often at the receiving end of the contempt of the latter. This is symptomatic of the derision by which modern Western science looks at any other knowledge system whose conceptual structures are alien to it. Ayurveda not only has a strong empirical component but it also has a complex theory and philosophy of the human body as well as the notion of health and cure. Valiathan, himself a prominent allopathic doctor, wrote three books on three important Ayurvedic physicians and also a good introduction to a modern understanding of Ayurveda (Valiathan 2003; 2007; 2010; 2013). However, these theories are often dismissed as being unscientific by allopathic doctors and very often this dismissal is based as much on the ignorance of what constitutes Ayurvedic science as much as their ignorance about what constitutes the nature of science.

Mathematics plays a very important part in science. In fact, we could claim that without mathematics there is no possibility of modern science. However, we should also remember that mathematics itself was imported to Europe through the Arabs who synthesized mathematics from the Indian as well as the Greek civilizations. India had a flourishing alternate tradition of mathematics and many seminal ideas arose from this culture (see Plofker 2009; Seshadri 2010). Yet, it would be difficult to find serious reference to these works in mathematical textbooks even in India, let alone the remainder of the world.

In other words, Western hegemony over science has seriously impacted what is being taught as belonging to science (on science education in the Indian context, see Kumar 2009). Not only does this privilege only certain cultures who supposedly had the capacity to do science, it also hides the historical truths about the scientific contributions from other non-Western cultures to the creation of modern science.

One way to understand this erasure is through understanding the importance that modernity in the West gave to logic and rationality. Since mathematics was an exemplar of the rational mind, particularly for extremely influential philosophers like Descartes and Leibniz, it became a marker for Western rationality and thus its presence in non-Western civilizations was fundamentally problematical since it would have challenged the claim of the European mind to rationality. Thus, it should not be a surprise to note how almost all the great writers of Europe negated the mathematical, scientific and logical contributions by Asian societies. In spite of the presence of highly developed philosophical systems as well as systems of logic, particularly in Indian philosophy, there were committed efforts by European scholars to negate the presence of these disciplines in Asian thought (on Indian logic and its rational traditions, see Matilal 1985; Mohanty 1992; Sarukkai 2005, 2012).

In saying this, we should also note that these practices of science and mathematics in India offer an important challenge to modern science as we know it today, and thus to what should be taught as science in our schools and colleges. There are two main differences, which I want to discuss briefly here. One is the view of nature that informs Indian and Chinese responses to the world, and the other is the set of beliefs and practices about mathematics, which sets it apart from modern mathematics. There is much to learn from carefully analysing these two points.

It is well known that there is an extremely close relation between the nature of science and the understanding of nature. Francis Bacon's view of nature as hiding secrets which have to be pried loose from it has often been seen as a watershed in the development of modern science, since it led to active intervention in nature in order to discover its secrets. If the task of science is to discover the secrets of nature, then such a view legitimizes certain ways of doing science, and of destroying nature, in order to recover those secrets. This conflictual engagement with nature as part of the origin of modern science runs into major conflict with Asian perspectives on nature (see e.g. Barnhart 1997; Chapple and Tucker 2001). These perspectives often describe nature in more syncretic terms and as embodying continuity with the human, thus making the task of extracting secrets from nature more difficult. Nature is worshipped in many different ways even today in India. There are various other narratives of nature (including the continuity and contiguity between animals and humans), which has a potentially serious impact on the practice of science according to modern science. One such major difference can be discovered in the approach to medicine in Indian systems of healing, including Ayurveda, as against the allopathic practice. On the one hand, we have medicines that are part of food habits like in Ayurveda, whereas in the modern scientific sense of medicine there is an attempt to extract the chemical agents that are seemingly efficacious in herbs and other food items.

These cultural views towards nature are rejected by Western science and through this there is also a rejection of the sciences that are based on different views and perspectives on nature.

Another interesting example is mathematics and the culturally different ways of doing mathematics. Indian mathematics was significantly different from Greek mathematics in one important sense: the metaphysics that characterized the Greek view of mathematical entities like numbers was not found in Indian thought. The metaphysics of numbers, as in Platonism, which elevated numbers to almost a theological domain, is not one that informs numbers in Indian mathematics. For example, numbers in Indian mathematics were only a device that was used in measuring and constructing, and thus had little theological influences like having an independent existence and independent truth values (see the diverse articles in Seshadri 2010). Moreover, mathematics was also written in prose and poetic forms. Such expressions of mathematics make the task of learning and teaching mathematics quite different from a symbolic representation of mathematics, as is usually done in textbooks today.

While we cannot at this moment claim what the consequences of these different views are, we should nevertheless note how these radically different cultural views towards nature, world and mathematics all contribute to a significant new understanding of science and science education. Unfortunately, the colonial system of education and the instrumentalist understanding of science in post-independent India have contributed to the erasure of such possibilities in the teaching of science. I do believe that bringing these elements into the teaching of science and mathematics will have a significant impact on the learning and practice of science in India (see Sarukkai 2014).

Current tendencies and trends in STEM

While there is now increased support for STEM education, the community of scientists and technologists feel that it is not enough. The government has started new teaching and research institutes in science that are very well funded and have good faculty. However the demand and projected need of scientists and engineers outweighs the production of these graduates. The projection is also based on global trends and the continued participation of Indian companies in the global market.

At the same time, there is a terrible sense of anxiety about the quality of science and technology in the country today, as constantly articulated by science administrators and the government. The last Nobel Prize winner in the sciences for work done in India (and for a scientist residing in India) was C.V. Raman, before independence. Very few Indians have won the Nobel Prize in the sciences, and even those that have were all working in institutions outside India.

It is not only the lack of Nobel Prize or other major international prizes that is of concern. Scientometric data consistently shows that India's contribution to global knowledge is quite low even when compared with much smaller countries like South Korea and Japan. Unlike China, for example, the overall scientific publications from scientists in India lack both quality and quantity. The impact of Indian scientific contribution is still too negligible despite many excellent institutes supported by the government. In terms of innovation and patents, the situation is not much better. This is ironic, considering that some of the world's best innovation laboratories, like GE and Microsoft, have established their research centres in India. So whether the problem is institutional, cultural or social will only be known after we see the impact of these initiatives (see Madhan, Chandrasekar and Arunachalam 2010; Garg, Dutt and Kumar 2006; Arunachalam 2002).

On the other hand, India's fascination with science has led to serious social repercussions, which ultimately may pose new challenges for STEM education. In India, there is little social responsibility, and negligent accountability to the larger society, in the practice and use of science. This has led the government and scientists to take an elite view about science. The public debates on big dams and the nuclear programme, for example, are not about dialogue about science but are more diatribes about the irrationality of non-scientists. But it is impossible for science education to be sustained meaningfully in this heavy-handed manner in any society. The social responsibility exhibited by scientific institutions in Europe and the US is a good example of how these institutions have at least begun to engage with these questions of responsibility and accountability.

This indifference to the social responsibility of science has led to another serious problem in India, which is that there is almost no presence of the history, philosophy and sociology of science and technology anywhere in the country. It is ironic that for a country with one of the largest number of scientists and engineers, there is a marked absence of science and technology studies in the country. The implications of this will be far reaching and will be felt in the years to come. And where there have been attempts to establish such programmes, it is the more powerful scientific establishment which attempts to appropriate them.

One of the fall outs of the hegemonic imposition of science as well as a lack of meaningful public debate about science is the increased challenge to science from tradition. The challenge comes from two directions: from religion and another from a more serious engagement with earlier Indian knowledge systems. In the absence of an open space for discussion about science and technology, these challenges make it easier for people to attack science without understanding it. Given the increased religiosity around the country, and scientists' ambivalent response to it, we can expect more serious challenges to the dominant government view of modern science as the only means of progress, rationality and development.

There are also serious challenges to science education when we carefully reconsider the nature of earlier knowledge traditions. In particular, there is tremendous scope for a meaningful way of making ethics integral to knowledge formation, as was the practice in pre-modern traditions, both in India and Europe (see Sarukkai 2009). In the context of science education, it is extremely important to integrate the ethical imagination with questions of fact and knowledge. We also have to consider the exclusiveness inherent in science education, particularly mathematics education. If there are other cultural models of doing and learning mathematics, it might make mathematics learning more egalitarian and, through this process, we might even be able to diffuse the epistemological power of mathematical knowledge. Thus, earlier ideas of science and technology, in which India had made great contributions, can become a source of discontent with current practices of doing and learning science. But in doing so, they will also become a source of alternate reflections on science and technology, and on STEM education. Whether these alternate reflections are worth doing or not can only be answered after initial attempts are made to develop them.

Notes

1 For further information see the website of the Sikkim Manipal University (SMU) and its Directorate of Distance Education, available from http://smude.edu.in/ [Accessed 13 October 2014].
2 For further information see the website of the Department of Science and Technology, available from http://dst.gov.in/scientific-programme/ser-index.htm [Accessed 10 November 2014].
3 This term has been invoked in the Indian constitution.
4 German philosophers, including Hegel and Husserl, were quite consistent in their view that Indians did not have the capacity for rational discourses like philosophy, theory and science. The belief that even the idea of knowledge was available only to the Greeks and not to other cultures like the Indian has been repeatedly stressed by philosophers such as Gadamer. Most popular books on a general history of science and mathematics also continue the myth that these disciplines were not discovered by any culture other than the Greeks and the later Europeans (see e.g. Gadamer 2001 or Sinha 1971; for an account of the historical reception of Indian logic in Europe see Ganeri 2013).

Bibliography

Adas, Michael (1989): *Machines as the Measure of Men: Science, Technology, and Ideologies of Western Dominance*. Cornell University Press, Ithaca and London.

Alvares, Claude (1991): *Decolonizing History: Technology and Culture in India, China and the West: 1492 to the Present Day*. The Apex Press, New York and the Other India Press, Goa.

Arunachalam, Subbiah (2002): Is Science in India on the Decline? *Current Science* 83 (2). Pp. 107–108.

Bala, Arun (2006): *The Dialogue of Civilizations in the Birth of Modern Science*. Palgrave Macmillan, New York.

Barnhart, Michael G. (1997): Ideas of Nature in an Asian Context, *Philosophy East and West* 47 (3). Pp. 417–432.

Chapple, Christopher Key and Mary Evelyn Tucker (eds.) (2001): *Hinduism and Ecology: The Intersection of Earth, Sky, and Water*. Oxford University Press, New Delhi.

Department of Higher Education (2013): All India Survey on Higher Education 2010–2011. Ministry of Human Resource Development, Government of India, New Delhi. Available from http://mhrd.gov.in/sites/upload_files/mhrd/files/statistics/AISHE201011.pdf [Accessed 27 October 2014].

Gadamer, Hans-Georg (2001): *The Beginning of Knowledge*. Continuum, London.

Ganeri, Jonardon (ed.) (2013): *Indian Logic: A Reader*. Routledge, London and New York.

84   *Sundar Sarukkai*

Garg, K.C., B. Dutt and Suresh Kumar (2006): Scientometric Profile of Indian Science as seen through Science Citation Index, *Annals of Library and Information Studies* 53. Pp. 114–125.

Kapila, Shruti (2010): The Enchantment of Science in India, *Isis* 101 (1). Pp. 120–132.

Kumar, Krishna (1988): Origins of India's Textbook Culture, *Comparative Education Review* 32 (4). Pp. 452–464.

Kumar, Krishna (2009): *What is Worth Teaching?* Orient Blackswan, Hyderabad.

Madhan, Muthu, G. Chandrasekar and Subbiah Arunachalam (2010): Highly Cited Papers from India and China, *Current Science* 99 (6). Pp. 738–749.

Matilal, Bimal Krishna (1985): *Logic, Language and Reality: Indian Philosophy and Contemporary Issues.* Motilal Banarsidass, New Delhi.

Mohanty, Jitendra Nath (1992): *Reason and Tradition in Indian Thought: An Essay on the Nature of Indian Philosophical Thinking.* Clarendon Press, Oxford.

Murray, Seb (2014): Hundreds of Indian B-Schools are Forced to Close as Business Bites, MBA India, May 21. Available from http://www.businessbecause.com/news/mba-india/2558/hundreds-of-schools-forced-close-as-indian-business-bites [Accessed 10 November 2014].

Plofker, Kim (2009): *Mathematics in India.* Princeton University Press, Princeton (NJ).

Sangwan, Satpal (1990): Science Education in India under Colonial Constraints, 1792–1857, *Oxford Review of Education* 16 (1). Pp. 81–95.

Sarukkai, Sundar (2005): *Indian Philosophy and Philosophy of Science.* Motilal Banarsidass, New Delhi.

Sarukkai, Sundar (2008): Culture of Technology and ICTs. In: *ICTs and Indian Social Change*, edited by Ashwani Saith, Manimegalai Vijayabaskar and Vasudevan Gayathri. Sage, New Delhi. Pp. 34–58.

Sarukkai, Sundar (2009): Science and the Ethics of Curiosity, *Current Science* 97 (6). Pp. 756–767.

Sarukkai, Sundar (2012): *What is Science?* National Book Trust, New Delhi.

Sarukkai, Sundar (2014): Indian Experiences with Science: Considerations for History, Philosophy, and Science Education. In: *International Handbook of Research in History, Philosophy and Science Teaching*, edited by Michael R. Matthews. Springer, Dordrecht. Pp. 1691–1719.

Sebastian, Meryl (2014): ISRO Successfully Places Mangalyaan in Mars' Orbit: India Makes Space History. September 24. Available from http://www.dnaindia.com/scitech/report-mars-orbiter-s-crucial-engine-test-successful-all-you-need-to-know-about-india-s-mars-mission-2020646 [Accessed 23 October 2014].

Seshadri, C. S. (ed.) (2010): *Studies in the History of Indian Mathematics.* Hindusthan Book Agency, Gurgaon.

Sinha, Debabrata (1971): Theory and Practice in Indian Thought: Husserl's Observations, *Philosophy East and West* 21 (3).

Valiathan MS (2003): *The Legacy of Caraka.* Orient Longman, Himayatnagar, Hyperabad.

Valiathan MS (2007): *The Legacy of Susruta.* Orient Longman, Himayatnagar, Hyperabad.

Valiathan MS (2010): *Legacy of Vagbhata.* Universities Press, Himayatnagar, Hyperabad.

Valiathan MS (2013): *An Introduction to Ayurveda.* Orient Blackswan, Himayatnagar, Hyderabad.

7 Corporate social responsibility programmes for STEM education

Cases from the Indian technology cluster city of Hyderabad

Nagalakshmi Chelluri and Mohan V. Avvari

Introduction

Corporate social responsibility (CSR) and the role of businesses in India is now quite clear, with the Indian government passing the Companies Rules of 2013 (Ministry of Corporate Affairs 2014) and offering a list of activities that can be included as CSR. The list includes many activities that contribute to the improvement in quality of life for the less privileged in society, as well as addressing concerns of environmental degradation. It also includes education and provision for associated infrastructure.

In India, education—including the field of STEM education—is considered to be the most important source of social mobility for the people. Furthermore, science and technology are considered the means to bringing about development and have been the cornerstones of the higher education system (see also the contribution by Sundar Sarrukkai in this book, Gundemeda 2014). According to the All India Survey on Higher Education (Department of Higher Education 2013), the Gross Enrolment Ratio (GER) in higher education is 20.4 per cent for young people age between 18 and 23. The 'highest number (34 per cent) of students is enrolled in the Arts followed by Engineering & Technology (19 per cent), Commerce (14.5 per cent) and Science (12 per cent)' at the undergraduate level (Department of Higher Education 2013: ii). The above data is significant for the business organisations in India, as much of the human capital required to drive the growth engines comes from the above-mentioned institutions. It is widely acknowledged that business organisations play a key role in the social sector and work in partnership with the government (Avvari, Ejnavarzala and Lakshmi 2012).

In general there have been concerns raised regarding STEM education, especially considering the issue of employability of the graduates—stating there is a need to 'retrain' these graduates to 'fit' into their jobs, etc. (Avvari, Ejnavarzala and Lakshmi 2012). While there should be efforts from all concerned stakeholders (government departments, universities, etc.), in this paper we are interested in, and hence intend to investigate, how the industry is trying to support STEM education through CSR programmes. The paper sheds some light on CSR in India and current developments and then presents some examples of CSR activities by three companies as a basis to identify patterns of different types of programmes that technology companies have developed for STEM education. The study focuses on information and communication technology (ICT) firms in the city of Hyderabad, which has emerged as one of the key technology clusters in India.

The policy of CSR and its current status in India

The role of business organisations in contributing towards building a better society has been acknowledged worldwide. Caroll is one of the well-known writers on CSR, who developed a popular model of CSR (Carroll 1991). He presented a pyramid structure of CSR consisting of four different components. The basic building block of every CSR initiative is economic responsibility, focusing on the idea that something has to be profitable. This is then followed by the legal responsibilities, ethical responsibilities and, finally, philanthropic responsibilities (Carroll 1991: 42, Figure 3).

The trend of corporate philanthropy as a voluntary act has been institutionalized, and the last few decades have seen further transformation in the practice of CSR. This has been described by Peter M. Senge and colleagues with reference to the new challenges of building sustainable enterprises (Senge, Carlstadt and Porter 2001). The authors explain the transition of the interests of business from rationalism to naturalism to humanism. This process is also reflected in the orientation of the businesses, which shifted from profits to people in terms of their human resource development and also focuses on sustainable aspects concerning the earth. The changing relationships between civil society organizations and businesses are also discussed, especially their cooperation in the field of sustainable development. Porter and Kramer (2006, 2011) state that while businesses have done a lot in terms of social responsibility, they find that businesses are pitched against society (though interdependent), and CSR is seen as generic instead of being congruent with the firm's strategy. They see that CSR will be important for businesses to gain competitive advantage and postulate that NGOs, governments and business organizations should change the way they see each other. It should not be merely CSR but rather 'corporate shared value'— postulating businesses working together with society.

In India, businesses are mostly engaged in some form of CSR either as philanthropy or in a systematic way, implemented through a department and dedicated staff. But these efforts have not always been documented in an organised way, and were not a subject of discussion in the past (PriceWaterhouseCoopers 2013). As recently as 2013, India became the first country to legally mandate expenditures on CSR. The Ministry of Corporate Affairs passed the Companies Act 2013, which requires larger companies to spend at least two per cent of their net profits, averaged over the three preceding financial years, on CSR (PriceWaterhouseCoopers 2013). The act also defines a set of activities which are eligible for CSR, including programmes eradicating extreme hunger and poverty, reducing child mortality, ensuring environmental sustainability or improving education (see also Turaga and Kandathil 2014). Even though there are some open questions about how these regulations will be implemented, the Act remains, in our opinion, a major step in promoting CSR practice for the corporate world.

CSR activities have also been implemented in the overall Indian information technology (IT) and business process outsourcing (BPO) industry, which provides direct employment (as employees) to about 3 million and indirect employment (as consultants and vendors based on contracts) to about 9 million people (NASSCOM 2013). The scale of CSR activities in general and related to STEM education is difficult to discern, but given the new regulation it is expected to grow much more. These CSR activities to support STEM could be in cooperation with the government (education institutions) and/or independent activities supplementary to what the government does. Most of these companies invest in different types of activities, which are usually individual or team based ones and are sometimes taken up by the human resource departments. As mandated in the Companies Act 2013, much of the information about their CSR activities can be found on the companies' websites. Furthermore, there are variations in the ways in which CSR in education has been implemented by the business organisations. Firstly, there are some large corporates, which have independent CSR departments and chart out their yearly plans. Secondly, some corporates establish independent foundations and, through these, channel their activities. The third way is through collaboration with leading non-governmental or civil society service organizations, which are then supported by the companies through cash payments or other tangible or intangible resources and means. Fourthly, smaller businesses adopt a school or educational institution and offer infrastructure provisions such as drinking water in schools or toilets, or offer in kind through donations for notebooks, pens and other recurring expenditures.

The next section provides three examples of firms that are involved in CSR at different levels and gives instances of their STEM supporting programmes.

Cases of CSR for STEM education in Hyderabad ICT cluster

The establishment of the IT hub in Hyderabad, named Cyberabad, occurred during 1994. HITEC City (Hyderabad Information Technology and Engineering Consultancy City) is one of Asia's largest IT clusters and has well-known multinational IT firms including Microsoft, Infosys, Oracle, Dell and others (Kshetri and Dholakia 2005). With the objectives of building and promoting the state of Andhra Pradesh (Brand AP) as the most preferred destination for the IT and ITES sectors in India, the independent institution ITsAP (Industry Association of Andhra Pradesh) was established in 1991 and consisted of members of all companies.[1] ITsAP also gives awards every year for products and services, along with the best companies for their CSR activities. Thus this can be seen as one aspect of the spirit of CSR in the IT sector being nurtured in Hyderabad.

One of the largest information technology (IT) companies located in Hyderabad is Tata Consulting Services (TCS), which was established in 1968

(Tata Consultancy Service 2012). TCS specializes in offering software services, business consulting and solutions to domestic and international clientele. CSR activities in the field of STEM address school students offering skill development activities (e.g. IT WIZ a Quiz competitions on IT) but also programmes which try to increase the awareness of the IT sector (e.g. InsighT) (Tata Consultancy Service 2012). Much of the expenditure goes towards the prizes distributed and in organizing the events. The reach for this initiative is quite high—over 200,000 students in 5,000 schools, located in 12 cities across India. At the higher educational level, there are two initiatives. *Ignite* is tuned to the requirements of science graduates and software professionals and aims to provide knowledge on computing, core technological skills, tools, communication and team skills, business literacy and cultural awareness. There is also a provision for a 'live' project experience to provide skills for growing minds. *Soft skills development* is initiated for raising employability through skill enhancement among rural graduates from the marginalized sections of society. Training in speaking English, communication and soft skills, computer skills are provided to improve the performance of the beneficiaries. During the financial year 2011–2012, the number of trainees was as high as 7,828 candidates, out of which 717 were subsequently employed by TCS. The company also has a Business Process Outsourcing unit that has been employing physically challenged persons, such as visually challenged persons, through the Advanced Computer Training Centre since 2008.

Earlier known as Infotech Enterprises, Cyient Limited, headquartered in Hyderabad, offers engineering services, networks and operations to domestic and international clientele. The company has been engaged in quite a strong corporate social responsibility activity for a long time, and works with an aim of contributing to sustainable community and promoting holistic community development. The company's CSR activities are worked out through the Cyient Charitable Trust (CCT). Activities of CSR range from adopting schools to promoting primary education and providing relief funds. To enhance the quality of education for the underprivileged students in India, the CCT started the 'Adopt a School' initiative, which is primarily about adopting government-run high schools. So far they have adopted 13 government schools across India and supported about 7,000 children. CCT's contribution to schools include developing physical infrastructure (sanitation facilities, classrooms, play area, etc.), recruiting qualified teachers, distributing educational aids (notebooks, school bags, exam kits, uniforms, etc.), conducting meetings with parents and the local community or organizing career guidance programmes.

Another example is the Microsoft India Development Center (MSIDC), which was set up at Hyderabad in 1998 by Microsoft India (R&D) Private Limited, a subsidiary of Microsoft Corporation headquartered in the USA.[2] The centre is one of Microsoft Corporation's largest R&D centres outside its headquarters in Redmond.[3] One important programme is the DPE (Deployment and Product Evangelization), which is basically about adopting colleges that are not of very high academic standards. The company's strategy is to deploy its technology to these colleges through the setting up of the MIS—Microsoft Innovation

Centres—so that students are trained and asked to test the products. The use of these technologies by the students yields a fresh testing arena among the novices and generates interest among students and valuable feedback for the company.

Among other activities, MSIDC also arranged a training programme in the year 2013, on 'Windows-8 Application Development' for undergraduates in their third year of engineering. The tools and skills that were offered in the training were: C#.net, Blend Tool, SQLLite and ASP.net. The students were able to start developing the Windows 8 apps, which were meant to be published in the Windows Market Place.

All these programmes do not actually yield any monetary return, but serve as education tools for Microsoft technologies. It may also be noted that these Microsoft Student Partners are taken to some technology conferences held across the country for a first-hand exposure to the academic and technological environment. The entire cycle of training and development is treated as an education initiative of the MSIDC. After training it was also conceived that these students could be absorbed into the company positions. However, it was learned through the interview that none of these students qualified for the positions.

Considerations resulting from the cases and beyond

The three cases of global and Indian multinational corporations (MNCs) illustrate that the organizations are involved in CSR programmes for skill development in the STEM area. The two large ones (TCS and Microsoft) work through multiple programmes, while the slightly smaller India-based MNC, Cyient, works through its own foundation to implement education promotion and related activities in local schools. In other cases, not presented in this paper, it has been noted that there is also work being done with non-governmental organisations (NGOs). The following table summarizes the types of CSR programmes adopted by the three case organizations for supporting STEM education.

The modes of CSR programmes to support STEM education are quite varied— in the cases of the large transnational companies, TCS and Microsoft, they have formal divisions set up for these activities while also working with/through different organizations for the CSR programmes. In the other case, the CSR for STEM programmes are implemented through foundations. The cases also reveal the different forms and levels of support that the organizations are trying to provide for STEM education—there are programmes at the school level and higher education level. Some are directed towards infrastructure provision and some towards skill provision. In the case of TCS, the objective of their CSR programmes is to 'help science graduates transform into software professionals'—while also developing employability for the many science graduates. TCS is also creating a talent pool for itself while identifying possible talent through its quizzing competitions in higher education institutions.

The Cyient case aims at working with schools to develop the infrastructure and to improve school and therefore the overall quality of education. Even though it was stated that the MSIDC case was clearly working towards generating

Table 7.1 Initiatives of the IT companies and their possible impact

Name of the Company	Type of CSR	Approach	Possible Impact – STEM
TCS—Indian MNC	Company driven events, awareness, training	Direct initiatives by the organization	Raising employability, skill enhancement, soft skill development
Cyient Limited— Indian MNC	Cyient Charitable Trust—adopting schools and promoting primary education	Promoting educational and infrastructure activities through foundation	Indirect improvement in school environment through infrastructure
Microsoft— global MNC	Direct training and skill development, student partnerships in technology skill sharing	Training and tools for Microsoft technologies, skill development in software and project experience	Raising employability, skill enhancement, technological knowledge development

Source: Edited by the authors

a talent pool for itself, it was observed that these trained student partners have yet to make it to the company as employees.

While it can be inferred from the cases that these CSR programmes could help the beneficiary organizations in terms of infrastructure support and training to students in technology, there could be a bias in terms of each organization 'pushing' its own agenda, i.e, for the propagation of its technologies or to cater to its own needs rather than a broader development of STEM interests. Thus, understanding the long-term implications of these activities, and also the impact of the new regulation on the CSR investment, will require time as well as more intensive study at different levels—employees of the organizations with CSR programmes and the leaders and students of the recipient educational organizations.

Conclusion

This paper elicits different types of practices of CSR for STEM education among ICT firms in the technology cluster of Hyderabad. There are clearly different approaches or patterns among the CSR programmes adopted by different companies. While the different patterns provide ideas for new firms that would like to start off their CSR programmes to support STEM education, it is not yet clear which approaches could have the best impact, in terms of benefits to the intended recipient, to society as a whole and also to the firm that is organising it. The following diagram illustrates the possible flows or benefits in terms of resources and knowledge:

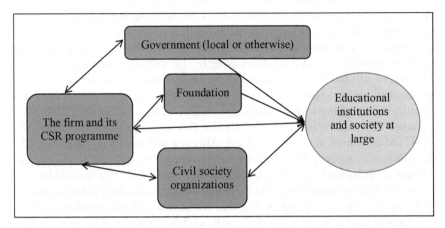

Figure 7.1 CSR programmes for STEM and its linkages and impacts among different organizations

The figure represents how CSR as a programme and also as a platform on which the associated institutions—the firm (CSR Programme), the foundations established to conduct the CSR–STEM, the government institutions monitoring the programme (the Ministry of Corporate Affairs to whom the programme is accountable) and the independent civil society organizations (or NGOs)—and the beneficiary educational institutions, schools, colleges and institutes are constantly interacting. The resources and knowledge are shared on this interactive platform, with the specific regulations for each of these institutions. As shown in the figure, the relations and interactions are two-way for the institutions, in spite of the fact that they operate in frameworks that are specific to them. This indicates a dynamic and beneficial relationship for all the institutions, as they can interact with a contingency approach from time-to-time and are fulfilling their needs in a mutually beneficial manner so far. This was evident during the interview process. The impact on the private sector is yet to be determined, as the regulation only came to be in 2013. However, companies involved in CSR for a longer duration are well versed in the activities and the outcomes, while it may be a smaller but emerging factor for the other STEM beneficiaries. The governmental institutions are more in the monitoring position, with a partnership approach for fulfilling their mission in imparting education to all eligible beneficiaries. CSR has grown beyond a philanthropic activity and is now mandatory for most of the firms. It is not just a privately driven programme for the larger firms and those aspiring to grow. Business organizations have now acknowledged and are drawing up strategies to leverage the same with publicity/PR overtones, as well as a creation of the most essential manpower pool in the region. The larger picture is yet to emerge at the national level and the data on impact is not accessible as of this period.

There is a need to understand how the different types of CSR programmes—like the direct help to educational institutions, working through foundations, etc.—impact the organization involved. It is still unclear how the flow of knowledge resources influences and has an impact on the culture of the donors and recipient organizations and its development. The spill over into the society or community still has to be examined. A factor that emerges in the case studies are the civil society organizations (CSOs); there is a growing number of business organizations working with or working through CSOs as part of their CSR programmes. It would be interesting to explore this aspect in the context of CSR for STEM education at the society level. Also, it is still hard to say if these CSR programmes to support STEM education are unique to India or to the region (cluster of Hyderabad) from which the cases are conducted—but it could be safe to say that CSR programmes could be similar among technology firms located in 'tech clusters' across India, given that they compete for talent/specialized skills.

Demographers now tell us that India will overtake China by 2040 as the world's most populous nation, with almost 1.5 billion people.[4] The implications of this are staggering, with additional demands for food, water, housing, health care and education. It is here that CSR can play a crucial role with business organizations working together with government and civil society for synergistic or mutually beneficial solutions. And as discussed in the article by Porter and Kramer (2006), CSR, if done strategically and integrated internally in the business and externally with stakeholders and society, can become a source of tremendous social progress. This paper could be the starting point for future studies to see the role of business organizations contributing to social progress while seeking economic benefits for their shareholders and employees with a particular focus on support for development of STEM education in different sectors or geographies.

Notes

1 For further information see the Association's website, available from http://www.itsap.org/index.php [Accessed 22 September 2014].
2 The following information is based on an interview with an HR division employee at the MSIDC and also refers to the company's website.
3 For further information see the starting page, available from http://www.microsoft.com/en-in/msidc/default.aspx [Accessed 22 September 2014].
4 See Population of India vs. China by indiaonlinepages.com, available from http://www.indiaonlinepages.com/population/compare-india-china-population.html [Accessed 14 September 2014].

Bibliography

Avvari, Mohan V., Haribabu Ejnavarzala and C. Naga Lakshmi (2012): University Linkages in Technology Clusters of Emerging Economies; Exploratory Case Studies from Cyberjaya, Malaysia; a Greenfield Development and Cyberabad, India; a Brownfield Development. *World Technopolis Review* 1 (1) 42–55.
Carroll, Archie B. (1991): The Pyramid of Corporate Social Responsibility: Toward the Moral Management of Organizational Stakeholders, *Business Horizons* 34 (4). Pp. 39–48.

Department of Higher Education (2013): All India Survey on Higher Education 2011–2012 (Provisional). Ministry of Human Resource Development/Government of India, New Delhi. Available from http://mhrd.gov.in/sites/upload_files/mhrd/files/AISHE2011-12P_1.pdf [Accessed 14 August 2014].

Gundemeda, Nagaraju (2014): *Education and Hegemony: Social Construction of Knowledge in India in the Era of Globalisation*. Cambridge Scholars Publishing, Newcastle upon Tyne (UK).

Kshetri, Nir and Nikhilesh Dholakia (2005): The Upper-Echelons Effect on the ICT Development of the Andhra Pradesh State of India: A Historical Analysis. College of Business Administration: University of Rhode Island, Kingston. Available from http://www.cba.uri.edu/research/workingpapers/documents/2006/TheUpper-EchelonsEffectontheITCDevelopmentoftheAndhraPradeshStateofIndia.pdf [Accessed 14 August 2014].

Ministry of Corporate Affairs (2014): Notification. Controller of publications, New Delhi, available from http://mca.gov.in/Ministry/pdf/CompaniesActNotification2_2014.pdf [Accessed 8 August 2014].

NASSCOM (National Association of Software and Services Companies) (2013): Indian IT-BPM Industry—FY2013 Performance Review, FY2014 Outlook. Mumbai. Presentation available from http://www.nasscom.in/sites/default/files/userfiles/file/FY13%20Performance%20Review%20and%20FY14%20Outlook.PDF [Accessed 22 September 2014].

Porter, Michael E. and Mark R. Kramer (2006): Strategy and Society: The Link between Competitive Advantage and Corporate Social Responsibility. *Harvard Business Review* December. Available from http://hbr.org/2006/12/strategy-and-society-the-link-between-competitive-advantage-and-corporate-social-responsibility/ar/1 [Accessed 22 September 2014].

Porter, Michael E. and Mark R. Kramer (2011): The Big Idea: Creating Shared Value, Rethinking Capitalism. *Harvard Business Review* January-February. Available from http://boost-afrique.weebly.com/uploads/2/5/0/7/2507823/hbr-creating_shared_value-developing_countries-abstract.pdf [Accessed 22 September 2014].

PriceWaterhouseCoopers (PwC) India (2013): Handbook on Corporate Social Responsibility in India. Available from http://www.pwc.in/assets/pdfs/publications/2013/handbook-on-corporate-social-responsibility-in-india.pdf [Accessed 9 September 2014].

Senge, Peter M., Goran Carlstadt and Patrick P. Porter (2001): Innovating Our Way to the Next Industrial Revolution. *MIT Sloan Management Review* 42 (2). Pp. 24–38.

Tata Consultancy Service (2012): Corporate Sustainability Report 2011–12. Tata Consultancy Services Limited, Mumbai. Available from http://www.tcs.com/SiteCollectionDocuments/About%20TCS/TCS_Corporate_Sustainability_Report_2011-12_3.pdf [Accessed 8. August 2014].

Turaga, Rama Mohana R and George Kandathil (2014): Defining the Social Responsibility of Businesses. Whose Business is it? Economic & Political Weekly XLIX (7), February 15. Available from http://www.epw.in/web-exclusives/defining-social-responsibility-businesses.html [Accessed 14 August 2014].

8 Highlights of STEM education in Egypt

Ghada K. Gholam and Nasser Mansour

Status of STEM education in Egypt

The educational system in Egypt is considered one of the largest in the world with more than 18 million students, 1.8 million teachers and around 45,000 schools. According to Ministry of Education (MoE) statistics, around 39 per cent of students at secondary education level were enrolled in the science sector (including biology, chemistry, physics and mathematics) for the secondary exam (level 2) in 2012/2013, and 86 per cent of them successfully passed the official examination (known as the Thanaweya Amma) (CAPMAS 2013).

However, the World Competitive Report of 2013 shows that based on the quality of its scientific research institutions in 2012, Egypt held only the 127th position out of 148 countries in an international ranking. Additionally, Egypt was ranked only 145th with regard to both the quality of the educational system and the quality of maths and science education in the same 2012 international comparison of 148 countries (Schwab 2013: 177).

In general, education is a major challenge for Egypt. Illiteracy levels remain high and the country's socio-geographical infrastructure means that Egypt continuously needs to address the quality of its education (UNESCO Cairo Office 2002). While education in Egypt is free[1], the system requires reform as schooling facilities and quality do not match the population growth and the requirements of a globalized world. In general, the educational system in Egypt is extremely hierarchical, with the MoE at the top. It is also well known for being bureaucratic, teacher-centred, authoritarian and extremely competitive (Hassaneen 2003). In describing the status quo of the Egyptian education system, Gahin draws the following picture:

> The Egyptian educational practice faithfully follows the principles of Freire's (1993) 'banking concept' of education [. . .] The role of the teacher is to 'deposit' in the 'bank' (the student). Students' greatest concern is to store and maintain all the information handed to them by the teacher and keep it in good condition so that when the time comes, it would be at their access to easily restore and pour it out in exams [. . .]. The communication pattern

in the majority of classrooms is that of an active teacher and passive learners. The teacher is the only authority figure determining the 'what' and the 'how' of the teaching process.

(Gahin 2001: 31f)

Over the last three decades in particular, the education system has been marked by instability and weakness. The economy was directed to cover the costs of war, which had direct effects on the Egyptian economy and caused a huge drop in education allocations. Thus schools were not able to meet society's demand for access to education, and this resulted in high class numbers and a widening in educational gaps between rural and urban communities (above all: the metropolitan areas of Cairo and Alexandria) on the one hand, and between males and females on the other.

Since the beginning of Egypt's Arab Spring Revolution in February 2011, the country has been in a state of constant flux as it seeks a new political order and leadership. On the whole, public enthusiasm and scientists' hopes have been high. Since the first year of the Arab Spring the situation has been as follows: 'Government prioritisation of science, as well as the launch of huge science-related projects such as the Zewail City of Science and Technology, has launched an unprecedented public discussion on the need to develop science and technology in Egypt' (Dickson and Osama 2012: see section on popular and government support).

It remains to be seen whether this new enthusiasm will trigger improvement and development in the field of science and technology in Egypt. Reliable data and literature on the last few years will soon be available. Therefore, this report is based on literature that focuses on the years before the Arab Spring.

Since the 1960s, science has been a basic subject in the central National Curriculum (NC). At primary and preparatory level, it has been part of integrated science lessons, in contrast to secondary level where science is divided into separate fields such as chemistry, physics and biology (Mansour 2010a).

Egypt has an educational system that is divided into the secular educational system and the Al-Azhar educational system. The curricula are very similar, with the exception of a stronger focus on religious studies in the Al-Azhar system.

This bifurcation of the education system can be traced back to the nineteenth century, when Muhammad Ali (considered the father of modern Egypt) introduced modern European education alongside the existing traditional system, which focused on religious study and Islamic teaching (Ali 1989). Sayed Ismail Ali argues that the division was not simply an ideological difference between traditional religious schools and those representing 'modern civilization,' but that the division extended far deeper into Egyptian awareness and led to the development of two different cultural styles (Ali 1989). We will give further insights into cultural and religious aspects that inform the education system in the next chapter, and will now continue with some information on the education system in general.

The secular educational system consists of three different phases: preschool education, basic education and secondary education. Preschool education is made up of two years in private institutions for children between the ages of four and six. Basic education is compulsory and includes primary (six years of schooling) and preparatory (three years of schooling) education beginning from the age of six. There are mixed-gendered schools, but the majority of the schools are gender segregated. Then follows secondary education, which offers the possibility to continue schooling in one of three different fields: general, technical or vocational. General secondary education lasts for three years, of which the first year serves as a preparatory year and contains both humanities and scientific subjects. At the end of the first year, students enter one of three streams for another two years (humanities, science or mathematics) on the basis of their grades. Nevertheless, some subjects, such as Arabic and religious education, are taught across all streams. Technical secondary education refers to schooling in any one of three distinct fields—industrial, commercial or agricultural—for either three or five years. The field of vocational secondary education is divided into the two separate streams of paramedical sciences and tourism and hotel management. Both specifications are offered as three- or five-year programmes.

The Azharite education system is supervised by the Supreme Council of the Al-Azhar Institution under the supervision of the Egyptian prime minister. The Al-Azhar schools include the same primary, preparatory and secondary stages as the secular educational system but have a stronger focus on religious study and on the study of the Arabic language (Groiss 2004: Chapter One).

Since the 1990s, the MoE has formed committees in order to further develop and improve the curriculum throughout all stages of education. As Groiss observes: 'The main changes included the introduction of technology in both teacher training and in preparing the students to deal with technology' (Groiss 2004: 18).

In 2003, the MoE announced the National Standards for Education in Egypt (NSEE) as a national project. The overall goal was to set up comprehensive quality educational standards in Egypt and to raise awareness about quality learning. It also included the consolidation of the central administration and its ability to set up educational goals and standards for accountability (UNESCO 2006). The NSEE emphasized three dimensions of the relationship between science, technology and society: science and technology, science from a societal and personal perspective and the history and nature of science. Emphasis is placed on including interactive relationships between science, technology and society throughout all grades of science education in Egypt, and hence encouraging interdisciplinarity among these fields.

Table 8.1 shows that university enrolment in STEM subjects in the practical faculties[2] is still low, though increasing compared with figures for 2007/2008 and 2011/2012. However, the majority of the students are still more attracted to arts and theoretical subjects[3].

Table 8.1 University graduates by faculty and sex 2007/08 and 2011/12

Faculty	Year	Total theoretical and practical faculties	Male	Female
Total	2007/08	324,284	145,396 44.8%	178,888 55.2%
	2011/2012	334,203	156,202 46.7%	178,001 53,3%
Theoretical faculties	2007/08	254,482	107,730 42.3%	146,752 57.7%
	2011/12	253,451	113,174 44.6%	140,277 55.4%
Practical faculties	2007/08	69,802	37,666 53.9%	32,136 46.1%
	2011/12	80,752	43,028 53.3%	37,724 46.7%

Source: Adapted from CAPMAS 2013: 61, 69, 75

Different perspectives on the field of STEM and STEM education

The field of education is embedded in a broad sociocultural context that influences and informs science teachers' practices in classrooms, but also guides the decision makers' plans and visions for STEM education in Egypt. In order to understand the situation of STEM education it is therefore essential to provide an insight into the different influences that form the sociocultural context. Referring to Lemke (2001), focusing on a sociocultural perspective on science education means: '[. . .] viewing science, science education, and research on science education as human social activities conducted within institutional and cultural frameworks' (Lemke 2001: 296). Lemke asserts that it is also necessary to give weight to 'the role of social interaction: seeing it, as in the Vygotskyan tradition[4] [. . .] to be central and necessary to learning' (Lemke 2001: 296).

The following section is based on this theoretical approach and uses different perspectives to explore the sociocultural context and its influence on science education. Additionally, we would like to expand this focus from science education to the overall field of science and technology and its role and meaning to Egyptian society.

The perspective of culture and religion

Religion in Egypt frames many aspects of social life: 'Islam is not a religion in the same sense that Christianity or Buddhism is a religion. For Muslims, Islam is much more than a moral philosophy of life, system of belief or a spiritual order;

it is a "complete and comprehensive way of life"[5] (Leavitt Center 2013: citation given by the Provost Cook in the section on Islam's Unique Attributes: And How They Can Challenge Democracy).

Therefore, a religious framework informs both culture and the educational system. However, the different historical attempts at reforming Islam also influenced educational *content*, particularly during recent decades, where the strong alliance between Islam and science is explicitly emphasized. When compared to how much educational content has changed in Egypt, the modernization of educational *practices* has fallen behind.

Furthermore, Islam forms a cultural base for identity on both the national and international level, uniting the different countries which understand themselves to be 'Islamic' (from the Maghreb region in the West to Malaysia in the East). Hence, not only in Egypt, there is the challenge of differentiating between 'modernization' and 'westernization,' the latter most commonly being seen as critical for identity building. The great increase in trade between Egypt and the West and the growth in communication through travel, books, the press, cinema and, more recently, through satellite television and Internet, are gradually bringing some new discoveries in science and new advances in technology from the West to the Egyptian people. This influence of Western technology, intertwined with the values of Western culture, raises a question with regard to the relationship of Islam and science in Egyptian society: to what extent can Western culture and technology be assimilated without compromising the integrity of Islam?

Moreover, European colonial expansion into the Muslim world, beginning in the early 19th century, ignited a cultural crisis regarding the unity and identity of the universal Islamic community (umma) and has since generated a vigorous internal debate as to the situation of the umma in the modern world.

Toronto (1992) remarks that one of the greatest challenges for both Muslim and non Muslim politicians, scholars, educators and planners in the Islamic world is the achievement of a synthesis between the development needs of a modern world and the moral imperatives of a religious society.

Cook (2000) also drew attention to the influence of western technological and scientific progress on the identity of Egyptian society: 'The West's accent on technological development may exact a spiritual and moral cost if not kept in proper perspective. [. . .] Many Egyptian educators draw a direct correlation between an insufficient emphasis on *tarbiyya* and the painful and lingering question of identity for Egyptians' (Cook 2000: 487, emphasis in original).

For a genuinely integrated pattern of educational development to occur, educational policy should reflect the shared goals expressed through the local community. The value of any national education system is ultimately contingent upon whether the educational philosophy matches the internal rhythm of the society's sociocultural value system. Islam remains central to Egyptian identity and practice and an educational system that does not accommodate Islam, as interpreted by most Egyptians, will do so at the risk of being irrelevant (Cook 2001).

During discussions among experts on Egypt at the Delphi workshop held at the Berlin Brandenburg Academy of Sciences in December 2013 (see Part III in this book)[6], it became clear that the challenge to integrate Islam in the education system—especially in the field of science and technology—is still very much an on-going concern. Especially with regard to science education, Nasser Mansour (2011) points to the situation faced by science teachers, who on the one hand have to transfer knowledge on evolution, cloning, abortion and genetic engineering, but also seek to teach and inform in accordance with Islamic views and its beliefs. In his conclusion, Mansour suggests that participants' views of the relationship between science and Islam confirmed that personal religious beliefs of the teachers influence their beliefs and views about the nature of science and its purpose. This situation seems to lead teachers to hold an ambivalent relationship towards science and religion, which might also lead to the creation of a contradiction between science and Islam. However, this tension is experienced by science educators in countries with Christian culture as well.

Thus, with the central role that Islam plays within Egyptian society, the question remains open: can Egypt develop an educational system that adequately reflects and perpetuates the social order in which it functions? The above arguments reflect an on-going debate between proponents of western secularization and Egyptian Islamic culture. It further leads to the question: how should and could this debate contribute to the development of the education system in Egypt?

The examination system

Another key issue related to the culture of science education in Egypt is the culture of examination, which will be discussed in this section. The examination system in Egypt works as part of the social-cultural context of Egyptian teachers, students and parents. Examinations in Egypt affect the educational system in general, and STEM education and careers in particular. Examinations in Egypt serve as an important certificatory and selective instrument for students, parents and teachers. The submission of exam results fulfils an accountability purpose for government, along with reports from inspections; this puts the Egyptian government into a powerful position over individuals in schools. Exams in Egypt create a competitive atmosphere and place the emphasis on the accountability of individual schools and individual teachers instead of on the monitoring of national standards in Egyptian education. One facet of that competition is to find a place at university. Competition for places at university increases in line with population growth, and grade requirements for priority subjects—medicine and engineering—continue to rise. Therefore, examinations in Egypt motivate students to learn by heart in order to achieve high marks in written examinations (Mansour 2010a, 2013).

Exams are administered to students in grades 2, 4, and 6. A student must pass the successive levels of examination before proceeding on to the next one. Then a student's score determines the type of secondary school to which a student may be admitted. Only the top scoring students are eligible for secondary schools and, later on in their career, universities. In light of the importance of the examination system, a highly competitive and anxious atmosphere prevails. This has also led to the creation of a market for private tutoring and in turn affects all those involved in the educational process in Egypt, including decision makers, curriculum experts, teachers, students, parents, etc. As argued by Rissmann-Joyce and El Nagdi (2013), the cost of tutoring for maths and sciences is much higher than that for the arts and humanities, and the grades needed for admission to universities in the former subject areas need to be far more competitive than in the latter. This also explains why the proportion of students enrolling in the science section at secondary level is declining.

The educational system in Egypt restricts teachers' creativity and professional freedom through a variety of methods (including the examination system and school inspections). School inspectors are extremely rigid and tend to be very traditional, forcing teachers to stick to the book and not allowing them to be creative or use innovative approaches. These methods limit and control teachers' ways of knowing about issues related to STEM. Teachers angle textbooks to achieve their schools' policy on student achievement and to help their students pass exams.

In addition, science educators face many other problems: low social status, low student standards, insufficient professional and academic training and limited availability of labs. The quality of science education is low due to outdated curriculum and teaching methods, lack of access to ICT (information and communication technology), focus on theoretical science education and neglect of hands-on and practical activities, lack of teacher support and, most importantly, lack of sufficient budget necessary to improve the quality of science education (see e.g. Boujaoude 2008: 11).

Overall, science teaching is unappealing and children tend to distance themselves from this discipline to join arts that seem more attractive, easier and requiring less effort. The education system may not be geared to create scientifically literate Egyptian citizens.

In brief, the reason behind the decline in those going into science education is more strongly linked to economic, rather than cultural or philosophical, factors, taking into account that shadow education or private tutoring for science courses is more expensive than for arts courses, and that despite the professional prestige for medical doctors and engineers, these professions are still not financially promising.

The gender perspective

In Egypt, young adults (17–22 years old) spend about nine years in school. In contrast, 'women are twice as likely as men to have fewer than four years of education—four times as likely if they are poor women' (UNESCO 2010: 8). Furthermore, the proportion of women who enter science education is declining more significantly than among men. This can be traced back to cultural, economic and social aspects of Egyptian life. This incidence of deprivation among women in Egypt is higher than in other developing countries in Africa such as Uganda or Zambia. Because of income differences, but also because of the rural and urban divide, gender disparities are enforced. Communities in Upper Egypt are among the poorest and most disadvantaged areas. According to a UNESCO survey which includes data on the deprivation and marginalization in education in Egypt it has been shown that 'over 40 per cent of the population lives in poverty and poor rural females average just over four years of schooling' (UNESCO 2010: 8). In addition, many parents and a considerable number of husbands do not want women to work too far away from the family home or on night-shifts (views that hold particular significance in medical and engineering professions).

UNESCO has focussed on this gender imbalance and worked on strengthening the position of girls and women in science through several projects, programmes and initiatives. In 1998, UNESCO and the company L'Oréal joined forces to support women whose research contributes to moving science forward, in order to encourage young women to pursue science careers. They founded the programme For Women in Science (FWIS) to encourage the world's female scientists through L'Oréal-UNESCO awards. Additionally, the UNESCO Cairo Office launched the Pan Arab Regional Fellowship Programme in 2010 to support female scientists in the Arab region, and to award fellowships to exceptional female scientists. Since 2010, and over the past three years, twenty-two fellows from the Arab region have each received $20,000 in recognition of their contributions to the advancement of science and to further progress their career.

Another project to encourage female involvement in science at the school level was also launched by UNESCO. This project, which involved building capacity in gender-inclusive scientific and technological literacy for life skills, was launched in 2004 with the Egyptian MoE. The main objective of the project was to give equal opportunity for males and females to learn STEM subjects without discrimination. It also tried to support links between learning maths, science and technology, and progressing towards STEM education. Furthermore, it also encouraged the civil society to be more involved in the learning process and spread the culture of gender equality in science.

The main recommendations of this project to the Egyptian MoE included: building new curricula in mathematics and science depending on technological development and facilitating using technological tools for students; developing curricula contents that enhance life skills linked to society and market needs; training teachers to use strategies for problem solving and for gender equality; encouraging creative thinking and student participation in scientific and technological competitions; the teacher's in-service development programmes should contain topics about gender equality; and finally, the media should play a role in spreading the culture of women in science (UNESCO Cairo Office 2004).

The influence of technology

According to the Ministry of Communications and Information Technology, the number of Internet users in Egypt grew by around 15 per cent over a twelve-month period between 2012 and 2013, reaching 36 million in June 2013. Mobile subscriptions in Egypt reached 96.8 million during the same period of

2013, a 4.7 per cent increase compared with 92.4 million in June 2012 (Ahram Online 2013).

With regard to social networking utilities, Facebook is the most popular website in Egypt. The Arab Knowledge report of 2010/2011 (MBRF and UNDP/RBAS 2012) shows the following data with respect to Egyptians' access to information and communications technology (Table 8.2).

The Internet's astonishing influence in Egypt triggered the government to shut Internet services down in 2011. In light of the public protests that began on 25 January 2011, the government blocked Twitter—and later Facebook—in an attempt to stop mobilization for anti-government protests. All five major service providers in Egypt went dark (Storck 2011: 23). The general public sees computer-related technologies as positive and as a means for democratization. In a recent report on the status of ICT in school education comparing five Arab countries, Isaacs states that the social movements that arose in 2011 in the Arab States demonstrated the potential of ICT for playing a catalytic role. Isaacs stresses that: 'Arguably, the Arab Spring ranks among the most significant, informal, ICT-assisted "learning" phenomena in 2011. Thousands of youth used social media—accessed via their mobile phones—as a space for self-identification, self-assertion, contestation and mobilisation around democracy, human rights and civil liberties' (Isaacs 2012: 6). With regard to the Middle East as a region, however, the potential for significant changes in education and, ultimately, in society, vary (see also UNESCO, UNESCO Institute of Statistics and Talal Abu-Ghazaleh Organization 2013: 5).

With regard to the situation in Egypt, it was found that 'although the number of computers available in Egypt is not keeping pace with enrolment [. . .] the country nonetheless continues to emphasise the integration of CAI (computer-assisted instruction). [. . .] Older types of ICT-assisted instruction are not a priority in Egypt, even though large populations live in rural or remote areas where they are frequently found to serve a useful function' (UNESCO, UNESCO Institute of Statistics and Talal Abu-Ghazaleh Organization 2013: 22).

To sum up, in Egypt it could still make sense to invest in 'outdated' learning technologies in order to overcome the digital divide between the rural and the urbanized areas, between younger and older individuals and between men and women. A long-term goal should be to develop a better Internet structure that

Table 8.2 Access to information and communications technology in Egypt in 2010

HDI rank	101
Mobile and fixed-line phone subscriptions (per 100 persons)	65
% Population covered by mobile phone network	95
Internet (per 100 persons)	16.6
Subscribers—Services Broadband subscriptions (per 100 persons)	0.9
PC (per 100 persons)	3.9

Source: Adapted from MBRF and UNDP/RBAS 2012: 77

provides access to learning technologies on par with the geographic scale of the country, and also in the classroom.

Trends and initiatives that support STEM education

According to pre-university Act No 139 in 1981, the overall goal of education was to provide learners with culture, science, nationalism, behaviour and sport components in such a way that it ensured their understanding of values and theoretical and practical studies (Ministry of Education, Egypt 1996).

In the new Egyptian Constitution of 2014 (The Arab Republic of Egypt) Articles number 19 to 25 deal with education and scientific research. It is the first time in history that the constitution mentions scientific research, critical thinking and creativity. For example Article 23 related to scientific research states: 'The State shall ensure freedom of scientific research and encourage scientific research institutions as a means to achieve national sovereignty and build a knowledge economy. The State shall sponsor researchers and inventors and allocate a percentage of government spending to scientific research equivalent to at least 1% of the Gross National Product (GNP), which shall gradually increase to comply with international standards' (The Arab Republic of Egypt 2014: Article 23).

For the past two decades there has been a widespread consensus in Egypt, as in the rest of the world, on the need for change in science education and its stronger integration in schools. The 1999 study by Egypt's National Specialised Councils (NSC), entitled Science Education for the 21st Century, stated that: 'Science education should be modernized in order to be compatible with requirements in the future' (NSC 1999: 57). The NSC also stated clearly that science education should aim to promote scientifically literate citizens, and should therefore among other things: provide students with scientific and creative thinking and to help them realise the massive extent of scientific and technological progress and improve their environmental behaviour.

This suggests that the main aim of science education in Egypt, as it is worldwide, is to prepare young people to be 'scientifically literate citizens' (Mansour, 2010b: 92) and to qualify them to contribute to shaping the world in which they will live. This is a challenge for school science education, and raises questions with regard to how science education can prepare students as citizens. In this respect, Kolstø (2001) notes that scientific literacy is necessary to produce citizens who know the important role that science plays in their personal and professional lives and in society.

Pre-university decree No. 139 in 1981, and its modifications, specified education and its goals and objectives in Egypt in the National Report of Arab Republic of Egypt from 1990 to 2000 (NCERD 2001). These goals and objectives are formulated culturally, scientifically and nationally, according to successive affective, cognitive and behavioural levels and aspects. The purpose is to provide the Egyptian citizen with suitable values, applied practical studies and qualities that give him or her a sense of humanity and dignity, and, in addition, helps the citizen to develop a strong character capable of meeting the challenges of the future and contributing efficiently to production processes and activities. Speaking at the annual conference of the National Democratic Party on 29 September 2003, (then-) President Mubarak commented that education reform was one of the topics targeted by the knowledge society. It could be achieved by encouraging social participation and non-centralism, improving teacher training, encouraging research and technological development, developing educational infrastructure and setting up systems to measure the extent to which this policy conforms to the development requirements for the country's employment needs.

The MoE identified a group of scientific and technological changes, including new discoveries in genetic engineering, nano-technology and artificial intelligence that constituted what is known as scientific literacy, with the potential to affect Egyptian society. The form and content of education should therefore reflect the characteristics and features of these changes, so that Egyptian students would be knowledgeable and become good scientifically literate citizens. The Ministry also pointed out that education's role was to help students to develop an understanding of the relationship between science, technology and society. Education has to emphasize the positive aspects of technology in different fields (e.g., the great advances made in medicine with regard to diagnosing, treating and performing critical operations), while at the same time highlighting its negative effects (especially if directed against human welfare), in order to form the learner's intellect and his/her ability to control and direct technology towards benefiting humanity (Ministry of Education, Egypt 2007).

In 2003, the Egyptian MoE developed National Standards that placed great emphasis on science, mathematics, technology and society at all education levels, as part of its efforts to pursue quality education and develop scientifically literate citizens. It also underlined the need to develop scientific literacy, including scientific culture, critical thinking, integrated science, life skills, laboratory work, social contexts, systemic knowledge, problem solving, reaching proofs, communication, disposition, use of technology, practical manipulations, efficiency in using computers and the ethics of technology (UNESCO 2005).

A new project being carried out by the MoE is the creation of specific STEM Schools. The first two STEM Schools for gifted boys and girls in science and technology opened in Cairo in 2011 and 2012. Both schools were designated for gifted and talented high school children. The government plans to establish twenty-seven STEM Schools between 2012 and 2017. The project is funded by USAID and aims to create a classroom community of learners focussed on communication, critical thinking, collaboration and creativity.

Subsequently, there has been an ongoing internationalization of higher education, such as at Cairo's renowned public universities that specialize in the fields of science and engineering (Ain Shams University, Helwan University). This internationalization is also apparent in the existence of various international schools and universities such as the American University in Cairo (AUC), which has a modern School of Science and Engineering, and the German University in Cairo (GUC), which offers (among others) programmes in Biotechnology and Engineering (incl. Civil Engineering and Mechatronics) up to PhD level.

However, these institutions are not part of the public educational system and therefore give priority to students with appropriate financial resources. With regard to the differentiated educational system and the various problems it faces on its different levels, it remains a future challenge to create quality education that is equally distributed across the country, works across social classes and guarantees suitable candidates' upward mobility from kindergarten to university. One way to push forward quality and the improvement of the educational system is to engage the private sector in higher education goals and to more strongly integrate and collaborate with the private sector to improve the educational system (Bond *et al.* 2013).

Since 2000, UNESCO's Cairo Office has been working towards improving the quality of teachers' education by training teachers and trainers on the use of ICT in science and mathematics education in secondary schools in Egypt. The main objectives of the training were to establish a model for the training of teachers to use ICT in teaching; to provide easy access to ICT resources for students; and to provide first-class software and Internet resources in Arabic (UNESCO Cairo Office 2002: 5). The training was very successful and much appreciated. However, it had two shortcomings. With respect to the training of trainers (ToT), once trained, the majority of the trainers were then able to find good jobs in the Gulf and left Egypt for better opportunities and higher salaries.

As for the training of teachers, although the teachers learned new strategies and practical approaches, they were not able to use them as supervisors insisted that they stick to traditional methods of teaching. The lesson learnt from this was to include supervisors in the training, so they were updated on new approaches to science teaching, along with the teachers.

Creative Science Education Initiative (CSEI) (ERP 2005) is a programme that uses creative approaches to science education and community participation. Its main objective is to support the development of critical thinking skills; introduce creativity in the learning and application of science; and encourage community participation in the education process. The CSEI material provides a platform for linking the sciences (biology, chemistry and physics) together, and shows how the different STEM fields are related to each other but also to other academic disciplines, such as ethics, history, geography, sociology and psychology.

Since 2006 around 950 students in grades 4 and 5 science classes have been participating in this initiative. The intended impact of the programme is that students will become active participants in improving their daily lives by applying scientific knowledge, critical thinking and problem solving skills to address community issues. The material developed consists of a set of thirty-six fables. Each fable includes a systems message and aims to give students grounding in science, enabling the students to use scientific knowledge as a creative tool.

The monitoring and evaluation report indicated the following results. Teachers observed that 'students are making links on their own; achieving higher learning rates; attendance is better; and CSEI helps students to concentrate more.' Whereas the supervisors observed that 'students understand the lesson through the story linked to it; students like the class more because they are participating;

performance of teachers has changed; and CSEI encourages the students to read more scientific articles' (ERP 2005: 20).

Another existing challenge is the ongoing brain drain of qualified high-skilled graduates, already mentioned in the context of the ToT. In light of an unsafe environment in today's changing Egyptian political and social system, and given the high numbers of unemployed, qualified graduates (especially from the middle class) leave the country. Ways must be found to prevent this kind of immigration, not least because these skilled people are needed for the improvement of the Egyptian economy and the overall long-term development of the country (Abdelbaki 2009).

Conclusion

The growing emphasis on STEM and Inquiry-Based Learning (IBL) initiatives and their impact on student learning and their engagement in the science classroom is informed by research evidence and has been well documented. However, despite a growing consensus regarding the value of inquiry-based teaching and learning and STEM, the implementation of such practices continues to be a challenge. If science teachers are to use inquiry-based science education to develop students' inquiry practices and encourage them to think as scientists and of STEM careers, a better understanding of factors and settings that can influence their attitudes towards STEM is very much needed, as discussed earlier. This knowledge can inform planning and practices at different levels or settings to develop STEM Schools. Roberts and Cantu (2012) argue that STEM integration in the classroom requires science teachers to use integrative approaches and be knowledgeable about other STEM disciplines, but teachers often struggle to instruct through integration. Teachers may become 'rigid' on specific subject matters, limiting the incorporation of other content.

The local culture of the students, including peers, family, industries, career models and the use of technology in everyday life, can induce students' interests in studying science and understanding STEM and in working towards professions in STEM. Therefore, to promote STEM education at schools and IBL, it is important to take advantage of local culture and raise awareness of the applications of STEM through science lessons. This STEM school culture requires collaboration among stakeholders and it requires building a collaborative and supportive STEM community in school (see e.g. Holman and Finegold 2010; Stohlmann *et al.* 2012). On this note, the review by Roberts (2002) argues that the views of parents, teachers, career advisors and society in general towards study and careers in science and engineering can play a significant role in shaping pupils' choices as to whether to study these subjects at higher levels. Therefore, it is important to develop STEM activities or IBL projects that can engage teachers, parents and industries or universities in the local areas of the students to understand STEM initiatives, but most importantly to raise awareness about STEM careers and subjects. These recommendations are supported by numerous research projects and reports (see for example: DCSF 2008; Hutchinson and Bentley 2011; Roberts

2002; Stohlmann *et al.* 2012). Taking this into account, we advocate that schools and universities should encourage and enable STEM teachers to keep up to date with cutting edge developments in their fields through: professional development; research; work placements; sabbaticals; or flexible working. Industry, universities and businesses should offer participation in research or industrial projects in ways that make it easy for teachers to engage, including use of social media and new technologies. Stohlmann *et al.* (2012) claim that through partnering with a local university or a nearby school, attending professional development, having common teacher planning time and encouraging open communication with the STEM local communities, science teachers can be assisted to feel that they have the support they need to implement STEM successfully in their classroom.

It is recommended that successful programmes or projects such as the STEM Schools project or the CSEI initiative should be replicated, scaled up and spread widely to include more schools and to reach out to a larger number of students. In addition, in recent years, the Egyptian MoE has begun to actively engage the private sector in educational projects. Continuing these steps would be a positive move towards the integration of STEM culture and would make a significant stride towards the reform of science education and the new approach to linking science. If this is achieved with the help and support of government authorities, then we can really say that Egypt is on the right track to STEM education. We would like to conclude with the following quote by Perzigian, which envisions higher numbers of Egyptian STEM students in the near future, and summarizes how this can be achieved: '[. . .] To be more globally-competitive in a high-tech world driven by scientific innovation, Egypt must attach a national priority to increasing the number of STEM students as well as the proportion of females. This, of course, will require major improvements in the quality of pre-college education in Egypt. And it will also require a major re-thinking and reform of the current university admission system now under the severely-limiting constraints of the thanaweya amma which measures rote memorization. Egypt must devise a more sensible, flexible and thoughtful system, a system that opens more doors than it closes to students aspiring to study in the STEM and other disciplines. If we can reform the system by allowing universities more discretion and control of student admissions and by allowing students more choice in what and where they study, Egypt can increase the number of STEM students. This will redound to the success of the nation and a more viable economy' (Perzigian 2014).

Notes

1 Public education in Egypt is understood by the different governments of Egypt to be free from primary to university education. Nevertheless, in the light of the increasing number of students and the pressure through the system of examination, families spend tremendous amounts on tutorship and private tuition. Many also send their children to private schools and universities that follow non-governmental, often international quality assessment and accreditation standards.
2 Practical faculties include medicine; pharmacy; dentistry; engineering; agriculture; sciences; veterinary medicine; petroleum and mining; athletic education; fine and applied

arts; agriculture and environmental sciences; nursing; physiotherapy; technology; constructive planning; and medical sciences.
3 Theoretical faculties include arts and humanities studies; commerce; law; administration and information systems; education; economic and political sciences; sharia and law; and languages.
4 Lev Vygotsky (1896–1934) mainly worked in the field of developmental psychology. In his most important contribution (*Thought and Language* published in 1963), Vygotsky presents a concept, which explores the interrelationship of language, development and thought, Lemke (2001) refers to this particular contribution and concept in his citation speaking about the Vygotskyan tradition (see also Vygotsky *et al.* 1978).
5 The term 'complete and comprehensive way of life' is similar to the German term 'Lebensform'.
6 The Delphi process including the workshop has been part of the activities conducted by the research group TECHcultures in 2013. The overall process and its results are presented in the third part of the book.

Bibliography

Abdelbaki, Hisham H. (2009): Estimation Of The Economic Impact Of Brain Drain On The Labor Expelling Country, *International Business & Economics Research Journal* 8 (12). Pp. 53–66.
Ahram Online (2013): Egypt Internet Users Reached 36 Million in June 2013: MCIT. October 28. Available from http://english.ahram.org.eg/news/84996.aspx [Accessed 17 September 2014].
Ali, Syed Ismail (1989): *Humum al-Ta 'lim al-Masri* (Concerns of Egyptian Education). Al-Awla, Cairo.
Arab Republic of Egypt, The (2014). Constitution of The Arab Republic of Egypt. Unofficial translation. Cairo. Available from http://www.sis.gov.eg/Newvr/Dustor-en001.pdf [Accessed 17 September 2014].
Bond, Michael *et al.* (2013): Science and Innovation in Egypt. Available from https://royalsociety.org/~/media/policy/projects/atlas-islamic-world/atlas-egypt.pdf [Accessed 10 September 2014].
Boujaoude, Saouma (2008): Improving Science Education in the Arab States: Lessons Learned from Science Education Practices in Four Developed Countries. UNESCO Cairo Office, Cairo. Available from http://unesdoc.unesco.org/images/0021/002173/217363e.pdf [Accessed 10 September 2014].
CAPMAS (Central Agency for Public Mobilization and Statistics) (2013): *Egypt, Statistical Yearbook*. Available from http://www.capmas.gov.eg/book.aspx [Accessed 10 September 2014].
Cook, Bradley James (2000): Egypt's National Education Debate, *Comparative Education* 36 (4). Pp. 477–490.
Cook, Bradley James (2001): Egyptian University Students: Religion, Change and the Politics of Protest, *Middle East Affairs Journal* 7 (1–2). Pp. 79–104.
DCSF (Department for Children, Schools and Families) (2008): STEM Careers Awareness Stakeholder Guide. London. Available from http://www.shu.ac.uk/_assets/pdf/cse-STEM-stakeholder.pdf [Accessed 10 September 2014].
Dickson, David and Bothina Osama (2012): Egypt: From Revolutionary Spirit to Scientific Progress, January 27. SciDev.Net. Available from http://www.scidev.net/global/innovation/editorials/egypt-from-revolutionary-spirit-to-scientific-progress-1.html [Accessed 17 September 2014].

ERP (Education Reform Program) (2005): Creative Science Education Initiative (CSEI) (unpublished brochure). Cairo.

Freire, Paulo (1993): *Pedagogy of the Oppressed*. Continuum, New York.

Gahin, Gamal Hamed Mohamed Ali (2001): An Investigation into EFL Teachers' Beliefs and Practices in Egypt: An Explanatory Study. Ph.D Thesis, Graduate School of Education, University of Exeter.

Groiss, Arnon (2004): Jews, Christians, War and Peace in Egyptian School Textbooks. Impact: SE (Institute for Monitoring Peace and Cultural Tolerance in School Education). Available from http://www.impact-se.org/research/egypt/index.html [Accessed 10 September 2014].

Hassaneen, Amany Ahmed Elmohamady (2003): Perceptions of Science Teacher Education in Egypt: A Comparison of Policy and Practice. Ph.D thesis, Graduate School of Education, University of Exeter.

Holman, S. John and Peter Finegold (2010): STEM Careers Review. Report to the Gatsby Charitable Foundation. Available from https://esero.org.uk/res/documents/page/STEM%20CAREERS%20REVIEW%20NOV%202010.pdf [Accessed 5 May 2014].

Hutchinson, Jo and Kieran Bentley (2011): STEM Careers Awareness Timelines: STEM Subjects and Jobs: A Longitudinal Perspective of Attitudes among Key Stage 3 Students, 2008–2010. International Centre for Guidance Studies (iCeGS), University of Derby, Derby. Available from http://www.derby.ac.uk/files/icegs_stem_subjects_and_jobs_march2011.pdf [Accessed 10 September 2014].

Isaacs, Shafika (2012): Turning on Mobile Learning in Africa and the Middle East: Illustrative Initiatives and Policy Implications. UNESCO, Paris. Available from http://unesdoc.unesco.org/images/0021/002163/216359e.pdf [Accessed 12 September 2014].

Kolstø, Stein D. (2001): Scientific Literacy for Citizenship: Tools for Dealing with the Science Dimension of Controversial Socioscientific Issues, *Science Education* 85 (3). Pp. 291–310.

Leavitt Center (2013) Islam and Democracy. Blog post of the Michael O. Leavitt Center for Politics & Public Service, February 18. Available from http://leavittcenter.org/tag/democracy/ [Accessed 17 September 2014].

Lemke, Jay L. (2001): Articulating Communities: Sociocultural Perspectives on Science Education, *Journal of Research in Science Teaching* 38 (3). Pp. 296–316.

Mansour, Nasser (2010a): Impact of the Knowledge and Beliefs of Egyptian Science Teachers in Integrating a STS Based Curriculum: A Sociocultural Perspective, *Journal of Science Teacher Education* 21 (5). Pp. 513–534.

Mansour, Nasser (2010b): The Representation of Scientific Literacy in Egyptian Science Textbooks, *Journal of Science Education* 11 (2). Pp. 91–95.

Mansour, Nasser (2011): Science Teachers' Views of Science and Religion vs. the Islamic Perspective: Conflicting or Compatible? *Science Education* 95 (2). Pp. 281–309.

Mansour, Nasser (2013): Modelling the Sociocultural Contexts of Science Education: The Teachers' Perspective, *Research in Science Education* 43 (1). Pp. 347–369.

MBRF (Mohammed Bin Rashid Al Maktoum Foundation) and UNDP/RBAS (The United Nations Development Programme/Regional Bureau for Arab States) (2012): Arab Knowledge Report 2010/2011: Preparing Future Generations for the Knowledge Society. Dubai. Available from http://arabstates.undp.org/content/dam/rbas/report/AKR2010-2011-Eng-Full-Report.pdf [Accessed 10 September 2014].

Ministry of Education, Egypt (1996): *Implementing Egypt's Educational Reform Strategy*. Book Sector, Cairo.

Ministry of Education, Egypt (2007): National Strategic Plan for Pre-University Education Reform in Egypt (2007/08–2011/12). Cairo. Available from http://planipolis.iiep. unesco.org/upload/Egypt/EgyptStrategicPlanPre-universityEducation.pdf [Accessed 10 September 2014].

NCERD (National Center for Educational Research and Development) (2001): Education Development. The National Report of Arab Republic of Egypt from 1990 to 2000. Cairo. http://www.ibe.unesco.org/international/ice/natrap/Egypt.pdf [Accessed 10 September 2014].

NSC (National Specialized Councils of Egypt) (1999): Report of the National Council for Education and Scientific Research and Technology: Science Education for the 21st Century, President's Office. Period 29 Cairo. Pp. 51–63.

Perzigian, Anthony J. (2014): Higher Education Reform in Post-Revolution Egypt. Egypt Independent Live Blog, April 3rd. Available from http://www.egyptindependent.com/ opinion/higher-education-reform-post-revolution-egypt [Accessed 10 September 2014].

Rissmann-Joyce, Stacie and Mohamed El Nagdi (2013): A Case Study – Egypt's First STEM Schools: Lessons Learned. Proceeding of the Global Summit on Education, Kuala Lumpur. Available from http://worldconferences.net/proceedings/gse2013/ papers_gse2013/025%20Stacie%20Rissmann-Joyce%20and%20Mohamed%20El%20 Nagdi.pdf [Accessed 10 September 2014].

Roberts, Amanda and Diana Cantu (2012): Applying STEM Instructional Strategies to Design and Technology Curriculum. PATT 26 Conference: Technology Education in the 21st Century, Stockholm. Linköping University Electronic Press, Linköping. Available from http://www.ep.liu.se/ecp/073/013/ecp12073013.pdf [Accessed 10 September 2014].

Roberts, Gareth (2002): Set for Success: The Supply of People with Science, Technology, Engineering and Mathematics Skills: The Report of Sir Gareth Roberts' Review. Available from http://webarchive.nationalarchives.gov.uk/+/http:/www.hm-treasury. gov.uk/d/robertsreview_introch1.pdf [Accessed 12 September 2014].

Schwab, Klaus (ed.) (2013): The Global Competitiveness Report 2013–2014. World Economic Forum, Geneva. Available from http://www3.weforum.org/docs/WEF_ GlobalCompetitivenessReport_2013–14.pdf [Accessed 10 September 2014].

Stohlmann, Micah et al. (2012): Considerations for Teaching Integrated STEM Education, *Journal of Pre-College Engineering Education Research* 2 (1). Pp. 28–34.

Storck, Madeline (2011): The Role of Social Media in Political Mobilization: A Case Study of the January 2011 Egyptian Uprising. University of St Andrews, Scotland. Available from http://www.culturaldiplomacy.org/academy/content/pdf/participant-papers/2012-02-bifef/The_Role_of_Social_Media_in_Political_Mobilisation_-_ Madeline_Storck.pdf [Accessed 10 September 2014].

Toronto, James Albert (1992): The Dynamics of Educational Reform in Contemporary Egypt. Ph.D thesis, Department of Middle East Studies, Harvard University.

UNESCO (2005): Capacity Building in Gender Inclusive Science & Technology Literacy (STL): Enhancing Life Skills in Egypt. Education for all (EFA) capacity building project, (January-December, 2004). UNESCO, Paris.

UNESCO (2006): Decentralization of Education in Egypt (Country Report). UNESCO Seminar: EFA Implementation: Teacher and Resource Management in the Context of Decentralization, Hyderabad. UNESCO, Paris. Available from http://unesdoc.unesco. org/images/0014/001470/147086e.pdf [Accessed 10 September 2014].

UNESCO (2010): Education for All: Global Monitoring Report 2010. Regional Overview: Arab States. Paris. Available from http://unesdoc.unesco.org/images/0018/001865/186558e.pdf [Accessed 10 September 2014].

UNESCO Cairo Office (2002): Report. Training of Trainers Workshop on use of ICT in Science and Math Education in Secondary Schools in Egypt. Ismailia (Egypt). Available from http://unesdoc.unesco.org/images/0021/002179/217966eo.pdf [Accessed 10 September 2014].

UNESCO Cairo Office (2004): Annual Report 2000: UNESCO Annual Report. UNESCO Regional Office for Science and Technology, Cairo.

UNESCO Institute of Statistics and Talal Abu-Ghazaleh Organization (2013): Information and Communication Technology (ICT) in Education in five Arab States. A Comparative Analysis of ICT Integration and e-readiness in Schools in Egypt, Jordan. Oman, Palestine and Qatar. UNESCO Institute of Statistics, Quebec. Available from http://www.uis.unesco.org/Communication/Documents/ICT-arab-states-en.pdf [Accessed 10 September 2014].

Vygotsky, Lev S. *et al.* (Eds.) (1978): *Mind in Society: The Development of Higher Psychological Processes.* Harvard University Press, Cambridge (MA).

9 Tertiary education in the GCC countries (UAE, Qatar, Saudi Arabia)

How economy, gender and culture affect the field of STEM

Nicole C. Karafyllis

Introduction

Much of what has been reported on science and technology education in Egypt by the experts Gholam and Mansour (in this book, see Chapter 8) is even truer for other parts of the Arab world, or the so-called MENA region (Middle East and North Africa): old-fashioned learning methods based on crude memorizing, weak teacher training, restrictive interpretations of Islam in relation to science education and so on. However, there are also promising initiatives, as the following examples show.

In order to interest more pupils and students in STEM subjects, the government[1] of the United Arab Emirates (UAE) in Abu Dhabi launched the TECH QUEST Leadership Programme for students in 2013, accompanied by school programmes for children, and a STEM Teacher Professional Development Programme that aims to equip teachers with skills and cutting edge strategies for a dynamic classroom. Children have to solve 'hands on' challenges, such as building small robots, carrying out biological experiments, etc. (The National, UAE 2013). For STEM students, bi-annual science camps offer the possibility of meeting peers who could facilitate internships and future employment. In addition, a parents' programme and widespread media coverage of TECH QUEST should work towards the shaping of very different attitudes towards science and technology—and towards what it means to be an Emirati. With this initiative, the UAE advances several economic and political strategies that have been implemented since the 1990s, but which have not yet had any great success: *diversification* of the economy by means of domestic innovations, and *emiratization*, i.e. nationalization of the labour market (Forstenlechner *et al.* 2012).

The countries of the central and southern Arabian Peninsula whose economies vastly depend on oil export and immigrant labour are termed GCC *countries* (GCC: Gulf Cooperation Council, founded 1974). The GCC countries, on which I will focus in the following, encompass the Kingdom of Saudi Arabia, the UAE, Kuwait, Qatar, Bahrain and Oman. Regarding the poor teacher training that has been such an issue throughout the Gulf region the UAE is again the first country to take strong steps. The UAE actively works to provide excellent teachers and to reduce the high number of school-dropouts (particularly among males) as part of the Education Strategy 2010–2020 (Ministry of Education, UAE 2010). At present, the Ministry of Education is working on a framework for a licensing test for schoolteachers (Dajani and Pennington 2014). There is political debate about this process, particularly with regards to unification of the curriculum: while the Minister wants to continue a system that includes 17 different curricula (among them British, German, Australian as well as local) in order to ensure an international landscape of education, other voices demand universal standards for education in Islam and Arabic language (i.e. also in private schools). Indeed, the increasing lack of skills in Arabic, even among nationals, is a looming problem in a country where English and Urdu have become the languages most commonly spoken. In this ongoing emotional debate about Arabic identity, STEM subjects seem to fall into second place. With this in mind, it was a prudent strategic move when Qatar showed its big exhibition '1001 Inventions' (Doha 2012/13), through which numerous children were inspired to practically connect with their culture's scientific past, in the country's Museum of Islamic Art (Doha News Team 2012).

These examples should highlight some of the educational challenges at a glance. Other than adding comparable single initiatives, I will now focus on some systematic arguments. As far as the limited reliable data allows,[2] I will paint a picture of tertiary education in the rich GCC countries and its ambivalent preconditions for engaging in STEM with regard to economy, politics, culture and gender. For comparative reasons, I will also consider trends in the general MENA region.

Due to high birth rates, the developing MENA region hosts one of the largest cohorts in the world of young people in proportion to population. Given that the average inhabitant of the region cannot be regarded as poor, and primary as well as secondary school enrolment is high (except in Yemen), the MENA region is a challenging market for higher education (Altbach and Knight 2007). However, in the GCC region, in recent years, tertiary enrolment rates barely reached 30 per cent, and are thus not on equal levels with Lebanon or the West Bank/Gaza, which both exceeded 50 per cent, much akin to some European countries. In economic, political, cultural and thus also educational respects, the 'Arab world' is all but a homogenous category. For example, at the universities in the GCC region the language of instruction is commonly English.

Most remarkably, the Gulf's higher education problems have a predominantly *male* face. In the long run, the GCC economies will depend hugely on well-educated women who will work as engineers. Looking at the enrolment figures in engineering/technical subjects at the United Arab Emirates University (UAEU) and the Higher Colleges of Technology, they are obviously willing to do so. During the UAEU academic year 2013/14, out of a total 14,024 students, 1,468 women and 767 men were enrolled in the College of Engineering, 912 women and 283 men in the College of Science (UAEU 2014). According to the data provided by the UNESCO Institute of Statistics on the ratio of female to male tertiary enrolment in public and private schools, this may also be true for Saudi Arabia, which is the only GCC country in which (officially) the ratio of female to male tertiary enrolment has been declining over the last few years. In Qatar, approximately only one out of seven students is now male. For the UAE, the gender ratio can be estimated at one male out of every three students. While during the 1990s, GCC countries proudly displayed their increasing numbers of females in tertiary enrolment to the rest of the world in order to stress their efforts at empowering women, the current, never-before-seen high gender ratio in tertiary education has—as the lack of data shared with the UNESCO for the UAE, Kuwait and Bahrain suggests—turned into shame regarding the comparatively low ambitions of young domestic males. On top of this, the gender ratio also underlines the fact that men are allowed to study outside the country and women are usually not (UNESCO Institute of Statistics 2014a).

There is no reliable data yet as to whether this gender qualification advantage pays off in the job market, but it is more than obvious that actual employment of women is not in synch with their levels of tertiary enrolment. A recent World Bank report highlights that the entire MENA region is characterized by the world's lowest participation of females in the labour force (Gatti *et al.* 2013). Gonzalez *et al.* (2008: 119) state that, for example, the UAE has 'a labour force participation rate among males that has remained unchanged for 30 years.'

However, the gender situation in vibrant Qatar, which is an absolute monarchy like Saudi-Arabia and Oman, might be better than available data indicates, e.g. on the proportion of seats held by women in the national parliaments (IPU 2014), because women actually hold strategic positions for education in the country. For example in 2010, Dr. Sheikha Abdulla al-Misnad, a key figure in Qatari education and President of the federal Qatar University (QU) since 2003, was given the rank of Minister by decree of the Emir of Qatar. The head of the superrich Qatar Foundation for Education is also a woman, HH Sheikha Mozah bint Nasser, the former first lady. These women particularly engage in the STEM field and have established scientific collaboration programmes with international partners, both for educational and economic purposes (Scott 2014). Of course, the suspicion of symbolic gender politics remains when looking at the employment situation of women across the region and the social strata.

The GCC countries have been extensively expanding their educational infrastructure, simulating Western models, e.g. the private Masdar Institute of Science and Technology in Abu Dhabi (UAE). More than a hundred private higher education institutions now exist in the GCC region. Nevertheless, local parents still prefer to send their children to the (tuition-free) national universities such as UAEU and QU; not simply because this route saves money but because the national universities have international faculty *and* aim to educate students in keeping with the values of Islam. These values together with their local interpretation meant that the walls of UAEU's women's campus were topped with barbed wire until 2011, and that the new stylish campus has guards and electronic barriers preventing (unmarried) females from getting out and males from getting in.

In summary: for the young countries of the GCC region, education is a political matter of *how* to adequately handle decolonization in light of globalization. The issue of dependence on foreign *technology*, and, to an even greater extent, the need for a technological literacy that goes along with a 'spirit of craftsmanship' (Sennett 2008) have been given a lot of attention by GCC governments, but are not yet central to the process of public discourse.

High youth unemployment, nepotism and brain gain from industrialized countries

A general bottleneck for further developments in tertiary education is the increasing youth unemployment in the whole MENA region (approximately 26.5 per cent of young Arab graduates are unemployed at present) (Al-Wazir 2013), particularly among Arab engineers—a situation which is *also* rampant in the rich Gulf region (e.g. Saudi Arabia and Bahrain). Higher education does not yet pay off in the Arab world. As a World Bank study reveals for Tunisia and Egypt, 'unemployment rates among individuals with primary school education or below oscillate between 2 to 6 per cent compared with 16–19 per cent among individuals with a university degree' (Angel-Urdinola, Semlali and Brodmann 2010: 5; see also Gatti *et al.* 2013).

UAE-based economists Ingo Forstenlechner and Emilie Rutledge (2010) regard the growing unemployment of nationals[3] in the Gulf countries—where the rate of unemployment for the under 30 age group is in double digits in all six countries—as one of the key domestic policy challenges. This is also stressed by the country report on Saudi Arabia edited by the International Monetary Fund (IMF 2013), not least in terms of guaranteeing social harmony in this country. The high youth unemployment puts partially in doubt the idea of a general STEM shortage in the MENA region, though it highlights the importance of improving the quality of STEM education, and education as a whole. Policies for graduates' transfer from university to workplace remain insufficient (no standardized job-seekers-allowance systems exist). While many Arab newspapers continue to vote for stricter nationalization policies, and governments, likewise, have announced such policies, positions in the private sector have been increasingly occupied by expatriates. The situation in the GCC region has led to a considerable brain drain of engineers from Europe (but also from Egypt and India) who can expect a comfortable, untaxed salary in the growing economies of the Gulf. An important implicit factor contributing to the high unemployment rates among young Arabs is the *distrust in the national education systems* among national employers themselves (see next section).

A lot will also depend on a better appreciation of quality education degrees and the distribution of jobs according to a transparent system. Humanitarian activist Yaza al-Wazir gave her opinion on youth unemployment to the popular news channel broadcast *Al Arabiya*:[4]

> The running joke in the graduate job market in Europe is that postgraduate degrees are the new undergraduate degrees—without one, you won't get hired, I am told. The sad reality is that in the Middle East, degrees mean next to nothing without nepotism, or *wasta* as it is known in Arabic.
>
> (Al-Wazir 2013)

Whereas the *Arab World Competitiveness Report* (World Economic Forum and European Bank for Reconstruction and Development 2013) regards corruption as an important negative factor, particularly in the development of North Africa, it fails to see the (difficult to measure) influence of *nepotism*, which—based on the common tribal structures combined with relatively low population sizes—is particularly high in the GCC countries.

In fact, in the last two decades, most MENA countries have actively reacted to needs and effects of globalization, acknowledging international standards in university education as driving forces for economic growth and diversification. This is also true for Saudi Arabia[5], and even more for the UAE and Qatar, where within a very short time, a hitherto unseen number of institutions for science and engineering education have grown, many of them with cross-border collaborative arrangements with the Western world (e.g. in Education City in Doha, Qatar and Knowledge City in Dubai, UAE). The level of innovation in the GCC countries is still low, however.

Transforming resource-based economies into skills-based economies

The GCC countries have become well aware of the fact that oil is an exhaustible resource, and that 'because of instability of oil prices, the revenue from oil is uncertain and volatile' (Muysken and Nour 2006: 957). The future of these economies will heavily depend on education and domestic entrepreneurship, allied with structural policies that put patents into application. The overall aim is to transform the resource-based economies into *skills-based* economies and thereby reduce the strong dependency on the importation of almost all goods, though—given the natural resources of the countries—not heading for 'industrialization.' This economic need is a push for investing in STEM education, though not exclusively: creativity depends on minds that are able to think in an interdisciplinary way and make use of insights from humanities and social sciences.

How do the inhabitants of the GCC region react to this educational challenge? For example, Qatari families spent only 3 per cent of their monthly household on education in 2013, while the expat population spent 5.6 per cent (Walker 2014a).[6] In the GCC countries, education is free at all levels, though a majority of nationals send their children to costly private schools for primary education, but do so less commonly for secondary and even less for tertiary education, especially when educating their daughters. It is the still hesitant or even reluctant *attitude* towards higher education and skilled work that turns out to be the biggest problem.

In the GCC countries, once again in contrast with Egypt, population size is, in general, low (except Saudi Arabia with 28.29 million inhabitants in 2012, of which approximately 7 million were foreigners),[7] and the percentage of immigrant workers and expatriate employees is extremely high. In the small countries of UAE, Bahrain and Qatar this figure can increase, depending on the season, up to 90 per cent. Most of the immigrant workers from Pakistan, India, Bangladesh and South-East Asia are low skilled or even unskilled and many of them are illiterate and unable to speak either Arabic or English. As a consequence, World Bank figures on the very low illiteracy rates in the GCC countries should be interpreted as only referring to the national population (i.e. a minority in most countries). Likewise, income per capita in these countries is very high, although average figures hide the elitist employment structures that depend on nationality.

On mainly economic grounds, the educational study by Muysken and Nour paints a grim picture of the region and particularly the UAE (based on data that focuses mainly on the years leading up to 2003) because 'the educational system in interaction with the excessive share of unskilled foreign workers' has 'lead to, on average, a low skill level, serious skills mismatch and insufficient transfer of knowledge' (Muysken and Nour 2006: 959). The low skills and technology use on both the micro and macro level has led to a continuous dependence on foreign technology at the macro level. Gonzalez *et al.* (2008) view this situation negatively as well. However, the UAE is the country in the region that has most intensively taken action. It has been continuously increasing its expenditures on research and development (R&D) and is thus currently already regarded as an *innovative-driven* economy (having amended key impact factors for sophistication and innovation). As for competitiveness, the UAE is seen on the same level with Germany, the USA and South Korea (World Economic Forum and European Bank for Reconstruction and Development 2013: 9).

So far, Muysken and Nour (2006) have been right, however. Although the GCC countries have seen extensive economic growth rates that have rarely not exceeded 6 per cent over recent years, the countries' nationals in the labour market and the domestic technological development did not profit at similar levels. Most of the emerging jobs for holders of a university degree (particularly in science and engineering) are given to academics from highly industrialized countries (in Saudi Arabia 75 per cent of the jobs created in the last years; see IMF 2013: 5).

In part, this situation results from the lack of an adequately diversified private sector. Personal attitudes also have considerable impact. Educated youth in the GCC countries mostly aim for employment in the *public sector* or government, where expertise in the STEM field is rarely required. As Forstenlechner *et al.* (2012) have pointed out, youth in the UAE find higher personal value working for their own government, where they profit from high salaries and have colleagues of the same nationality, instead of in the more competitive private sector. Furthermore, the initiative to 'apply for a job,' as is usually necessary in the private sector, often seems odd to young nationals, given that governmental jobs are basically 'offered to you' (frequently based on nepotism according to the *wasta*-system).

In the light of these preferences, it makes sense for graduates to choose humanities/social sciences and business/economics rather than STEM as subjects for higher education—which has been the situation over the past decades. However, it also makes sense for job hopes in the private sector. Until recently, the aim of diversifying the private sector concentrated on the service sector (including jobs in IT, business and tourism), rather than on manufacturing and production.[8]

The *Arab World Competitiveness Report* (World Economic Forum and European Bank for Reconstruction and Development 2013: Figure 3) highlighted three generally problematic areas of doing private business in the Gulf area, other than in North Africa and the Levant: restrictive labour regulations, limited access to financing and an inadequately educated workforce. It might come as no surprise that human resource managers in the private sector of GCC countries still prefer to hire non-nationals, whereas it is remarkable that this also applies when the HR manager him-/herself is, for example, an Emirati (Al Waqfi and Forstenlechner 2010; Forstenlechner *et al.* 2012). An important finding is: successful Emiratis in the private sector do not trust either the education or the 'work ethics' (i.e. rigour and motivation) *of their own people.* This distrust is also paradigmatic for the other GCC countries. As a consequence, the public sector—among them schools and federal universities—have come under enormous pressure to hire more and more nationals, thereby undermining the high international level of educational workforce that had been reached. The above findings matter with regard to the *extrinsic motivation* for choosing a career in the STEM field. Obviously, the lack of promising job perspectives in the private sector does not motivate Arab students to engage in STEM subjects.

Despite the numerous political announcements on the importance of education, the GCC countries' expenditures on research and development is remarkably low (UNESCO 2014b), topped by the UAE which spent 0.49 per cent of its GDP on R&D in 2011 (and most likely also by Qatar, which has not yet contributed data to the World Bank Statistics). By percentage, the UAE is almost on the same level with Egypt (0.43 per cent in 2011), though not on equal footing with the USA, China or Germany. Saudi Arabia's expenditure on R&D of only 0.07 per cent of its GDP (2009) somehow resembles the monarchy's general attitude on the importance of educating Saudi nationals, particularly the women. Nevertheless, the IMF regards the Saudi investments in education as 'appropriate,' while highlighting the need for more efficacy and quality indicators, as, for example, 'the scores of Saudi students on internationally standardized tests in mathematics and science are still relatively low' (IMF 2013: 14, see also Figure 3). The percentage of eighth grade students reaching the TIMSS educational benchmarks in science is considerably higher in the smaller GCC countries Qatar and the UAE, which in 2011 performed very similarly to Italy and Iran in science scores, and slightly below those levels in mathematics scores, on a par with Norway. The winning countries identified by the TIMSS study 2011 were Singapore, China, South Korea, Japan and the Russian Federation (Martin *et al.* 2012).

Late development of universities and professional organizations in the GCC countries

Located at the confluence of Europe, Mediterranean Arab countries like Egypt historically have many cultural and political intersections with the 'Western' world, including the building of professional organizations and universities, which the GCC countries lack. Besides its highly established education in medicine, Egypt has a long tradition of educating scientists and engineers (e.g. Cairo University was established in 1908, American University of Cairo in 1919) and also hosts comparatively old engineering societies, foremost the Egyptian Society of Engineers, founded as the 'Royal Society of Engineers' in Cairo in 1920. The society and its sub-branches very much engage in promoting the STEM field, support education and training of engineers, and make up-to-date teaching and learning material available.[9] Moreover, Cairo is the city which hosts the international Federation of Arab Engineers (FAE),[10] founded 1963. The Mediterranean Arab countries have a 'technology culture,' which is still rare in the Gulf, though it is developing.

As professional organizations and societies were forbidden until about the 1990s by the suppressive laws of the GCC countries, societies for promoting the engineering profession have only been formed in recent decades. The countries' various new engineering societies are now united under the leadership of the Gulf Engineering Union (formerly the Forum of Gulf Engineers, founded 1997), which holds annual conferences on engineering topics and actively engages in training and quality assessment for engineers, in exchange with both private and public institutions. Thus, regarding employment and training opportunities for domestic STEM students, the future will surely be more positive than the present.

In recent years, the countries of the southern Arabian Peninsula have increasingly oriented themselves politically and economically towards the region of India and Pakistan, while in educational as well as security affairs they still depend greatly on the consultancy and manpower of their former colonizer, Great Britain, and their 'neo-colonizer,' the USA. The latter is also the model for university education in the GCC region, where universities have existed only since the second half of the twentieth century. In the Kingdom of Saudi Arabia, the Ministry of Education was founded in 1953. Early established science and engineering institutions are, for instance, the large King Saud University (founded 1957) in Riyadh, and King Fahd College of Petroleum and Minerals, established in 1963 (and transformed into a university in 1975, KFUPM). At that time, the UAE, Oman, Bahrain and Qatar did not yet exist as countries but were British protectorates.[11] Soon after having become independent (1971), two big public universities grew out of former colleges that had once primarily provided teacher education: Qatar University (QU, founded 1977)[12] in Doha and United Arab Emirates University in Al Ain, Abu Dhabi (UAEU, founded 1976). Today, both have science, engineering, IT and health/pharmacy colleges, and colleges of humanities/social sciences, law/Sharia, business/economics and education (the UAEU also has food/agriculture). The two federal universities are well-respected educational hubs in the region, for Saudi students, too. In 1986, the national Sultan Qabus University (SQU) in Muscat/Oman opened its doors. The University of Bahrain (UoB) was established the same year.[13] All above mentioned federal universities are under the patronage of a member of the Royal Family of its country and, looking at enrolment data, they are more popular by far than any of the numerous private universities with Western partnerships in the Gulf. Expansion is on the agenda. In 2019, QU wants to open its doors for 25,000 students from all over the world. In the recent past, Qataris have complained about QU not enrolling enough national students due to high admission standards (Walker 2014b). Aspiring to become an international flagship and serving the needs of the national population at the same time is not an easy task.

Lack of 'technology culture': the symbolic power of technology versus the weak appreciation of knowledge

Politically, the GCC countries now want to be acknowledged as 'global players' and hubs amongst advanced nations, adding reputation to their excellent economic performance within the G20 economies. This strong wish does not only result in both the *nationalistic* and the *symbolic* interpretation of technology (e.g. in the effort of having the highest building in the world, i.e. the Burj Khalifa in Dubai, or their own nuclear power plant, such as is under construction in Abu Dhabi at present), but also in very special educational politics. For example, a high value is set on ICT in the classroom, e-learning and impressive campus architecture in order to show the 'modernization' of the education system. Despite these obvious materializations of change at the surface, the underlying political structures of education have remained comparatively rigid, particularly in Saudi Arabia. Its intransigence in the face of change can be seen on the administrative and planning level, and particularly in the curricula. Not everyone responsible for educational changes has yet realized that ICT facilities are neither necessarily resulting in an increased technological literacy nor in a general 'edification' (German: *Bildung*) which could make use of tacit knowledge. After all, both matter for high achievements in the STEM field. As Forstenlechner and Rutledge (2010: 45) put it: 'the focus now is unambiguously the content of the curriculum, not the color scheme of the campus buildings.'

Remarkable efforts have been made in all GCC countries in the fields of improving *gender equality* (women's primary, secondary and tertiary education) and the implementation of *vocational training* institutions since the new millennium, which in the UAE have been set up in collaboration with Germany and Australia. Both can be seen as final acknowledgements of social stratification within the indigenous population, where not every national belongs to the tribal elite of the ruling dynasty and thus a 'middle class' has to be established. When it comes to the use of the Internet, the smaller GCC countries lead the way on the Arabian Peninsula, with the UAE strongly in the lead. It is one of the countries with the highest Internet density in the world, having already hit the level that Europe will only reach by the end of 2014 (ITU 2014). While the UAE introduced the Internet in 1999, Saudi Arabia remained suspicious for a long time and is still trying to catch up.

In the GCC countries, the tradition of *Wahhabi* Islam forms a stricter religious framework for educational issues than in North Africa. For example, the GCC region has no book culture.[14] Libraries and bookstores are still rare and poorly equipped (including at universities), other than with licenses for electronic resources. When Sheikh Mohammed Ibn Rashid al Maktoum, ruler of Dubai and Vice-President of the UAE, opened the Gulf Educational Supplies and Solutions Exhibition in Dubai on March 7, 2014, the focus was on everything except books or regional scientific publishing houses with high quality standards (though he himself is a bestselling author of poetry).[15] Educational methods that, in the STEM subjects, promote the incorporation of film and drama are not welcome yet, at least in Saudi Arabia. One has to keep in mind that the 'moral police' also operate in the neighbouring GCC countries. It is not just politics, but religion and the different Islamic schools and traditions that also affect the situation. Neighbouring Iran—with its highly advanced education system and internationally renowned academics—is observed with suspicion and viewed as a thorn in the side of the people on the Arabian side of the Persian Gulf who, being mainly Sunnites, generally want all but advice from the Iranian Shiites. Turkey with its laicism is also not seen as a model for education. On top of this, rulers of the Ottoman Empire were colonizers of the Arab world for centuries.

In *Al Arabiya*, journalist Mustapha Ajbaili (2012) recently summarized the educational traditions that might be overcome in the near future; as he hopes, with the help of foreign partners such as the European Union:

'[. . .] following the decolonization period, educational institutions in the Middle East and North Africa were viewed more as instruments of social control than agents of liberation. [. . .] Liberal curricula—which encourages critical thinking and promotes individual initiatives outside certain national and religious frameworks—were generally suppressed' (Ajbaili 2012).

Just in recent decades, education as such is seen as having a value in its own right and adding value to the 'human capital'. However, academic degrees count far less for status and reputation, compared with heritage (tribal descent), community spirit, religious virtue and monetary wealth—the crucial elements that form the Gulf Arabian *habitus*. This differs from the Mediterranean parts of the Arab world. However, today's Arab youth who grew up in the metropolitan areas of Dubai, Abu Dhabi, Doha and Riyadh understand the effort needed to relate the question 'who am I?' not simply to 'who were my ancestors?', but also to 'where do I want to get: in terms of both *myself and my country?*' In all educational strategies stated by the GCC countries, lately one comes across the term 'rootedness' (to avoid 'cultural heritage'). Thus education, in the STEM subjects, too, should contribute to forming a national and cultural identity that cherishes the land and is therefore genuinely territorial. Educational issues are framed within the pursuit of future independence from Western educators, technology and labour force.

However, dropout rates in secondary education remain high. It will be crucial to get parents (particularly the fathers) 'onboard.' In 2012, the UAE outlined a law that no longer allows parents to take their children out of school by the age of 14. It is a problem that particularly affects boys (Ahmed 2012). Therefore, the present enrolment figures in tertiary education predominantly result from the ambition of women and foreign students. Solutions are seen in more opportunities for vocational education that supports training in a profession, resembling Germany's so-called 'dual system.'

It will take even more time to overcome cultural restrictions regarding technology. As Haan (1999) has stated, the education systems of the GCC countries have a bias against technical subjects and manual work. Based on data from UNDP 2003, only 27 per cent of UAE's tertiary students were enrolled in technical subjects (Muysken and Nour 2006: 965). Even after having obtained a degree in science or engineering, many of them end up with white-collar jobs, avoiding 'dirty hands.' One should keep in mind that, other than in Egypt and Lebanon, white is the colour of traditional male garb in the Gulf States, and the purity of this whiteness is carefully maintained during the day. The women of the region who dress in black usually have less antipathy towards manual work, and have historically been more involved with it (agriculture, childcare). In Gulf Arabia with its Bedouin culture of trade and travel, there is a true lack of 'technology culture' in Western and also Far East terms. This can be seen in the Arabic language: no word that refers to technics and technology etymologically relates to the word for 'hand' (see Chapter 1 in this book) as, for example, in 'manufacture'. Gulf Arabs prefer to delegate manual work to the many foreigners, not seeing that this leads to a general decrease in skill level and prevents the country from increasing its own skill knowledge.

What to study? Subject choice, tertiary enrolment and curriculum development

The GCC countries have, in formal academic terms, an increasingly well-educated youth, though the federal universities predominantly provide undergraduate education. On a closer look, a considerable, exclusively male part of the national populations has been educated *outside* the country, usually in the US and the UK. Preferred subjects are social sciences, humanities and business/economics, but not engineering or science.[16] In fact, engaging in social sciences and humanities makes sense, as the GCC region is characterized by rapid social change under restrictive cultural and religious conditions (Tibi 2005). In addition, modern social sciences and humanities are weakly established and belong to the most politically controlled inside the country. Moreover, this field increases the understanding and training of social interpersonal skills, reflective practices and language habits, i.e. soft-skills employers in the MENA region see lacking in Arab graduates (Angel-Urdinola, Semlali and Brodmann 2010: 7f; Gonzalez *et al.* 2008).

However, economic observers and consultants from outside the GCC region constantly stress that higher tertiary enrolment *and* achieving a university degree in STEM subjects will be crucial to form a skill-based economy that could, for example, domestically manufacture petrochemicals on a large scale. Chemistry and chemical engineering are STEM fields that the GCC countries particularly need to expand, and the long Arabic tradition in alchemy should ease this culturally. Looking at the enrolment numbers for STEM at the bigger universities, the GCC countries have reasonable, although still not high, enrolment figures for engineering, but they desperately lack sufficient university enrolment in the *sciences*. The trend to choose more 'applied' subjects because of the better job prospects (as can also be found in Europe) will, in the long run, endanger the foundations of basic research which generates knowledge to be applied later. According to data collected by Gonzalez *et al.* on graduates of UAEU, 'there has been a steady decline in post-secondary graduates majoring in technical fields (sciences, engineering) despite a growing demand for individuals with specializations in these fields' (Gonzalez *et al.* 2008: 191).

In general, it is agreed that children should be interested in STEM subjects as early as possible. Again the UAE has taken the initiative and, in late 2013, merged the once-separated tracks for arts and science in public schools (Salem 2013). Like in Saudi Arabia, pupils were as old as 15 when they were faced with the choice in the UAE's decade-old two track system, and most pupils opted for arts rather than science. The new change will not only make secondary education students more suited for the job market but will also increase the *intrinsic motivation* for studying STEM subjects: because technology is appreciated through the lens of art in Arabic culture.

Still not enough secondary education graduates enter university or other higher education institutions (Muysken and Nour 2006: 962). Many secondary school graduates have to take two- to four-semester preparatory or remedial courses before being admitted to university (e.g. termed as 'foundation years' at the UAEU). Even worse: more than the indicator 'enrolment in tertiary education' reveals, the *university life expectancy* is very low, for example, in the UAE: 'only few obtain the first university degree or higher (4%), falling far behind China (48%) and South Korea (41%)' (Muysken and Nour 2006: 962). This is not only due to a lack of ambition, given that for many nationals there is no economic need for social upward movement (or having a job at all), but also because some want their sons to engage in the family's business affairs as early as possible, and see the effort and time needed for achieving a university degree not paying off in terms of money and status.

In 2012, the UAE raised admission scores for their seventeen federal Higher Colleges of Technology (HCTs) whose degrees are seen as equivalent to those of the two other national universities. This became necessary due to the low English skills of secondary school graduates. The hope is that schools will react to this 'top-down' change with better teaching and learning outcomes in English. One typical reaction has already happened: demands for university curricula in Arabic only (Swan 2012). However, the new admission scores for English are still not very ambitious.

Figures on university degrees among domestic nationals (which have not been provided yet) would at present probably be higher than in the study of Muysken and Nour (2006). More women from the GCC countries study now than fifteen years ago, and they usually outnumber male students in achieving a degree, foremost in order to have their own income later. Nevertheless, women from very traditional families still cannot hope to actually work in their profession. As a consequence, some see their university studies as the only time of their life that they can be 'free' and want to prolong it for as long as possible. Some female students also delay obtaining a degree to postpone marriage.[17] Newer figures provided by the Commission for Academic Accreditation in Abu Dhabi (CAA 2011) seem to show a positive trend in tertiary enrolment in the UAE (though the numbers of nationals are not provided; neither is the increasing percentage of the population's youth visible, nor how many actually earn a degree).

One step towards international tertiary education was establishing cross-border collaborative private universities, as this facilitates the needed international accreditation of Masters Programmes and also enables easier grade transfer for those who want to continue studying abroad. As a result, enrolment in non-federal institutions in the UAE increased continuously between 2006 and 2011, and the trend continues—however, enrolment in federal institutions has not gone down. In 2009, 49 out of the UAE's 96 higher education institutions in the UAE were international, i.e. non-Emirati (British Council Abu Dhabi 2009: 6), and concentrated in the emirate of Dubai. The British Council Abu Dhabi, whose range of private institutions analysed included the non-licensed international ones, found only 11 per cent of Emiratis (a total number of 2,754) enrolled in private *international* higher education institutions for the academic year 2008/09. However, the British Council did not take into account the several private institutions that are, according to the survey's criteria, *not* international and provide, for instance, education in Islamic Law and Arabic-Islamic Studies. Above all, the low number of students engaged in international higher education shows that most Emirati students still prefer to study at the federal institutions where students can graduate with mediocre English skills. The bias against English language education is not true of Asian students who, at 51 per cent, make up the majority of students enrolled in tertiary private international education institutions in the UAE.

The UAE's most popular institutions, outside the dominant federal universities, are the American University of Sharjah, the American University in Dubai, the University of Wollongong (Australia), the Manipal Academy of Higher Education (India) and the Birla Institute of Technology and Science, Pilani (India), which together account for 48 per cent of the total student population in private international higher education institutions in the UAE. When students were asked why they study at a *private* university, most mentioned that their degrees were more prestigious, and a belief in the superiority of education with regard to quality of faculty and teaching methods. Other reasons mentioned were the wish to migrate abroad and improve academic English (British Council Abu Dhabi 2009: 10–23).

In order to strengthen the UAE's three federal universities, since autumn 2013, they have been regulated by the Commission for Academic Accreditation in Abu Dhabi (CAA). Educational programmes licensed by the CAA include engineering and health science, but a category for the sciences as such (physics, chemistry, biology) or mathematics is missing (CAA 2011: 6). Investigating the *non-federal*, i.e. *private international* universities in the UAE,[18] the picture of enrolment by subject again shows the comparatively high amount of students enrolled in business/administrative studies (59 per cent of undergraduates, 76 per cent of graduates, mostly doing MBA-programmes) which are relatively cheap to implement compared with medicine, science and engineering, the last of which is chosen by 13 per cent of undergraduates. At the bottom end of both offered and chosen subjects are: education, sciences (particularly biology), history and philosophy (British Council Abu Dhabi 2009: 16). This data from the private international universities allows one more to draw inferences from the foreign mother institutions' motives and their investment policies in the UAE rather than to draw conclusions with regard to local students' actual interests and preferences.

When looking at the federal UAEU, the picture of enrolment by subject changes. In medicine, the UAEU in Al Ain is allied with the big Tawam hospital as a training hospital and university clinic. A total of 575 medicine and health science students were enrolled in the academic year 2013/14, 422 of them female. The numbers for engineering (in the UAEU including architecture) are considerably higher and show an interesting gender ratio: from 2,235 engineering students, 1,468 are female (see Table 9.1). For women in the UAE, engineering is the third most popular field of study after humanities/social sciences and business/economics. For male students, business/economics are in first place, on the same level as engineering, followed by law and the sciences. From the 14,024 total of students enrolled in 2013/14, only 3,240 students were male. This highly uneven percentage can be found in all federal universities in the UAE, like in most GCC countries.

Note that in Table 9.1 the limited number of students enrolled in graduate studies (not even 8 per cent of total students) shows—all of a sudden—a considerably higher percentage of male students (335 of 786). In the disciplines of engineering and science, gender-segregated education faces severe challenges, as students are required to work in laboratories together, i.e. as *teams*. Often there

Table 9.1 Numbers of students enrolled according to subject and gender at the UAEU in the academic year 2013/14

College	Male Students	Female Students	Total
Humanities & Social Sciences	280	3,110	3,390
Sciences	283	912	1,195
Education	0	528	528
Business & Economics	769	2,097	2,866
Law	368	721	1,089
Food & Agriculture	98	556	654
Engineering	767	1,468	2,235
Medicine & Health Sciences	153	422	575
Information Technology	131	410	541
Graduate Studies	335	451	786
Doctorate	48	95	143
Professional Doctorate	8	14	22
Total	**3,240**	**10,784**	**14,024**

Source: UAEU 2014

is not enough financial provision to establish 'double' graduate programmes to ensure gender segregation. This situation favours male students when it comes to upward academic mobility.

For male nationals from the richer parts of the UAE (Abu Dhabi, Dubai, Sharjah) there is almost always the option to study abroad. However, as many of the male students from the GCC area sent abroad have not been coming back home (or only do so after a long time), or, since 9/11, do not want to study in the US anymore because they fear discrimination, the issue of educating the nation's male youth *inside* the country looms. The British Council Abu Dhabi study (2009: 35) highlighted that out of students enrolled in private international tertiary education in the UAE, 23 per cent had considered studying at the parent institution abroad rather than at a UAE branch (28 per cent male, 18 per cent female). Out of Emirati students, only 11 per cent had thought likewise (gender ratio not provided). Out of expatriate students from other Arab countries, only 14 per cent had considered doing so, whereas 33 per cent of Asian expatriate students would have liked to study 'abroad,' i.e. mostly in the UK and the US. Asked for the reasons why they then did not study abroad, 26 per cent of all the students who had considered doing so gave the answer 'objection of family members.' Among other answers were: 'cultural constraints' (3 per cent), 'did not get admission' (5 per cent), 'was not offered subject/course of choice' (6 per cent) and 'did not get visa' (9 per cent) (British Council Abu Dhabi 2009: 36).

Altbach and Knight (2007: 303) have pointed out that political realities and issues of national security may affect higher education in the future: 'tightened requirements in the US and other countries, security restriction on the subjects that can be studied, and fear of terrorism expressed by potential international students may affect cross-border student flows.' Both the UAE and Qatar have reacted to this trend and are building a higher education market for students who do not easily get a visa or admission to a university in North America or Europe. More and more students from other Arab countries and Asia now study in the GCC region.

Situation for researchers and educators: why PhD programmes are still lacking

Problems with the concepts of equality and academic rigour frame another area of friction within the educational fabric of the region. Nationals employed in the academic systems (and in other fields) of GCC countries get triple salaries for the same or less work[19] as an expatriate teacher from Europe or North America. This is, if at all, justified by the living costs and large family size nationals tend to have. Tenured positions for foreigners do not exist. Four-year contracts on a rolling basis are standard in academia, making the renewal dependent on constant evaluation (of teaching and research quality), institutional demand and, most importantly, current individual reputation. Not having a *tenure option* results in a lack of continuity within the educational system, as the younger professors are currently striving for better options on the international academic market, since job security is a concern. Expatriate professors in GCC countries are usually either very young or very old, adding a few years earning extra income after retiring in their home countries. One of the effects of the high turnover in human resources is *slow curriculum development*, which usually starts from scratch every few years. Poor planning is one of the severe failures of the university systems in the region.

Even if quality assessment of both students' and teachers' performances exists, special problems apply. Facing a generally unstable employment situation increases the tendency of *grade inflation*, as expatriate professors are more inclined to give comparatively overly generous grades to the national students of whom a high percentage is tribally related to the countries' ruling families. Peer evaluation of faculty by expatriates most often skips the national faculty out of the same concern.

Another result of no-tenure is that students do not get the opportunity to academically *engage* with their peers over a longer period of time. Moreover, they miss the cohort of the ambitious professors aged 40–55 that are usually both experienced in teaching and administration, and at the forefront of cutting edge research. For the STEM field this fact also matters regarding the lack of professors that spend sufficient time building up a laboratory for a specific research field and keeping it properly maintained. A high-impact researcher is faced with a double-bind situation: according to international standards, he or she is expected to have research projects with external funding, although a transparent funding structure in the region is still in development (as well as the administrative capacity to operate matching funds coming from outside the country). One funding institution to be highlighted is the Qatar National Research Fund (QNRF), which has implemented a cross-border peer-review system on a state of the art electronic basis and launches regular funding cycles with specific proposals and initiatives, accompanied by international conferences held in Doha.

The governmental concept of getting internationally recognized high-quality education for the national youth is usually outweighed by the desires and economic pressure to hire more national academics, some of whom, however, have degrees from well-known Western universities. Particularly since North Africa's Arab Spring revolutions in 2011, the tendency to stick to their 'own people' (though not to the national police for security issues) has grown in the GCC countries. For example, since 2011, the national UAEU has rigorously increased its 'emiratization' policy. All positions in higher administration and faculty management (e.g. deans, provost) are now held by nationals, which was not the case before—according to my own observations while working there from 2008 to 2010 under an Australian provost and a Canadian dean. In spring 2014, the UAE issued a decree that stated that nationals hired at the public universities will get a salary increase of 25 per cent, whereas the salary for expatriates has stagnated since 2008, despite the high rate of inflation.

The only institution in the country that holds a real PhD programme is the Masdar Institute of Science and Technology, a small but research-intensive university that accompanied the opening of the eco-model city Masdar near Abu Dhabi in 2009. The uniqueness of this programme is stressed by national voice, the Emirati writer Mariam Al Hallami (2014), who also complains about the government's low expenditures on funding research that would really build a knowledge-based economy. In general, the idea that research, teaching and learning are intertwined has still to be developed in the Gulf region, including the idea that employment and funding structures for university faculty—who have to spend most of their time teaching and grading rather than doing research—are related. At the UAEU three main restrictions for the PhD programme, which was set up in 2009, applied and still apply. First, the governmental scholarships for PhD students, though amounting to what an assistant professor would earn in the US, were too low to get male Emiratis interested in a PhD track, compared to salaries they would get when, for instance, working for the police. Second, no extra faculty was hired for the programme. Last but not least, the English writing skills of students at the public universities are still too low to create a longer thesis.

Conclusion: science and technology topics of interest in the GCC area

To conclude, engaging in the STEM field is both unattractive and politically desired in the GCC countries. The most severe problems in tertiary education result from a lack of respect for teachers/lecturers who are, at the same time, both researchers and professors, and actually need time for their research. Moreover, problems result from a lack of transparent and appropriate funding structures, low expenditures on research and development, students' poor English skills and restrictive labour market policies that urge the public sector towards nationalization. Particularly for the STEM field, there is a general lack of a science and technology culture, which has negative effects. Such a culture should be established, starting with a different attitude towards S&T. Thus it not only would improve intrinsic motivation but at first would *require* intrinsic motivation, such as a fascination in scientific explanations and solutions. In addition, a private sector where employers have a strong bias towards hiring nationals, particularly those with a domestic degree, triggers reduced interest in choosing the STEM field for study. Moreover, the high unemployment rate of Arab STEM graduates negatively influences the extrinsic motivation for studying a related subject. The intrinsic motivation might change with new curricula that makes STEM interesting to children as early as possible, and by active talent scouting that is able to overcome the hidden employment structures of nepotism and cultural bias. More important, though, will be the effort to link contents of STEM to cultural traditions and histories of the region, which would imply the creation of interdisciplinary curricula where STEM is taught together with insights from the arts and humanities, and could make use of textbooks that are adequately culturally adapted.

For a look to the future, I will highlight important areas of STEM in which the GCC countries have begun to invest and which might raise the number of domestic STEM students. For example, the newly founded Saudi Arabian King Abdullah University of Science and Technology (KAUST) focuses on four research areas: water, energy, food and environment. In general, these research areas are highlighted in most Gulf universities. Solar technology, in particular, in combination with 'intelligent' water and agricultural technologies (incorporating research findings from nano and material science) should boost technological development in the various countries and thereby trigger economic growth and diversification. Environmental management and *sustainability* also play a crucial part in academic institutions, as the region has already been hit by the effects of climate change (e.g. increased desertification and so-called 'coral bleaching'). Moreover, the high rate of food imports affects GCC economies and the countries are thus striving to improve their agricultural systems. Another science area of common interest is *genetics*, particularly human genetics, addressing the significant problem of high rates of hereditary diseases and infant deaths due to first-cousin marriages.[20] Thus, genetics is one of the main areas where a scientific worldview contrasts strongly with the cultural practices of the region. Still, this might be seen as challenging. Another dominant field of research is Arabic language technologies (ALT), uniting research in informatics and computational design with insights from linguistics and sociology.

So far, only one country in the region, Qatar, has publically announced that arts, social sciences and humanities are of vital interest.[21] Despite all the economically motivated interest in pushing the STEM field, one must not forget that the GCC area is geopolitically fragile and affected by terrorism. Therefore, investments in education are seen by the GCC countries and further afield as a general means for peace. GCC charity organizations are the biggest donors to causes that improve education in the poorer Muslim countries (e.g. Pakistan and Yemen; see IMF 2013 for the vast charity funds of Saudi Arabia).[22] On these grounds, Qatar University, in line with Qatar National Research Strategy, is planning to increase quality research on international affairs, human rights and governance. This will lead to the establishment of new disciplines, which might enable students to critically reflect on the different goals that the STEM field is striving for. A discipline the region probably needs most is, however, peace studies.

Notes

1 See the website http://www.techquest.ae [Accessed 15 June 2014]. Advanced Technology Investment Company (ATIC), a daughter of the Emirati MUBADALA Company that heads for diversification of the Emirati economy and is engaged in several economic fields (from solar energy to real estate), is responsible for TECH QUEST. As in the GCC countries a private sector in the true sense hardly exists, I count TECH QUEST as a governmental initiative.
2 That much of the collected data in the GCC countries is purposely hidden from public scrutiny is highlighted by Forstenlechner and Rutledge (2010: 39).
3 Note that all unemployment data on the GCC countries address the unemployment of nationals, as non-nationals losing their job face termination of visa and have to leave the country.
4 Al Arabiya was founded in 2003 in Dubai Media City (UAE) and is majority-owned by investors from Saudi Arabia. In the Arab world, it is the biggest competitor to the news channel Al Jazeera, based in Qatar.

5 On recent transformations in Saudi Arabia, see Niblock (2007) and Freitag (2010).
6 Figures quoted in this newspaper article originate from the Qatari Ministry of Development and Planning Statistics, based on a survey 2012/2013.
7 UAE: 9.206 million, Qatar: 2.051 million, Bahrain: 1.318 million, Oman: 3.314 million inhabitants for 2012 (World Bank Statistics 2014).
8 This is stressed by the recent country reports of the IMF (2013) and by the World Economic Forum and European Bank for Reconstruction and Development (2013).
9 See e.g. the English webpage of the *Egyptian Society of Mechanical Engineers* (ESME) at http://www.esme-egypt.com/index.php?option=com_k2&view=item&layout=item&id=92 [Accessed 19 June 2012].
10 See the website http://www.arabfedeng.org [Accessed 15 October 2014].
11 Kuwait became independent in 1961.
12 See the webpage of Qatar University and its history, available from http://www.qu.edu.qa/theuniversity/history.php [Accessed 23 June 2014].
13 University of Bahrain grew out of the College of Arts, Sciences and Education and the Gulf Technical College (founded 1968)/Gulf Polytechnic.
14 This traces back to a special understanding of *holiness* of scripture (see Diner 2010) and an *oral* culture of communication.
15 See the regional daily newspaper *Al Khaleej Times*, 7 March 2014, title page.
16 Forstenlechner and Rutledge (2010) highlight these preferences for domestic students of the GCC region.
17 These statements are based on many conversations I had with national students while teaching as a professor at the UAEU 2008–2010.
18 The study by the British Council Abu Dhabi also considers institutions that have not been licensed by the CAA at that time.
19 The same household ratio has been reported for Qataris, where the monthly salary only accounts for two thirds of the household income, and other benefits (e.g. health insurance, electricity, etc.) apply (Walker 2014a). Figures quoted in this newspaper article originate from the Qatari Ministry of Development and Planning Statistics Report (MDPS Report), which will include the data from the new *Household Expenditure and Income Survey* 2012/13 already announced to the media in June 2014.
20 According to the Centre for Arabic Genomic Studies based in Dubai (UAE), at least half of all present Gulf Arab marriages are between cousins; and at least 35 per cent of Qatari marriages are between first cousins, mainly in order to sustain the economic wealth of the tribe. In the Gulf countries, premarital testing (e.g. for the common sickle cell anaemia) has become mandatory and public awareness campaigns try to inform the society about the genetic risks of intermarriage (Doherty 2012).
21 For further information see the Qatar National Research Strategy and a Strategic Plan for Implementation (2012), available from http://www.authorsqscience.com/qfarc2013/QNRS-2012-Brief-Final.pdf [Accessed 15 October 2014].
22 For the UAE, the charity initiative Dubai Cares (in collaboration with UNICEF) is very involved with its poor neighbour Yemen.

Bibliography

Ahmed, Ajshan (2012): Compulsory School Leaving Age Raised in the UAE. *The National*, UAE, July 24. Available from http://www.thenational.ae/news/uae-news/education/compulsory-school-leaving-age-raised-in-the-uae [Accessed 15 October 2014].

Ajbaili, Mustafa (2012): EU Program Seeks to Modernize Higher Education in Middle East and North Africa. *Al Arabiya News*, May 1. Available from http://www.alarabiya.net/articles/2012/05/01/211514.html [Accessed 13 October 2014].

Al Hallami, Mariam (2014): A Knowledge Economy Begins with Funding for Research. *The National*, January 9. Available from http://www.thenational.ae/thenationalconversation/comment/a-knowledge-economy-begins-with-funding-for-research [Accessed 13 October 2014].

Altbach, Philip G. and Jane Knight (2007): The Internationalization of Higher Education: Motivations and Reality. *Journal of Studies in International Education* 11 (3–4). Pp. 290–305.

Al-Waqfi, Mohammed and Ingo Forstenlechner (2010): Stereotyping of Citizens in an Expatriate-dominated Labour Market: Implications for Workforce Localisation Policy. *Employee Relations* 32 (4). Pp. 364–381.

Al-Wazir, Yara (2013): What about the Middle East's Unemployed Graduates? *Al Arabiya*, October 11. Available from http://english.alarabiya.net/en/views/news/middle-east/2013/10/11/What-about-the-Middle-East-s-unemployed-graduates-.html [Accessed 15 October 2014].

Angel-Urdinola, Diego F., Amina Semlali and Stefanie Brodmann (2010): *Non-Public Provision of Active Labor Market Programs in Arab-Mediterranean Countries: An Inventory of Youth Programs*. World Bank, Washington (DC). Available from http://siteresources.worldbank.org/SOCIALPROTECTION/Resources/SP-Discussion-papers/Labor-Market-DP/1005.pdf [Accessed 13 October 2014].

British Council Abu Dhabi (2009): TNE in the UAE. Research Findings. UAE Country Partnership Meeting 5 June 2009. PowerPoint Presentation (67 slides) by Alison Devine. Available from http://slideplayer.us/slide/700550/ [Accessed 15 October 2014].

CAA (Commission for Academic Accreditation) Abu Dhabi (2011): *Annual Report 2011*. Abu Dhabi. Available from https://www.caa.ae/caa/images/AnnualReport2011.pdf [Accessed 13 October 2014].

Dajani, Haneen and Roberta Pennington (2014): New Licensing System for Teachers in the UAE. *The National*, June 4. Available from http://www.thenational.ae/uae/education/new-licensing-system-for-teachers-in-the-uae [Accessed 13 October 2014].

Diner, Dan (2010): *Versiegelte Zeit. Über den Stillstand in der islamischen Welt*. List, Berlin.

Doha News Team (2012): New Exhibitions at the MIA Encourage Kids to be Inspired by Science. *Doha News*, October 18. Available from http://dohanews.co/new-exhibitions-at-the-mia-encourage-kids-to-be/ [Accessed 14 October 2014].

Doherty, Regan (2012): First-Cousin Marriages Come Under Scrutiny. *The Independent*, April 8. Available from http://www.independent.co.uk/news/world/middle-east/firstcousin-marriages-come-under-scrutiny-7626995.html [Accessed 15 October 2014].

Forstenlechner, Ingo and Emilie Rutledge (2010): Unemployment in the Gulf: Time to Update the "Social Contract". *Middle East Policy* 17 (2). Pp. 38–51.

Forstenlechner, Ingo *et al.* (2012): Emiratisation: Determining the Factors that Influence the Recruitment Decisions of Employers in the UAE. *The International Journal of Human Resources Management* 23 (2). Pp. 406–421.

Freitag, Ulrike (ed.) (2010): *Saudi-Arabien: Ein Königreich im Wandel?* Ferdinand Schöningh, Paderborn.

Gatti, Roberta *et al.* (2013): Jobs for Shared Prosperity: Time for Action in the Middle East and North Africa. World Bank, Washington (DC). Available from http://documents.worldbank.org/curated/en/2013/04/17659009/jobs-shared-prosperity-time-action-middle-east-north-africa [Accessed 13 October 2014].

Gonzalez, Gabriella C. *et al.* (2008): *Facing Human Capital Challenges of the 21st Century: Education and Labor Market Initiatives in Lebanon, Oman, Qatar, and the United Arab Emirates*. RAND Corporation, Santa Monica (CA).

Haan, Hans Christiaan (1999): The UAE: Assessment of Technology use in some Selected Sectors: Towards Introduction and Explaining Capital and Skill Intensive Technologies. *Specialist Report* No. 6. National Human Resources and Employment Strategy Project, Dubai and Amsterdam.

IMF (International Monetary Fund) (2013): Saudi Arabia. IMF Country Report No. 13/229. Washington (DC). Available from http://www.imf.org/external/pubs/ft/scr/2013/cr13229.pdf [Accessed 13 October 2014].

IPU (Inter-Parliamentary Union) (2014): Proportion of Seats Held by Women in the National Parliaments (%). Available from http://data.worldbank.org/indicator/SG.GEN.PARL.ZS [Accessed 13 October 2014].

ITU (International Telecommunication Union) (2014): ICT Facts and Figures. Geneva. Available from http://www.itu.int/en/ITU-D/Statistics/Documents/facts/ICTFacts Figures2014-e.pdf [Accessed 15 June 2014].

Kingdom of Saudi Arabia, Ministry of Higher Education (2006): Educational System in Saudi Arabia. Saudi Arabian Cultural Mission (SACM). Washington (DC). Available from http://www.sacm.org/publications/58285_edu_complete.pdf [Accessed 14 October 2014].

Martin, Michael O. *et al.* (2012): TIMSS 2011 International Results in Science. TIMSS & PIRLS International Study Center, Lynch School of Education, Boston College, Chestnut Hill (MA).

Ministry of Education, UAE (2010): The Ministry of Education Strategy 2010–2020. Ministry of Education, Abu Dhabi.

Muysken, Joan and Samia Nour (2006): Deficiencies in Education and Poor Prospects for Economic Growth in the Gulf Countries: The Case of the UAE. *Journal of Development Studies* 42 (6). Pp. 957–980.

The National, UAE (2013): Emirati Students Take Tech Quest Opportunities, August 14. Available from http://www.thenational.ae/news/uae-news/technology/emirati-students-take-tech-quest-opportunities [Accessed 15 October 2014].

Niblock, Tim (2007): *The Political Economy of Saudi Arabia.* Routledge, Abingdon (Oxon).

Salem, Ola (2013): UAE Public School Students will not have to Choose Between Arts and Science, FNC hears. *The National*, November 23. Available from http://www.thenational.ae/uae/education/uae-public-school-students-will-not-have-to-choose-between-arts-and-science-fnc-hears [Accessed 15 October 2014].

Scott, Victoria (2014): Sheikha Moza Seeks Scientific Collaboration During Visit to Japan. *Doha News*, April 24. Available from http://dohanews.co/sheikha-moza-promotes-scientific-collaboration-visit-japan/ [Accessed 14 October 2014].

Sennett, Richard (2008): *The Craftsman.* Yale University Press, New Haven (CT).

Swan, Melanie (2012): Hundreds of UAE Students Face College Rejection. *The National*, July 21. Available from http://www.thenational.ae/news/uae-news/education/hundreds-of-uae-students-face-college-rejection [Accessed 15 October 2014].

Tibi, Bassam (2005): *Islam Between Culture and Politics.* Palgrave Macmillan, Houndmills.

UAEU (2014): UAEU Facts & Figures. Available from http://www.uaeu.ac.ae/en/about/facts_and_figures.shtml [Accessed 15 October 2014].

UNDP (2003): *Human Development Report 2003.* Oxford University Press, Oxford and New York.

UNESCO Institute of Statistics (2014a): Ratio of Female to Male Tertiary enrollment (%). Available from http://data.worldbank.org/indicator/SE.ENR.TERT.FM.ZS [Accessed 13 October 2014].

UNESCO Institute of Statistics (2014b): Research and Development Expenditure (% of GDP). Available from http://data.worldbank.org/indicator/GB.XPD.RSDV.GD.ZS [Accessed 15 October].

Walker, Lesley (2014a): Report: Qatari Families Earn Almost Three Times as Much as Expats. *Doha News*, June 18. Available from http://dohanews.co/ministry-stats-show-average-qatari-household-earns-qr72000-monthly/ [Accessed 15 October 2014].

Walker, Lesley (2014b): Qatar University Undergoes Massive Expansion. *Doha News*, May 8. Available from http://dohanews.co/qatar-university-undergoes-massive-expansion/ [Accessed 15 October 2014].

World Bank Statistics (2014): Population, Total. Available from http://data.worldbank.org/indicator/SP.POP.TOTL [Accessed 15 October 2014].

World Economic Forum and European Bank for Reconstruction and Development (ed.) (2013): *Arab World Competitiveness Report*. World Economic Forum, Geneva. Available from http://www3.weforum.org/docs/WEF_AWCR_Report_2013.pdf [Accessed 13 October 2014].

10 Science culture in Brazilian society

Simon Schwartzman

Introduction

In recent decades, Brazil has invested significant amounts of resources and energy into expanding its science, technology and innovation sector. Expenditure on science, technology and innovation reached 1.21 per cent of GDP in 2012, the largest percentage in absolute and relative terms in the Latin American region. This is a comparable figure to 1.74 per cent in Canada or 1.84 per cent in China but remains far below that of Germany, South Korea and Japan, all of which spent 3 per cent or above. Currently, Brazil has about 100,000 researchers and 71,000 students enrolled in 1,600 doctoral programmes, producing 12,000 graduates every year, 45 per cent of them in STEM fields (natural sciences and engineering) (Viotti and Pinho 2010: 98). In 2009, Brazilian authors published 32,100 papers in indexed publications internationally, comprising 54 per cent of total papers from Latin America and 2.7 per cent of those worldwide.[1]

Graduate and research programmes, however, are just part of a much larger and very differentiated higher education sector. Only about 13 per cent of the adult population holds a higher education degree, and this number is not undergoing a very significant increase. The net enrolment rate (percentage of persons ages 18–24 in higher education) is approximately 15 per cent. Brazil does not have undergraduate colleges like the US or UK. All students enter a career programme that can last from four to six years, working for a teaching licence or a bachelor's degree, and some then move up to master's, doctoral or specialization course programmes.

The higher education census of 2012, carried out by the Ministry of Education, identified 7 million first-degree students (including 1.1 million students in distance education courses and 1 million students who graduated in the same year) (INEP 2014). The survey shows that 63 per cent of students are enrolled in the social sciences, humanities and teaching, and 18.7 per cent in engineering, computer sciences and mathematics. Sixty per cent of the students are women, heavily concentrated in education, health and welfare, while men predominate in mathematics, computer sciences and engineering. In postgraduate education, the distribution by field shows a stronger emphasis on the natural sciences, particularly in health.

The impressive developments in graduate education and academic research, however, should be seen in light of the fact that they have occurred mostly

Table 10.1 Enrolment in higher education by gender and field in 2012

Enrolment in higher education by gender and field, 2012

	Total	Percentage	% of women
Education	1,371,600	19.4%	72.5%
Humanities and arts	161,745	2.3%	55.9%
Social sciences, business and law	2,916,189	41.3%	56.6%
Sciences, mathematics, computation	433,836	6.1%	30.9%
Engineering, production and construction	891,712	12.6%	30.3%
Agriculture and veterinarian sciences	165,075	2.3%	44.2%
Health and well-being	961,915	13.6%	76.6%
Services	153,427	2.2%	60.6%
Total	7,058,084	100.0%	60.6%

Source: Adapted from INEP 2012

Table 10.2 Number of postgraduate degrees granted in 2012

	Doctoral	Master's
Agrarian sciences	13.3%	11.7%
Biological sciences	10.2%	7.7%
Health sciences	18.7%	15.6%
Exact sciences and earth sciences	9.7%	8.8%
Humanities	16.5%	17.1%
Applied social sciences	9.2%	13.3%
Engineering	10.9%	11.2%
Linguistics, literature and arts	5.4%	6.8%
Multidisciplinary	6.0%	7.8%
Total	100.0%	100.0%

Source: Adapted from Ministério da Ciência, Tecnologia e Inovação 2014

within academic institutions. Brazil's science and technology field has been largely disconnected from the country's broader social and economic institutions, with weak ties to the productive sector. Thus, most people with doctoral degrees work either in universities (66 per cent) or in public administration (18 per cent), and only 1.6 per cent in industrial or agricultural activities (Galvão, Viotti, and Baessa 2008: table 5). The small number of patents produced in Brazil also provides evidence of this deficient scenario (see Pedrosa and Queiroz 2013).

Public appreciation of science and technology

Brazil does not have a culture that is resistant or opposed to science. Technological gadgets and services are widely used, and access to computers and the Internet is growing rapidly. Public opinion surveys, as well as questionnaires administered to students in different contexts, show that the general population believes in the benefits brought about by science and technology (S&T). At the same time, however, people neither really understand nor participate in the scientific under-pinnings of developments in S&T, and are therefore not concerned about their potentially harmful effects.

Access to technological devices and communications in Brazil occurred simultaneously with the country's rapid transition from a mostly rural to a pre-dominantly urban society. Today, about 85 per cent of the population lives in urban areas, compared with just 50 per cent in the 1950s. Rural settlers were and still are among the poorest in the country, and for many of them, migration to the urban cities meant better access to jobs and services, even if conditions were far from ideal. At the same time, agricultural productivity increased with the growth of large-scale, mechanized agriculture. Up until the year 2000, less than 40 per cent of households had telephones and less than 10 per cent had computers, in part because of the public monopoly on telecommunications. With privatization and the development of new communication technologies, access to cell phones became universal (Figure 10.1), and today, about 50 per cent of households have access to computers and the Internet. In the 1980s, hyperinflation forced the banks to adopt sophisticated technologies to keep bank accounts adjusted for daily currency devaluation, whereas most banking

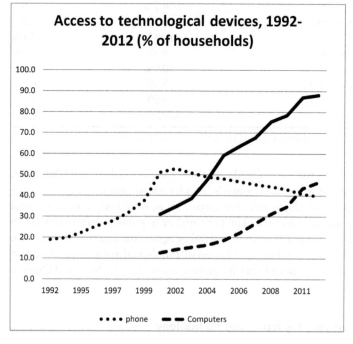

Figure 10.1 Access to technological devices, 1992–2012
Source: Adapted from IETS 2012

transactions are now done through the Internet and automated tellers. Since 2000, voting has been done electronically, and most of the government's tax procedures, including the collection of individual income-tax returns, are also done online.

In 2010, the Brazilian Ministry of Technology conducted a survey on the population's perceptions towards S&T that revealed an interesting paradox (Ministério da Ciência e Tecnologia 2010): most respondents were unaware of any scientific research institution in the country and could not even name a single Brazilian scientist, but, at the same time, 25 per cent of respondents said they were well informed about S&T issues, compared with 11 per cent for Europe as a whole in similar surveys (see Figure 10.2 below).

The survey showed that Brazilians are particularly interested in scientific issues related to the fields of environment, health and medicine and religion, and believe that they are mostly beneficial; the most important benefits are perceived to be in healthcare and better living conditions. When asked for their sources of information on S&T, TV is mentioned as the most frequent source, followed by reading newspapers and talking frequently with friends about S&T issues. The most credible sources of information are medical doctors, journalists and religious priests, and the least credible are politicians. Scientists are mentioned as credible sources by just 5 per cent of respondents.

The reference to religious priests made by some respondents can be linked to the current state of religiosity that prevails in Brazilian society. Brazil is the

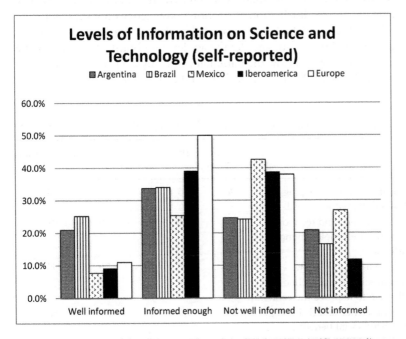

Figure 10.2 Levels of information on science and technology (self-reported)

Source: Adapted from Polino 2012: 83

largest Catholic country in the world, but African religions and practices have also survived among former slaves, and, in the last decades, different branches of evangelical religions have grown very rapidly among the urban poor (barely any other religious traces from the original native population have survived). Although most Roman Catholics are not active churchgoers, the religiosity practised by Evangelists, African cults and Spiritists share a common deep belief in revelation, magic and the presence of the dead among the living, a world of mysteries that many would expect science to eventually confirm, rather than to demystify.

A similar appreciation for science appears in the Brazilian results of the Program for International Student Assessment (PISA) assessment carried out by the Organization of Economic Co-Operation and Development (OECD) in 2006 (OECD 2007). The respondents were 15-year-old students then at the same educational level in each country. The table below presents the main results of appreciation of science by students in a few selected countries. The survey shows that the students most optimistic about the social benefits of science were those from Thailand, China, Tunisia, Brazil and Jordan, while those most pessimistic were from Northern Europe, including Germany and Denmark.

Science proficiency

In contrast to their high appreciation for science, Brazilian students actually had much less scientific knowledge than their counterparts in other countries. The graph below shows the distribution of scientific proficiency on a six-point scale developed by OECD, in which zero means below the minimum expected, while five means outstanding performance for the age level. In Brazil, 28 per cent of the 15-year-old students were below the minimum, and only 0.5 per cent were at the top, far worse than the OECD average, but also below Chile.

Table 10.3 Percentage of students agreeing or strongly agreeing with the following statements

	China (Taipei)	Brazil	OECD average	Germany	Denmark
Science is important for helping us to understand the natural world.	96	96	93	91	94
Advances in science and technology usually improve people's living conditions.	98	94	92	89	91
Science is valuable to society.	96	93	87	76	93
Advances in science and technology usually help to improve the economy.	94	77	80	73	73
Advances in science and technology usually bring social benefits.	93	84	75	67	56

Source: Adapted from OECD 2007: 129, figure 3.2

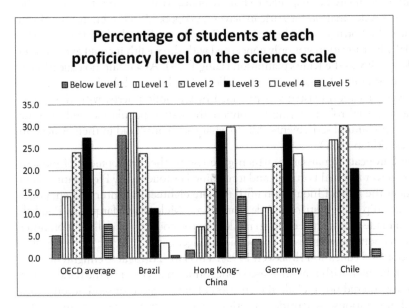

Figure 10.3 Percentage of students at each proficiency level on the science scale
Source: Adapted from OECD 2007: 49, figure 2.11a

The low achievement in science by Brazilian students is consistent with their low achievements in the PISA assessments of language and mathematics and also with the National Assessment of Educational Achievement ('Prova Brasil') on language and mathematics carried out by the Brazilian Ministry of Education every two years. According to the Brazilian data, only 11 per cent of students at the end of secondary education and only 5.8 per cent of those in public schools achieve the minimum proficiency in mathematics expected for their level (Todos Pela Educação 2012). This situation is made worse by the fact that at the age of 15, when all young people should be in their first year of secondary school, 47 per cent are still held in primary school, and 8 per cent have already left school. One year later, at age 16, retention in primary school is still at 27 per cent, and the percentage of dropouts rises to 14 per cent. Despite compulsory education, only 60 per cent of the Brazilian population ever finishes their secondary education.[2]

Historical roots – the King's plantation

The limitations of Brazilian education are rooted in the country's colonial past and the low priority given to education issues by Brazilian elites until only recently. Throughout its time of colonization by the Portuguese in 1500 to independence in the early nineteenth century, Brazil was a source of wealth for the colonizers, based on forced labour used to extract gold and produce sugar and other agricultural products for the external market. Most of the native population was either decimated or expelled to remote areas, while the country became the world's main destination for African slaves. As opposed to the English in North America, the Portuguese seldom came to Brazil to settle with their families. The colonial administration was only concerned with the wealth it could extract from its colony—it was the King's plantation (Lang 1979). As a result, no educational, scientific or cultural institutions were allowed to be established in the colony. Whatever education existed was provided by Catholic priests, with the Jesuits playing a special role in trying to convert the native population and organize them in agricultural settlements akin to what the Spanish did in their American colonies (Alden 1992).

The European Renaissance, which gave rise to the development of modern science, never reached Portugal, and it remained untouched by Protestant reform and under the grips of Inquisition until the late eighteenth century. Then, under the leadership of Sebastião José de Carvalho e Melo, the Marquis of Pombal, Portugal made a concerted effort to modernize the country, modelling it on other European countries with respect to public management, economic efficiency, secularization and education (Maxwell 1995). This late 'Portuguese enlightenment,' however, brought with it an increased concentration of power in the hands of the monarchy and did not include the creation of autonomous or semi-autonomous learned institutions—scientific societies, modern universities—or spaces for individual entrepreneurship associated with the development of modern capitalism elsewhere in Europe (Ben-David 1965).

In 1808, the Portuguese Court moved to Brazil fleeing the Napoleonic Wars and established a few education and research institutions, which were retained and expanded following independence in 1822. These included, for example, a military and engineering school in Rio de Janeiro, a medical school in Bahia and a mineral collection in Rio de Janeiro, which later became a national museum. Throughout the nineteenth century, Brazil was an independent monarchy ruled by a branch of the Portuguese Royal Family, with an economy based on slave labour working on the traditional sugar plantations and, later, in coffee production. Brazil's second emperor, Pedro II, who ruled from 1840 to 1889, was very interested in science and even became a member of the French Academy of Sciences (Schwarcz 1998). During his tenure, a few new research institutions and institutions of education were established, many of them overseen by French leaders, including an astronomic observatory and a mining school modelled on the French École de Mines (Carvalho 1978). Nevertheless, little or nothing was done to build up a public education system, and most of the population—slaves and former slaves, children born from the miscegenation of Brazilian Indians, Portuguese immigrants and slaves—remained illiterate, living in the countryside or in the outskirts of the emerging urban centres along the coast.

Things began to change in 1850, however, when the British succeeded in putting an end to the slave trade and the slave-based economy started to collapse. Slavery was officially abolished in 1888, and in 1889 a military coup turned Brazil into a republic. From the late nineteenth to the early twentieth centuries, Brazil became a significant destination for immigrants from Italy, Germany and other European countries, as well as from Japan, who came mostly as indentured labourers to work on the coffee plantations. The immigrants—about 4 million between 1884 and 1933—brought with them their cultural and religious institutions, including schools for the children. In the early twentieth century, the state of São Paulo, the hub of coffee production and the richest in the country, began creating public schools, as well as several professional and research institutions in engineering, medicine, agriculture and biology, some of them under the leadership of foreign immigrants. Tropical diseases plagued the country's main ports, and a tropical research institute was created in Rio de Janeiro in 1900 to deal with the problem, inspired by France's Pasteur Institute.

The 'Brazilian Enlightenment'

To some extent, the end of slavery and the monarchy can be viewed as the period of intellectual and cultural enlightenment in Brazil. The new generation of people educated in engineering and medicals schools, in Europe in some cases, searched for their place in society. They tended to stress the value and importance of specialized knowledge as an alternative to the more established ways of thinking based on religious and legal traditions (Schwartzman 1991a). Literature and knowledge of French positivism, as proposed by Auguste Comte, became mandatory for these new intellectuals. Positivist doctrine provided the engineers with the reassurance that they had the right and competence to rule society, which would be better and more civilized under their command. They campaigned against the monarchy, in favour of universal education and better salaries for the working class; they opposed the church and all forms of corporatist organizations (universities, with their pretences of self-regulation, were perceived as one of them), and, above all, organized themselves in secret societies and conspired for power. They were so successful that their motto, 'Order and Progress,' is still enshrined in the Brazilian flag (Nachman 1977). In order to modernize the country, they created a new planned city, Belo Horizonte, the forerunner of Brasilia, and led a sweeping urban reform of Rio de Janeiro, opening large avenues and destroying most of the old Portuguese-style city (Underwood 1991).

The notion that society should be ruled by enlightened despots was pursued by the Getúlio Vargas authoritarian regime, which had been in power in Brazil from 1930 to 1945 (Dulles 1967). Autocracy returned again in full force when the military regained power in 1964 and placed the country under the doctrine of national security. On the other side of the ideological divide were the Marxists, who also shared a fascination for rational planning, and important scientists educated in the 1930s and 1940s, inspired by the examples of Jean Frédéric Joliot-Curie in France and John D. Bernal in England, joined the Communist party.

Medical doctors too would not be left behind. They argued that Brazilian society should be cured of its ailments, which included not only the tropical diseases that plagued the population, but also 'racial degeneration' that many of them believed arose from racial miscegenation. At the turn of the century, Nina Rodrigues from the Bahia School of Medicine worked with biological theories that looked for links between physical traits and criminal behaviour. This research led directly to questions about the racial composition of the Brazilian population and the alleged problems people assumed to have derived from racial miscegenation. Character traits such as laziness, lust or lack of discipline were no longer explained by old environmental factors, but instead attributed to the new, biological and presumably more scientific theories. This diagnosis for the underpinnings of the Brazilians' troubles had to be followed by treatment and as such, eugenics became an important issue in Brazilian medical circles (Stepan 1991). In 1929 the first Brazilian Congress of Eugenics was held in Rio de Janeiro with participants from several Latin American countries. It was followed by the establishment of a Brazilian Commission of Eugenics in 1931. Interventions were called for in many areas, from prenuptial examinations for the control of vene-real diseases to the sterilization of alcoholics, syphilitics and those suffering from schizophrenia. Using the assumed superiority of the white race as their basis, some individuals within the field of eugenics worked on the expectation that there would be 'improvement' and 'correction' of the Brazilian population in the long term (Viana 1982). Others, less 'optimistic,' called for strict limitations on racial intermarriage. After World War II, all these theories and proposals became, of course, unacceptable, but the issues of sanitation, preventive medicine and universal healthcare, supported since 1915 by the Rockefeller Foundation, have remained strong among significant sectors of the medical profession up until today (Cueto 1994; Lima 2007).

The enlightenment also reached the field of arts, literature and education. In 1922, a famous 'week of modern art' took place in São Paulo, bringing together painters inspired by the European avant-garde and authors writing literature and poetry in language free of the strict academicism that had dominated Brazilian literary circles until that point (Resende 2000).

Public education also figured into the enlightenment agenda. In the 1920s, a series of national education conferences brought together intellectuals, reli-gious leaders and businessmen to discuss the establishment of a public education system that could at long last raise the population out of illiteracy. In 1932, a 'Manifesto of the Pioneers of the New School' was published, inspired by the ideas of John Dewey, proposing for the first time the creation of a national public education system. It would be a long time, however, before its actual imple-mentation (Azevedo 1932; Borges 1994). In 1931, the national government established the Ministry of Education, Culture and Health and approved a bill that regulated the creation of the first universities. The new ministry's energy was invested, for the most part, into the establishment of a national univer-sity and the regulation of secondary education in all its details (Schwartzman, Bomeny and Costa 2000). Local governments were supposed to build up and improve primary education, but did little. By 1950, 50 per cent of the Brazilian population over 15 was still illiterate.

Although most of the Brazilian economy remained based on agricultural prod-ucts and mining, starting in the 1930s, the national government and intellectuals became convinced that the country could only develop through industrialization and import substitution, to be fostered by public investments and central economic planning. This view gained new momentum in the 1950s under the influence of the economists of the United Nations Commission for Latin America (ECLAC) (Hirschman 1968). It is remarkable that, in reading through the economics literature of this period, there is no mention of education-related issues, in spite of the growing importance of the international economics literature on human capital (Becker 1964; Schultz 1960).

The roots of contemporary science

The first Brazilian university, the University of São Paulo, was inaugurated in 1934. It brought together pre-existing professional schools in engineering, medicine and agriculture, among others, and imported a small group of researchers from Germany, France and Italy to staff its new 'Faculty of Philosophy, Sciences and Letters.' Within this faculty, several of the most significant research traditions in the country in physics, chemistry, biology, mathematics and the social sciences were inaugurated. Other research lineages developed along older institutions such as the Oswaldo Cruz Institute for Tropical Diseases in Rio de Janeiro, the Butantã Snake Venom and the Biological Research institutes in São Paulo (Schwartzman 1991b). At each of these places, it was possible to identify a leader born or educated in Europe, and they all had to struggle to keep autonomous research alive in the face of limited resources, demands for short-term applied work and bureaucratic encroachment from government authorities and politicians.

It was not until 1949 that S&T gained the attention of the national government, through the creation of the National Council of Scientific Research and a National Centre for Physics Research. The expectation was that Brazil could rapidly acquire nuclear capabilities for energy and national defence, a project that did not prosper due to both international constraints on the transfer of nuclear technologies and the lack of technical ability in the country (Adler 1987). These aspirations subsequently lost relevance and visibility, but corresponding institutions continued to function with reduced budgets.

In 1964 a military coup ousted the Brazilian civilian government and many leading scientists who had been politically active, mostly from the left, demanding a stronger role for S&T in public policy, lost their jobs and were forced into exile. Then, gradually, several policies were implemented to improve the quality of the country's universities and to give more priority to scientific and technological research. In 1968, a new law was introduced that initiated the rearrangement of Brazil's public universities following the US model, with academic departments and graduate programmes, replacing the old 1931 university legislation. The Brazilian Corporation of Agricultural Research (EMBRAPA) was established in 1972 under the Ministry of Agriculture, and was instrumental in increasing the productivity of Brazil's crops. In 1973 the government enacted the first National Plan for Scientific and Technological Development, succeeded by a second plan in 1976.

Under the presidency of General Ernesto Geisel, Brazil undertook a very ambitious project for economic, technological and political self-reliance that was made possible through rapid economic growth in the 1970s, but would soon be thwarted by the changing international economic environment of the late 1970s and early 1980s. The project relied on the strengthening of public-owned companies in the fields of oil, energy, electricity and communications and on heavy investment in capital goods, infrastructure and also in the field of S&T (Castro and Souza 1985). An incomplete list of initiatives from those years in science and technology includes (see also Schwartzman 1994):

- The placement of S&T under the responsibility of the economic policy authorities, which allowed for a much higher influx of resources to S&T than ever before;
- The creation of a new federal agency for S&T under the Planning Secretariat, the Financing Agency for Studies and Projects (FINEP), which was unencumbered by civil service routines and restrictions and responsible for the administration of several hundred million dollars a year for S&T support;
- The establishment of a few large-scale centres for R&D, such as the Coordination for Graduate Programs in Engineering of the Federal University in Rio de Janeiro (COPPE) and the University of Campinas. These centres were geared towards technological research and graduate education in engineering and sciences;
- The beginning of several programmes of military research, such as the space programme and the 'parallel' nuclear programme, as well as the establishment of a weapons industry;
- The agreement with Germany for cooperation in nuclear energy, which was meant to create an autonomous capability in the construction of nuclear reactors based on locally reprocessed fuel;
- The establishment of a policy of market protection for the computer industry, telecommunications and microelectronics, linked to an emerging national private sector.

In 1984, during a period of economic stagnation, rising inflation and disorganization of the public sector, the military returned power to the civilians. By then, however, the institutional framework created by the military government had already been installed or was on its way, including the creation of a ministry of science and technology by the new civilian government, heralded by most of the scientific community as fulfilling their dream of placing S&T at the core of Brazil's national public policy. The new S&T bureaucracy associated with the scientists and researchers working in different institutions and organized in scientific and professional associations became a significant interest group; but although powerful enough to assure the maintenance and gradual increase of public resources allocated to them, it was not strong enough to actually place science, technology and innovation at the core of the country's education and public policies.

Education, science, technology and innovation in contemporary Brazil

The civilian governments that succeeded the military regimes after 1985 did not question or attempt to change the broad framework for S&T established by the Geisel regime of the 1970s, despite recommendations by an advisory commission that stressed the importance of adjusting the system to the more flexible and market-oriented features of more advanced economies (Schwartzman *et al.* 1995). The university model defined by the 1968 legislation created a small number of expensive public institutions, not all of them of good quality, which were unable to absorb the growing demand for higher education. This situation opened up the space for private institutions, providing mostly cheap undergraduate degrees by way of evening courses.

Today, more than 70 per cent of the students in higher education are enrolled in private institutions, while graduate education and research is concentrated in a few public universities such as the state universities of São Paulo and Campinas and the Federal Universities of Rio de Janeiro, Minas Gerais, Rio Grande do Sul and Pernambuco. CAPES, an agency within the Ministry of Education, regulates the country's graduate programmes through peer review committees and provides fellowships to graduate students. Support for scientific research is provided mostly by the National Council for Scientific and Technological Research (CNPq) and state science-supporting agencies.

The higher education legislation required that university professors have doctoral degrees, which the country did not produce, and this led to a rapid expansion of graduate programmes, and also to some efforts to send students abroad for graduate education. To control the quality of graduate education and research, the Ministry of Education implemented a strict assessment system based on publication, graduate education statistics and peer review. This assessment has been used to close down graduate programmes that are considered unacceptable, leaving very few programmes ranked at the top level required to keep up with international standards. Most of the doctors who graduate from Brazilian universities end up working in universities or are already working there when they get their degrees. The assumption is that the presence of professors with doctoral degrees who do research enhances the quality of undergraduate and professional careers, but, since research is concentrated in a few public universities and hardly exists in private institutions, most students do not benefit from it (Schwartzman and Balbachevsky 2014).

Brazil has some interesting examples of research institutions creating partnerships and doing work relevant for the economy and society (Schwartzman *et al.* 2008). The traditional Instituto Oswaldo Cruz in Rio de Janeiro, which is partnered with the Ministry of Health, produces vaccines used in public health programmes, and maintains several research programmes in the areas of pharmacology, tropical diseases and public health. Petrobrás, Brazil's national oil corporation, maintains large research programmes in partnership with universities, including the Faculty of Engineering of the University of Rio de Janeiro, for the development of deep-sea drilling technologies. The Catholic University in Rio de Janeiro also has a longstanding partnership with Petrobrás and other firms for the development of computer software and systems, and the Luiz de Queiróz School of Agriculture of the University of São Paulo works closely with EMBRAPA in agricultural research. The University of Campinas also has different research programmes associated with the private sector, and has generated a technological hub on its grounds; the Aeronautics Technological Institute (ITA), run by the Air Force, is at the heart of Embraer, a successful private producer of mid-range airplanes for the international market. However, most higher education institutions and research programmes tend to be isolated and inward looking, in part because they do not depend on external contracts to maintain themselves, but also because as part of the civil service, they have little flexibility to engage with external clients. In 2004 the Brazilian Congress approved an 'innovation law' to foster stronger links between universities and the productive sector (Matias-Pereira and Kruglianskas 2005), but this legislation does not seem to have changed the picture very significantly.

Higher education as a whole has been expanding in recent years, but the number of people with higher education degrees is still only around 13 per cent of young adults between 25 and 35 years, and much less for the older generation. Figure 10.4 shows the distribution of the population with higher education by age group, which gives a perspective on evolution. Forty-five per cent get their

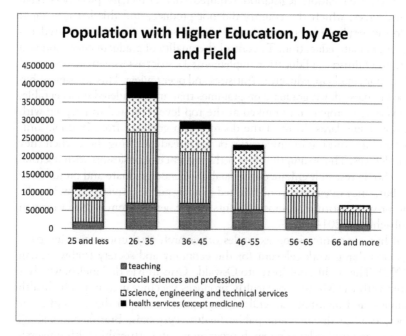

Figure 10.4 Population with higher education, by age and field

Source: Adapted from Instituto Brasileiro de Geografia e Estatística 2010

degrees in the social sciences and social professions (particularly management and law) and 22 per cent in fields requiring scientific and technical competence, including the traditional professions of medicine and engineering. The third largest group is that of schoolteachers. Until the 1990s, teacher education was done at normal schools and on secondary level, but in 1996, legislation was established that they should all get higher education degrees, in addition to their previous education, within the next 10 years, and that all new teachers should have a university degree. This target was not fully met, but led to the proliferation of evening and distance education courses in education and pedagogy that offered the teachers their required degrees (secondary school teachers need to have a higher education degree in their fields of specialization). The only sector that has been growing in relative size is that of healthcare services, with 7 per cent of the younger graduates.

Brazil did not develop vocational education as an alternative to the conventional secondary school courses, and also lacks a significant sector of post secondary, short-term courses. Officially, all higher education graduates, irrespective of the institution where they studied, have a four-year degree ('bacharelado' or a teaching license), which takes longer for careers such as medicine and engineering. Revenues associated with university degrees vary hugely between different careers, with the highest incomes going to the traditional professions— medicine, engineering and law—and the lowest for administration, health services and teaching, which are the largest (Figure 5) (Instituto Brasileiro de Geografia e Estatística 2010). The reasons so many people go into these careers is that, because of the inferior quality of their early education, they do not pass entrance examinations for the most prestigious fields and universities. Instead,

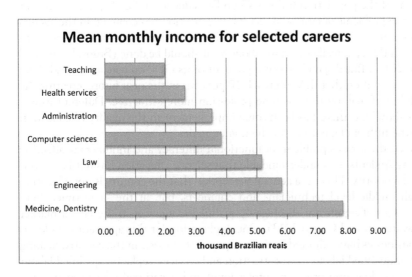

Figure 10.5 Mean monthly income for selected careers

Source: Adapted from Instituto Brasileiro de Geografia e Estatística 2010 (1 Brazilian real about 0.5 US$)

they often need to work, can only study in the evening and cannot pay to attend the best private institutions.

General education and STEM

The low status of the teaching profession is not the only reason students often do not excel, but it goes a long way towards explaining the low results obtained by Brazilian students in the national and international assessments mentioned earlier. In the past, primary school teachers were drawn from the middle classes, and studied in select public normal schools that may not have taught them much in terms of pedagogy and child development, but took care of their proficiency in language, mathematics and introductory sciences. Today, most teachers come from poor families and poor-quality public schools, and the programmes of teacher education emphasize broad sociological and teaching theory rather than the best teaching practices or the actual topics they are supposed to teach. Up to the fifth grade, there is one teacher per class, who is supposed to deliver all topics and classes to his or her students, including language, mathematics, science and the humanities. After the fifth grade, there is one teacher per subject based on the assumption that he or she is certified to teach their subject matter. In 2007 the Brazilian National Council of Education, a government body, estimated that the country had a deficit of about 250,000 specialized teachers. The deficit was particularly acute in the STEM subjects.

Only in the 1990s did Brazil reach the point where most children are in school, but many drop out before completing mandatory education: currently, only 60 per cent of the population finishes secondary education. Finally, in more recent years, the problems of basic and secondary education has come up in the agenda of national and state governments, and there is a flurry of initiatives trying to deal with these, as well as debates about what should be done (Bruns, Evans, and Luque 2012). Brazil spends about 6 per cent of its GDP on education, and there is the expectation that this will reach 10 per cent in the near future, creating the possibility of making the teaching profession more attractive. Different assessments show that there has been some improvement in the quality of education up to the fifth grade, but not for the higher grades.

Given the serious problems of functional illiteracy and innumeracy affecting so many students, it is understandable that science education has not been considered a priority. There is a general perception that the country is not educating enough middle-level technicians and engineers, but, at the same time, there are no signs of significant shortage of qualified manpower in the labour market (Schwartzman and Castro 2013). One explanation for this apparent paradox is that businesses have adjusted to the manpower that exists in the country, making use of unqualified labour for construction and services, replacing qualified labour with technology and providing professional and vocational education through the national system of industrial apprenticeship (SENAI) and similar institutions managed directly by the business sector.

There have also been several initiatives to introduce inquiry-based education in the earliest school years, including a project run by the Brazilian Academy of Science to apply the methodologies used by the La main à la pâte science education programme in France (Charpak, Léna, and Quéré 2005). A review carried out at the request of the Brazilian Academy of Sciences in 2009 found that, although many of these initiatives show promising results, they seldom go beyond the pilot stage, and are subject to vagaries associated with changes of education authorities and competing education programmes (Schwartzman and Christophe 2009).

Another significant initiative is the National Scientific Olympic competitions in different areas including biology, computer science, physics or geography, done with the participation of scientific societies in each of the fields. Of these, the most consolidated is the National Olympics of Mathematics, which has also been the subject of assessments on its impact. In these competitions, the schools are encouraged to participate by registering their students, who go through a series of tests from local to national and international competitions. One function of these competitions is to find and encourage talents that can then be supported to continue their education at high levels of excellence. The other function is to get the schools active concerning the issues of science knowledge and competence, which could have a positive effect on students' performance as a whole.

In 2009, 43,864 public schools, with 19 million students (about 37 per cent of the student population), enrolled in the competition and 33,000 received prizes. An analysis of the impact of this participation in Brazil's national assessment of education showed it increased the students' performance by 1.9 points on the 500-point scale of the national assessment (Biondi, Vasconcellos, and Menezes-Filho 2012). Another study showed that full participation led to an increase of 4.1 points on this scale (Soares and Candian 2011). These effects, while statistically significant, are very modest, and do not change the broader picture of the low quality of Brazilian public education in general, and in mathematics and sciences in particular.

In 2011 the Brazilian government launched an ambitious programme called 'Sciences Without Borders,' to provide fellowships to 100,000 Brazilian students in four years to study abroad in STEM fields and to attract foreign researchers to come to Brazil. Most of the fellowships were for undergraduate students to go abroad for a year or so. This signified a radical departure from the established practice of Brazilian S&T agencies only providing support for graduate education in selected institutions abroad. Twenty-five thousand of these fellowships were to be provided by the private sector. From the beginning, the programme was recognized as an important effort to break the prevailing insularity of Brazilian S&T, but was received with scepticism because of the emphasis on undergraduate fellowships and the improvised way in which it was implemented, without the participation of the country's education, scientific and technological institutions, and without a clear notion of what these students could accomplish during these brief spells abroad (Castro *et al.* 2012). In January 2014, the programme's website stated that 45,000 fellowships had been granted, 36,000 of those for undergraduate students, mostly to the US, UK and France (Ciência sem Fronteiras 2014).

For 2014, the estimated costs of the programme were about 1 billion Brazilian reais (US$400 million), and the Brazilian Association for the Advancement of Science (SBPC) expressed concern that this could lead to a reduction in the resources to support the National Research Council and regular scientific and technological research activities in Brazilian institutions (Escobar 2013).

Conclusion

We can summarize this overview by saying that the Brazilian population, and the Brazilian culture, is neither opposed nor resistant to the advancements of S&T, but scientific and technological culture has remained restricted to a small segment of its population and has not really penetrated the education system, in spite of the growth in student enrolments and the existing requirements of scientific education in school programmes. The problem is not related specifically to STEM but to the quality of public education as a whole. The root of this situation is the history of slavery, which left the country with very high levels of social inequality, and a disregard for education that dates back to centuries of Portuguese colonization and extends to well into the twentieth century. The assessments of education quality, which started in the 1990s, showed some modest improvements in some states for fifth graders, but practically no improvement for ninth graders and students completing secondary education.

At the other extreme, there is a significant scientific and technological establishment, with many scientists getting involved in issues of general education; there is more data and research on education; public expenditures in education are increasing; and there is a growing national awareness that general education should improve. It certainly will, but it will take some time.

Notes

1 Data on expenditures and publications comes from the Brazilian Ministry of Science, Technology and Innovation, available from http://www.mct.gov.br [Accessed 20 October 2014]. Publication figures are from the Thompson/ISI database.
2 Data from the Brazilian National Household Survey of 2011.

Bibliography

Adler, Emanuel (1987): *The Power of Ideology: The Quest for Technological Autonomy in Argentina and Brazil.* University of California Press, Berkeley.
Alden, Dauril (1992): *The Making of an Elite Enterprise: The Jesuits in the Portuguese Assistancy, 16th to 18th Centuries.* Associates of the James Ford Bell Library, University of Minnesota, Minneapolis.
Azevedo, Fernando (1932): *A reconstrução educacional no Brasil, ao povo e ao governo. Manifesto dos Pioneiros da Educação Nova.* Companhia Editora Nacional, Rio de Janeiro.
Becker, Gary Stanley (1964): *Human Capital.* Columbia University Press for the National Bureau of Economic Research, New York.

Ben-David, Joseph (1965): The Scientific Role: the Conditions of its Establishment in Europe, *Minerva* 4 (1). Pp. 15–54.

Biondi, Roberta Loboda, Lígia Vasconcellos and Naercio Menezes-Filho (2012): Evaluating the Impact of the Brazilian Public School Math Olympics on the Quality of Education, *Economia (LACEA)* 12 (2). Pp. 143–170.

Borges, Dain (1994): Review Essay: Brazilian Social Thought of the 1930s, *Luso-Brazilian Review* 31 (2). Pp. 137–150.

Bruns, Barbara, David Evans and Javier Luque (2012): Achieving World-Class Education in Brazil. The Next Agenda. The International Bank for Reconstruction and Development, The World Bank, Washington (DC). Available from https://open-knowledge.worldbank.org/bitstream/handle/10986/2383/656590REPLACEM0hieving 0World0Class0.pdf?sequence=1 [Accessed 20 October 2014].

Carvalho, José Murilo de (1978): *A Escola de Minas de Ouro Preto: O peso da glória.* Financiadora de Estudos e Projetos, Rio de Janeiro and Companhia Editora Nacional, São Paulo.

Castro, Antônio Barros de and Francisco Eduardo Pires de Souza (1985): *A economia brasileira em marcha forçada.* Paz e Terra, Rio de Janeiro.

Castro, Claudio De Moura *et al.* (2012): Cem Mil Bolsistas no Exterior, *Interesse Nacional* 5 (17). Pp. 25–36.

Charpak, Georges, Pierre Léna and Yves Quéré (2005): *L'enfant et la science: l'aventure de la main à la pâte.* Odile Jacob, Paris.

Ciência sem Fronteiras (2014): País de Destino do Bolsista. Available from http://www.cienciasemfronteiras.gov.br/web/csf/painel-de-controle [Accessed 24 October 2014].

Cueto, Marcos (1994): *Missionaries of Science: The Rockefeller Foundation and Latin America.* Indiana University Press, Bloomington.

Dulles, John W.F. (1967): *Vargas of Brazil: A Political Biography.* University of Texas Press, Austin.

Escobar, Herton (2013): Ciência sem Fronteiras ameaça 'canibalizar' investimentos em pesquisa científica. Blogs Herton Escobar, November 27. Available from http://blogs.estadao.com.br/herton-escobar/cnpq-x-csf/ [Accessed 24 October 2014].

Galvão, Antonio Carlos Filgueira, Eduardo B. Viotti and Adriano R. Baessa (2008): Características do Emprego dos Doutores Brasileiros: Características do emprego formal no ano de 2004 das pessoas que obtiveram título de doutorado no Brasil no período 1996–2003. CGEE, Brasília. Available from http://www.inova.unicamp.br/inovacao/report/inte_relatorio-doutores080825.pdf [Accessed 20 October 2014].

Hirschman, Albert O. (1968): The Political Economy of Import-Substituting Industrialization in Latin America, *The Quarterly Journal of Economics* 82 (1). Pp. 1–32.

IETS (Instituto de Estudos do Trabalho e Sociedade) (2012): Tabulações da PNAD elaboradas pelo IETS (1992–2012). Instituto de Estudos do Trabalho e Sociedade, Rio de Janeiro. Available from http://www.iets.org.br/dado/tabulacoes-da-pnad-elabora-das-pelo-iets-1992-2012 [Acessed on October 29 2014].

INEP (Instituto Nacional de Estudos e Pesquisas Educacionais Anísio Teixeira) (2012): Microdados para download. Available from http://portal.inep.gov.br/basica-levantamentos-acessar [Accessed 20 October 2014].

INEP (Instituto Nacional de Estudos e Pesquisas Educacionais Anísio Teixeira) (2014): Sinopses Estatísticas da Educação Superior – Graduação. Available from http://portal.inep.gov.br/basica-levantamentos-acessar [Accessed 20 October 2014].

Instituto Brasileiro de Geografia e Estatística 2010: Brazil National Population Census, 2010. Available from http://censo2010.ibge.gov.br/en/ [Accessed 29 October 2014].

Lang, James (1979): *Portuguese Brazil: The King's Plantation.* Academic Press, New York and London.

Lima, Nísia Trindade (2007): Public Health and Social Ideas in Modern Brazil, *American Journal of Public Health* 97 (7). Pp. 1168–1177.

Matias-Pereira, José and Isak Kruglianskas (2005): Gestão de inovação: a lei de inovação tecnológica como ferramenta de apoio às políticas industrial e tecnológica do Brasil, *RAE-eletrônica* 4 (2).

Maxwell, Kenneth (1995): *Pombal, Paradox of the Enlightenment.* Cambridge University Press, Cambridge (UK) and New York.

Ministério da Ciência e Tecnologia (2010): Percepção Pública da Ciência e Tecnologia no Brasil Resultados da enquete de 2010. Brasília. Available from http://www.mct.gov. br/upd_blob/0214/214770.pdf [Accessed 20 October 2014].

Ministério da Ciência, Tecnologia e Inovação (2014): 3.5.2. Brasil: Alunos matriculados e titulados nos cursos de mestrado e doutorado, ao final do ano, por grande área, 1998–2012. Available from http://www.mct.gov.br/index.php/content/view/7755/ Brasil_Alunos_matriculados_e_titulados_nos_cursos_de_mestrado_e_doutorado_ao_ final_do_ano_por_grande_area.html [Accessed 20 October 2014].

Nachman, Robert G. (1977): Positivism, Modernization, and the Middle Class in Brazil, *The Hispanic American Historical Review* 57 (1). Pp. 1–23.

OECD (2007): PISA 2006 Science Competencies for Tomorrow's World, Volume 1 Analysis. Paris. Available from http://www.nbbmuseum.be/doc/seminar2010/nl/ bibliografie/opleiding/analysis.pdf [Accessed 20 October 2014].

Pedrosa, Renato Hyuda de Luna and Sérgio Robles Reis de Queiroz (2013): Brazil: Democracy and the 'Innovation Dividend'. Available from https://archive.org/details/ BrazilDemocracyAndTheinnovationDividend [Accessed 20 October 2014].

Polino, Carmelo (2012): Información y actitudes hacia la ciencia y tecnología en Argentina y Brasil: Indicadores Seleccionados y comparación con Iberoamérica y Europa. In: *El Estado de la Ciencia 2012: Principales Indicadores de Ciencia y Tecnología Iberoamericanos*, edited by Mario Albornoz. REDES: Centro de Estudios sobre Ciencia, Desarrollo y Educación Superior, Buenos Aires. Pp. 81–92.

Resende, Beatriz (2000): Brazilian Modernism: The Canonised Revolution. In: *Through the Kaleidoscope: The Experience of Modernity in Latin America*, edited by Vivian Shelling. Verso, London. Pp. 199–216.

Ruiz, Antonio Ibañez, Mozart Neves Ramos and Murílio Hingel (2007): Escassez de professores no Ensino Médio: Propostas estruturais e emergenciais. Relatório produzido pela Comissão Especial instituída para estudar medidas que visem a superar o déficit docente no Ensino Médio (CNE/CEB). Conselho Nacional de Educação, Brasília.

Schultz, Theodore W. (1960): Capital Formation by Education, *Journal of Political Economy* 68 (6). Pp. 571–583.

Schwarcz, Lilia Moritz (1998): *As barbas do imperador: D. Pedro II, um monarca nos trópicos.* Companhia das Letras, São Paulo.

Schwartzman, Simon (1991a): Changing Roles of New Knowledge: Research Institutions and Societal Transformations in Brazil. In: *Social Sciences and Modern States: National Experiences and Theoretical Crossroads*, edited by Peter Wagner. Cambridge (UK) and New York. Pp. 230–260.

Schwartzman, Simon (1991b): *A Space for Science: the Development of the Scientific Community in Brazil.* University Park, Pennsylvania.

Schwartzman, Simon (1994): Catching Up in Science and Technology: Self-Reliance or Internationalization? International Sociological Association (ISA) World Congress;

Bielefeld (Germany). Available from http://www.schwartzman.org.br/simon/aant.htm [Accessed 24 October 2014].

Schwartzman, Simon and Micheline Christophe (2009): A educação em ciências no Brasil. Academia Brasileira de Ciências and IETS, Rio de Janeiro. Available from http://www.abc.org.br/IMG/pdf/doc-210.pdf [Accessed 20 October 2014].

Schwartzman, Simon and Cláudio de Moura Castro (2013): Ensino, Formação Profissional e a Questão da Mão de Obra Ensaio, *Ensaio: Avaliação e Políticas Públicas em Educação* 21 (80). Pp. 563–624.

Schwartzman, Simon and Elizabeth Balbachevsky (2014): Research and Teaching in a Diverse Institutional Environment: Converging Values and Diverging Practices in Brazil. In: *Teaching and Research in Contemporary Higher Education: Systems, Activities and Rewards*, edited by Jung Cheol Shin *et al*. Springer, Dordrecht. Pp. 221–235.

Schwartzman, Simon *et al.* (1995): *Science and Technology in Brazil (volume 1): A New Policy for a Global World*. Fundação Getúlio Vargas, Rio de Janeiro.

Schwartzman, Simon, Helena Maria Bousquet Bomeny and Vanda Maria Ribeiro Costa (2000): *Tempos de Capanema*. Paz e Terra, Sao Paolo and Fundação Getúlio Vargas, Rio de Janeiro.

Schwartzman, Simon *et al.* (2008): Brazil. In: *University and Development in Latin America: Successful Experiences of Research Centers*, edited by Simon Schwartzman. Sense Publishers, Rotterdam.

Soares, José Francisco and Julina Fizzoni Candian (2011): O impacto da OBMEP no desempenho dos alunos da Prova Brasil: Explicitação de condições de sucesso em escolas bem sucedidas. In: *Avaliação do impacto da Olimpíada Brasileira de Matemática nas Escolas Públicas* (OBMEP), edited by CGEE. Brasília. Pp. 73–94.

Stepan, Nancy (1991): *The Hour of Eugenics: Race, Gender, and Nation in Latin America*. Cornell University Press, Ithaca (NY).

Todos Pela Educação (2012): De Olho nas Metas 2011: Qiuarto Relatório de Monitoramento das 5 metas do Todos Pela Educação. Rio de Janeiro.

Underwood, David K. (1991): Alfred Agache, French Sociology, and Modern Urbanism in France and Brazil, *Journal of the Society of Architectural Historians* 50 (2). Pp. 130–166.

Viana, Oliveira (1982): Populações meridionais do Brasil e Instituições políticas brasileiras. Câmara dos Deputados, Brasília.

Viotti, Renato Baumgratz and Roberto Dantas de Pinho (2010): Doutores 2010: estudos da demografia da base técnico-científica brasileira. CGEE, Brasília.

11 Policy controversies in science education in Brazil

A brief overview

Elizabeth Balbachevsky and Edilene Cruz[1]

Curricula content and learning strategies in secondary education

Since the 1990s, the central controversy surrounding science education in Brazil has revolved around curricula content and learning strategies for the STEM fields, especially at the secondary level. The secondary level, which follows nine years of study in basic education, corresponds to secondary education or high school and consists of three years of study. This level is known in Brazil as *ensino médio*, which translates as 'middle school.' This translation is significant because it expresses how secondary education is traditionally regarded in public opinion and also by an important part of the elite: as a transitional step from primary education to higher education.

Traditionally, Brazilian secondary education emphasized teaching an extensive list of themes, organized along strict disciplinary lines. Curricula contents have been expanded in successive waves of curricula reforms. The current format includes 14 different mandatory subjects (e.g. mathematics, physics, chemistry, biology, sociology, world history, Latin-American history, etc.). Even more impressive is the fact that this framework applies to all students, even those attending the small sector of vocational secondary education. In addition to this large number of disciplines, within each discipline, the list of subjects is extensive.

Two different independent institutional dynamics are responsible for this particular situation. Firstly, there is the old Napoleonic model that organizes higher education in Brazil (Schwartzman 1992). According to this model, a bachelor's degree is, at the same time, both a diploma and a certification that allows the holder to have access to hard-to-access areas in the labour market. While there is some similarity between this ideal and the reality in well-defined career tracks, like medicine or law, there is a clear problem when it comes to considering bachelor programmes in more basic disciplines like chemistry, physics or sociology. Traditionally, the way to solve this issue is to define teaching at secondary education as the main closed market for professionals coming from the basic areas. This explains why well-organized advocacy groups from these areas are always fighting to secure and introduce new disciplines to the secondary level's curricular structure. It also accounts for the resistance to a more interdisciplinary focus, combined with problem-oriented learning.

Secondly, the other drive for the overloaded curriculum in secondary education comes from the pressure created by the exigencies posed by the entrance
examinations of the major universities in the country. In Brazil, access to higher
education is controlled by a *numerus clausus* policy with only a limited number of
positions open to freshmen. Entrance examinations, which determine whether a
student qualifies for a particular subject or not, are known in Brazil as *exames ves-
tibulares.* Preparing pupils to succeed in these exams is based on learning centred
on the memorizing of formulas and different types of exercises. These dynamics
also explain why students at secondary education are trained *not* to use calcula-
tors when solving exercises in physics and mathematics. Since using a calculator
is forbidden at the entrance examination held by the most prestigious universities, learning physics or mathematics with the help of a calculator is viewed as a
handicap by most secondary schools in Brazil.

The Ministry of Education and the National Council of Education are responsible for setting the curricula and, in this role, favour extensive curricula in all
disciplines. The rationality behind this dynamic is the egalitarian ideal of making
sure all students receive the same education. However, its successful implementation fails due to a lack of qualified teachers, the low social status attached to the
teacher's role in Brazil and the poor quality of public school infrastructure and
governance. Simultaneously, it exacerbates inequalities between public and private education, and among the latter between elite and mass education.[2]

Opposing perspectives on the current problems in the field of education

The policy arena of education in Brazil is central for a large number of stakeholders: NGOs of diverse ideological orientations, teachers' unions, scholars
and intellectuals from the education field, major scientific societies, private and
public universities, officials in charge of education policies at all federal levels,
families with young children, and business and journalists are all present and
have relevant issues in the field of education. In spite of this variety of stakeholders' profiles, it is possible to understand the major controversies that organize
the policy arena of education in Brazil using the concept of advocacy coalition,
as proposed by Paul Sabatier and collaborators (Sabatier 1988; Weible, Sabatier
and McQueen 2009). In this sense, it is possible to identify two major coalitions.
One organizes the most traditional stakeholders in Brazilian Education: educators, intellectual leaders from the pedagogical schools, some NGOs and teachers'
unions. The other includes a new generation of scholars coming from the fields
of economics and political science involved in the discussion of educational policies, some officials in charge of education policies at state and municipal levels,
leaders from some large NGOs and, to an extent, senior bureaucrats from the
Ministry of Education.

For the members of the first coalition, teachers' salaries and the low level of
public resources invested in education are the central issues. Members of this
coalition tend to support the current curricula format and also agree with the
prevalence of a secondary education focussed on a generalist curriculum.

While vocational education may be tolerated, it should complement the traditional extensive general curriculum, which should be the core of secondary education. Members of this coalition also oppose conceiving learning goals as skills and competencies. Instead, they emphasize the actual content of learning as a right of all children. For this coalition, the central issue for science education in Brazil is to ensure that all pupils will have access to the same general disciplinary curricula composed of the main disciplines in science and mathematics.

For the members of the second coalition, the core problem of Brazilian education is not lack of resources, but the poor management of available resources. According to the members of this coalition, more autonomy to schools and strong steering instruments for the government to direct schools towards better performance is the best alternative way of improving education. Members of this coalition recognize the low social standing attached to teaching in Brazil. However, for them, change in this picture should come with meritocratic policies, which would recognize and reward teachers' good performance. Members of this coalition also tend to support a more diverse and flexible curriculum design, where convergence is a product of assuring the student's access to a general set of skills and competences and not of specifying curricula contents. For the members of this coalition, the central issue of science education is to provide more diversified learning alternatives, which should bring science closer to the students' daily experience, improving its relevance and sustaining students' interest in learning science and mathematics.

Recent improvements—from rote learning to competence training

At the end of the 1990s, the new Education Law (namely the 'Lei de Diretrizes e Bases da Educacao' passed in 1996) initiated a new process in science education focussing on and defining competencies the student should master at all basic education levels, instead of listing topics that should be presented to the student in all disciplines. The new law also redefined secondary education as the final stage of Brazil's basic education, which should be available to all the country's youth. As a result, the final three years of the twelve-year cycle of basic education in Brazil should both train students for the labour market and finish the general learning process open to all Brazilian students. Since the adoption of this law, the Ministry of Education has developed a set of competencies and just published a revised version of minimal national curricula contents (Ministry of Education 2014) in 2014.

One would expect that the new approach would have opened a window of opportunity for diversifying the curricula in science education. However, this did not happen. The old institutional dynamics were never counteracted. In fact, the strategy adopted by the government to popularize the new approach ended up reinforcing the old patterns that make science education so dysfunctional in Brazil.

Another Ministry of Education initiative that accompanied the above-mentioned reform was the establishment of a major national evaluation exam in

1998 for secondary education (ENEM, Exame Nacional do Ensino Médio). The exam was proposed as an optional self-evaluation exercise, where students were exposed to problems contextualized into real-life situations, demanding a more interdisciplinary approach. Even though attending the exam was not mandatory, the Ministry of Education tried to influence public universities to accept the ENEM's scores as part of their entrance procedures in order to ensure visibility and legitimacy for the new exam (Castro 2001; Castro and Tiezzi 2005). With these measures, enrolment for the exam increased (4 million students in 2008) and the ENEM became a relevant driving force, on top of former dynamics, in defining curricula contents and learning approaches in secondary education.

In 2009, the ENEM experienced a radical change that ended up mitigating its effects in supporting the new approach to curricula content. During that year, the Ministry of Education proposed that the ENEM be used as a unified procedure for access to federal universities. The Ministry could not impose this system upon the universities, but tried to win their agreement with promises of resources, while negotiating changes in the ENEM in order to make it an acceptable substitute for the old entrance examination for the universities. With its new direction, the ENEM is organized on a matrix that combines competencies and abilities with disciplinary contents. The contents are organized into five different areas, of which two areas—'Mathematic and Its technologies' and 'Natural Sciences and their technologies'—are focussed on accessing the student's abilities and competencies in mastering contents of the STEM fields. Recent studies of the ENEM's contents in these areas produced mixed evaluations. While they acknowledge efforts made in producing more contextualized questions, which explore real-life applications of concepts and contents, they note the long list of contents students still need to learn in order to be successful in this exam and the prevalence of the old disciplinary approach (see e.g. Hernandes and Martins 2013; Gonçalves and Barroso 2014).

In spite of its advances, the ENEM proved to be a poor tool for promoting real change in science education in Brazil. It has no effect on the way teacher education is organized. Today, teacher education is still regarded as a by-product of disciplinary-oriented bachelor programmes. The government tried to impose a new framework for teacher education, but faces strong resistance from the universities. Most importantly, the ENEM has all the same problematic traits found in the old universities' entrance examinations. Nevertheless, the visibility and impact of this exam has grown rapidly. While some traditional universities still hold their own exams, almost all federal universities, most state-owned universities and many private institutions use the ENEM as the only alternative for selecting their freshmen. More recently, in 2013, the federal government took a new step towards broadening the impact of the ENEM in molding the future of the students: a basic performance in this exam is demanded from all students interested in participating in Brazil's major programme for international mobility—the Science Without Borders programme (see also the contribution by Simon Schwartzman, Chapter 10). Within these parameters, teachers, parents and schools have ample room to see secondary education as synonymous with intense training for succeeding in just one marathon: the ENEM exams, held only once a year and carried out in a concentrated, two-day effort. No matter the changes, learning strategy in this context stays disconnected from the way science and technology is built, works and advances. Additionally, it creates strong tendencies for homogeneity, erasing all centrifugal forces that support differentiation, experimentation and adaptation to local needs and circumstances at secondary education.

The dynamics that support an old-fashioned view of science education are still present in Brazil. The old debate between strict disciplinary orientations, focussed on learning an exhaustive list of contents, and a more interdisciplinary approach, highlighting learning competencies and abilities necessary for solving real-life problems and understanding the major science controversies, is still being fought in Brazil. While the rhetoric has bent towards the latter view, the former is still very much in place, in schools and teachers' practices and in parents' expectations.

Acknowledgement

The authors would like to acknowledge the financial support given by FAPESP, Fundação de Amparo à Pesquisa do Estado de São Paulo (11/50771-8).

Notes

1 The authors would like to thank undergraduate students Lilian Sendretti R. Macedo and Juliana Pagliarelli dos Reis for their work done in mapping the policy controversies from the point of view of the press and the NGOs in Brazil. Both students benefitted from scholarships from the Brazilian Federal Science Council (CNPq).
2 Popular imagination tends to equate private education with elite education: large, well-equipped and highly selective schools, where tuition easily costs upwards of 12,000 euro per year. However, Brazil also has a large number of small private schools catering for children from the lower middle class, where tuition can often be as low as 100 euro per month.

Bibliography

Castro, Claudio de Moura (2001): Parecer sobre a participação do Brasil no PISA. A penosa evolução do ensino e seu encontro com o PISA. In: *BRASIL. Relatório Nacional PISA 2000*. Brasília. Pp. 77–88. Available from http://www.oei.es/quipu/brasil/pisa2000.pdf [Accessed 22 September 2014].
Castro, Maria Helena Guimarães and Sergio Tiezzi (2005): A reforma do ensino médio e a implantação do Enem no Brasil. In: *Os desafios da educação no Brasil*, edited by Colin Brock and Simon Schwartzman. Nova Fronteira, Rio de Janeiro. Pp. 119–154.
Gonçalves Jr., Wanderlei P. and Marta F. Barroso (2014) As questões de Física e o desempenho dos estudantes no ENEM, *Revista Brasileira de Ensino de Física* 36 (1). Pp. 1402/1–1402/11.
Hernandes, Jesusney Silva and Maria Inês Martins (2013): Categorização de questões de física do Novo ENEM, *Cadernos Brasileiros de Ensino de Física* 30 (1). Pp. 58–83.

Ministry of Education, Brasil (2014): Parâmetros curriculares Nacionais. Ensino médio. Available from http://portal.mec.gov.br/seb/arquivos/pdf/ciencian.pdf [Accessed 9 July 2014].

Sabatier, Paul A. (1988): An Advocacy Coalition Framework of Policy Change and the Role of Policy-Oriented Learning Therein, *Policy Sciences* 21 (2–3). Pp. 129–168.

Schwartzman, Simon (1992): Brazil. In: *The Encyclopedia of Higher Education I*, edited by Burton Clark and Guy Neave. Pergamon Press, London. Pp. 82–92.

Weible, Christopher M., Paul A. Sabatier and Kelly McQueen (2009): Themes and Variations: Taking Stock of the Advocacy Coalition Framework, *Policy Studies Journal* 37 (1). Pp. 121–140.

12 Closing the achievement gap and building the pipeline through STEM education

A US perspective

Yvonne M. Spicer

Justifying the need for technological literacy

Technological literacy implies more than just knowing about technology and engineering. Just as the skill of reading is essential for language literacy and the capacity for inquiry is essential for scientific literacy, the ability to use the engineering design process lies at the heart of technological literacy. If today's students can learn to apply the engineering design process in the classroom, as adults they will be better equipped to address fundamental problems of the modern world such as global warming, depletion of natural resources, or the loss of biodiversity. Although science is essential for understanding the root causes of these problems, it will take teams of people with a wide variety of expertise—and a firm grasp of the engineering design process—to solve them. Arguments for increasing students' capability to think like engineers fall under two categories: the 'Pipeline Rationale' and the 'Technological Literacy Rationale.' These rationales, summarized below, promote engineering education as either an economic driver or a social necessity—topics that we consider complementary and equally important for the future health of our nation and world.

The Pipeline Rationale

Perhaps the most commonly cited argument for introducing technology and engineering in K-12 programmes, the 'Pipeline Rationale,' states that our nation's competition and leadership in technological innovation worldwide is dependent on producing more engineers and skilled technicians. By this theory, we must broaden the base of the metaphorical 'pipeline' that brings a steady stream of students through the K-12 education system and into post-secondary and graduate engineering degree programmes. We must introduce technology and engineering concepts to more children at earlier ages in order to interest them in the kinds of engineering careers that will help us solve pressing issues and remain competitive in the global innovation market into the future.

Over the past five years there has been a significant increase in the number of reports warning that the US workforce is losing its competitive edge. A study by the National Academy of Sciences and others and commissioned by Congress, framed the issue as follows:

The United States takes deserved pride in the vitality of its economy, which forms the foundation of our high quality of life [. . .] That vitality is derived in large part from the productivity of well-trained people and the steady stream of scientific and technical innovations they produce. Without high-quality, knowledge-intensive jobs and the innovative enterprises that lead to discovery and new technology, our economy will suffer and our people will face a lower standard of living.

(National Academy of Sciences, National Academy of Engineering and Institute of Medicine 2007: 1)

The report goes on to explain that a great many of today's engineers are reaching retirement age, and too few young people are prepared to replace them (about 6 per cent of undergraduates study engineering). This is a comparatively low number, as 12 per cent of undergraduates in most of Europe, 20 per cent in Singapore, and more than 40 per cent in China study engineering (National Academy of Sciences, National Academy of Engineering and Institute of Medicine 2007: 31). These statistics are a striking indication that the United States is falling behind in the field of engineering, with potentially serious consequences for future economic competitiveness.

Putting global competition aside, educators and policymakers are also focused on the higher wages earned by STEM professionals compared with non-STEM workers (see e.g. Carnevale, Smith and Melton 2012: 29ff). Encouraging enthusiasm in the STEM fields from an early age is a potential way to help students make the most of their degrees and careers.

The Technological Literacy Rationale

While the Pipeline Rationale emphasizes engineering primarily as an economic driver, we see in the Technological Literacy Rationale an equally compelling argument stating that everyone in our modern society—whether or not they choose to enter technical fields—needs to be technologically literate. That is, in order to be an informed global citizen, every person needs to be able to understand societal issues related to technology, such as global warming and sustainable development, as well as to understand and apply the engineering design process in order to solve problems in their daily lives.

By this rationale, every student needs to become technologically literate, not just those pursuing engineering and technology as careers. According to a report from the National Academy of Engineering (NAE) and the National Research Council (NRC) to face future challenges and also to benefit from technological improvements 'Americans must become better stewards of technological change' (NAE and NRC 2002: 12).

By encouraging technological literacy in every person, we can predict that individuals will have greater power to make decisions in their personal lives and will be in a better position to make positive contributions to society. They will also have a greater understanding and appreciation for the work that engineers and technicians do, and will therefore be more likely to support this work or even to pursue a career in engineering or technology. As our technical workforce gains strength, especially in such visible fields as aerospace, information technology and environmental engineering, the hope is that more people will see and appreciate the accomplishments of engineers and the essential role that they play in shaping modern society.

The state of STEM education in the United States

Now that we have outlined the reasons for strengthening our nation's engineering education efforts, we can discuss the current landscape of these efforts. In terms of formal education, we see a great need to understand what is happening during the school day that inspires or inhibits students in STEM fields: how and when are we introducing STEM topics in schools, and to whom? How can we improve this dialogue and incorporate science and engineering into curricula at every grade level in every school? How can we close the achievement gap, and ensure that every student, no matter his or her race, class, immigration status or gender, has the same access to quality STEM education?

These kinds of questions have lingered in the national consciousness since the 1983 report 'A Nation at Risk' commissioned by Terrel H. Bell, Secretary of Education under the Reagan administration (National Commission on Excellence in Education 1983). This document outlined contemporary policy efforts to solve the issues of the US educational system and included recommendations on school curricula, standards and expectations, school time and teaching. Now America has reached a new educational frontier: science and engineering education. Compounding the problem are shifting demographics: while minority groups are growing in population share, their participation in the science and engineering fields does not match their rate of growth (NAS, NAE and Institute of Medicine 2011), leading to an 'achievement gap' between historically privileged groups and marginalized minorities in science and engineering. This achievement gap has the potential to create long-lasting inequalities and impact future career choice and success in many underrepresented groups. There is an obvious need to close the gaps in our educational system and ensure high standards of STEM education for every student.

Educational leaders in the United States realize that the nation is falling behind in numbers of skilled workers in critical STEM fields; however, while this problem is national in scope, the United States legally does not possess a national education system due to the Tenth Amendment to the US Constitution.[1] Efforts to improve standards or curricula must therefore be adopted by individual states on a case-by-case basis. The onus is thus on US state leaders to upgrade curricula and adopt a common core of internationally benchmarked standards for grades K-12 that will give students a chance to compete globally. In developing standard recommendations, national leaders have made an effort to learn and borrow from their international peers. Top international performers in education can help provide a template for all nations to improve their own systems: within the United States, this means that individual states must step up to the challenge and adopt education systems that are internationally competitive in the STEM fields.

The US government has recommended standards in recent years, beginning with the Common Core State Standards which is intended to communicate clear benchmarks of success for all students in math and English language arts. Most recently, the Next Generation Science Standards, with a focus on science and engineering design, will address concerns that date back to 1983. As an incentive, states that adopt standards were eligible to apply for competitive grant funding from the Race to the Top fund, a part of the American Recovery and Reinvestment Act of 2009. States awarded a grant must demonstrate their commitment to fostering change by submitting a comprehensive proposal for education reform. This proposal must include:

- An emphasis on STEM
- Potential innovations for improving early learning outcomes
- Expansion of data collection systems
- Plans for increased coordination between schools, community partners, workforce organizations and post-secondary institutions
- School-level conditions for reform, innovation, and learning.

Notably, STEM is the only field singled out as a competitive preference priority (US Department of Education 2009).

Massachusetts is a useful model state to look at in terms of education reform, especially in the STEM fields. As the first state to develop engineering state standards and assessments in 2001, Massachusetts has historically been a national leader in STEM education. The 1993 Massachusetts Education Reform Law mandated curriculum frameworks and assessment statewide through the Massachusetts Comprehensive Assessment System (MCAS). In 1996, an initial statewide framework recognized 'science and technology' as an academic subject. The state continues to develop novel ways to overcome challenges such as implementation and teacher preparation (Foster 2009). Recently, Massachusetts has been singled out as a leader in research into pre-kindergarten education, a topic that is rapidly gaining importance on the national stage (Weiland and Yoshikawa 2013).

Common Core State Standards (CCSS)

The Common Core standards development started in 2009 with a focus on two subject areas: mathematics and English language arts. The mathematics standards emphasize depth of mathematical understanding and ability to use mathematical concepts in real-world situations, a necessary skill for engineering. The Common Core is not a curriculum, but a collective goal to be reached based on international comparisons and lessons learned from the past few decades on mathematics education (Common Core State Standard Initiative 2014). As of the spring of 2014, forty-three states have adopted common core standards; however, seven states have opted not to participate. According to its developers, the Common Core State Standards are 'informed by the highest, most effective standards from states across the United States and countries around the world' (Common Core State Standard Initiative 2014: last paragraph).

Next Generation Science Standards (NGSS)

The Next Generation Science Standards are based on the latest research into K-12 science education, outlined in a preliminary 2012 report by the National Research Council (NRC). Using the Framework, twenty-six states collaboratively developed these standards, led by Achieve, a bipartisan, non-profit organization dedicated to promoting college- and career-ready agendas nationwide. In spring 2014, ten states adopted the standards, which are based around three dimensions: Practices, Crosscutting Concepts and Disciplinary Core Ideas. The focus is on identifying major concepts that link the sciences, allowing students to create linkages between topics and apply their knowledge to real-world situations (Achieve, Inc. 2013).

Teacher development

The status of the United States' STEM education landscape calls for a greater number of teachers trained in STEM topics. A study by the Aspire Institute on the Foundations for the Future (Wheelock College Aspire Institute 2010) addresses the need for stronger teacher preparation programmes in STEM as well as time in the curriculum to deliver rich and engaging STEM activities for students. The report recommends teacher training with an eye to increasing engineering curricula as early as pre-kindergarten in order to engage students and familiarize them with engineering content as early as possible. The study proposes to increase the number of high-performing maths and science undergraduates for enrolment in masters programmes for PreK-6 education. They hope that beginning with scientifically competent students will result in scientifically competent elementary teachers, leading to higher quality STEM teaching in schools at all grade levels. A study by Cunningham, Lachapelle and Lindgren-Streicher, presented at the American Society for Engineering Education Annual Conference & Exposition, showed that the majority of elementary-level teachers held vital misconceptions regarding the role of engineers, most commonly that 'engineers construct buildings' (Cunningham, Lachapelle and Lindgren-Streicher 2006: findings, third paragraph).

In order to remain competitive in STEM fields, the United States must improve the state of its teacher training systems to ensure that all elementary teachers are prepared to actively engage with STEM topics. A study by Hill, Rowan and Loewenberg Ball (2005) found that teachers' mathematical knowledge was significantly related to student achievement gains. To address this challenge, the 100Kin10 movement has been making strides to build a cadre of teachers to ensure a well-educated STEM workforce for the future.[2]

Early childhood STEM education

A major focus in the United States in recent years has been increasing access to pre-kindergarten programmes. A 2012 report from the National Institute for

Early Education Research found that '[. . .] only high-quality pre-K has produced substantial gains in school readiness, achievement and educational attainment, higher productivity in the labor force, and decreases in social problems like crime and delinquency' (Barnett *et al.* 2012: 5). While pre-kindergarten has been shown to be a powerful predictor of future academic and economic success, these effects are impacted heavily by teacher quality, necessitating a focus on teacher training for early childhood educators. The necessity of high-level training for early childhood educators is a contentious topic nationwide, as limited resources prove a barrier to providing high-quality training. In Massachusetts, the Department of Early Childhood and Care (EEC) considers providing early childhood educators professional development in STEM critical to building best practices to provide quality training (Wheelock College Aspire Institute 2011).

Another issue facing early childhood educators is lack of access to appropriate technology in the classroom: while researchers are increasingly recommending introducing technology to children early, schools often reserve their newest science equipment for higher grades, leaving elementary school teachers to work with older, less-functional materials. These problems are particularly pronounced in schools with less funding, potentially contributing to the STEM achievement gap (Shamburg 2004).

However, several organizations are making strides towards creating age-appropriate engineering curricula and projects that early childhood educators can use in the classroom: research shows that engineering concepts are often readily accepted by children, as such concepts often mirror the way that children naturally think about and experience the world. Wyeth and Purchase have studied a system that uses interlocking blocks to demonstrate programming concepts for young children. Wyeth's and Purchase's (2002) work shows that abstract concepts can be made relevant to young children when presented in the right way. Marina Bers *et al.* (2002) recommend the introduction of constructionist pedagogies in technology education for students as young as pre-kindergarten, saying that 'Young children are natural engineers—they build forts, towers of blocks, sandcastles and take apart their toys to see what is inside' (Bers *et al.* 2002: 139). The engineering process is natural for children: if we can overcome the barriers to implementing this kind of learning in early childhood education, research shows that we should be successful in attracting students to STEM degrees and careers.

At the Museum of Science in Boston, the 'Engineering is Elementary team' has done considerable work to create curricula that link literacy and engineering skills for elementary-aged students. This kind of learning can be powerful, as it creates cross-disciplinary knowledge gain in students; additionally, it helps teachers who feel they must reach certain literacy goals in their curricula by integrating engineering concepts with reading skills. Similarly, the Center for Engineering Education Outreach (CEEO) at Tufts University is pioneering a number of efforts to make cross-curricular science and engineering learning accessible for students of all ages.

Attitudes towards STEM subjects in the United States

In the US there is a general lack of awareness of STEM education; moreover, the general public often underestimates the value of STEM education. The lack of consistency in defining STEM education is pervasive both in terms of what the content should look like in the classroom as well as teacher professional development. According to Provasnik *et al.* (2012), the US ranks eleventh among fourth graders and ninth among eighth graders in maths, and seventh among fourth graders and tenth among eighth graders in science worldwide.

To examine the issue further, it is important to analyse the data for measuring deep content learning in STEM fields. Laird, Shoup and Kuh (2005) developed the National Survey of Student Engagement (NSSE) that is administered at public and private colleges around the United States to measure deep learning in STEM fields at the higher education institutions. The authors contend that we can measure high-order learning, integrative learning and reflective learning of STEM content, which has implications for practices in instruction and skill development for the workforce. In Massachusetts, the survey will be used as a metric to evaluate the state's progress in achieving growth in STEM graduates (Governor's STEM Advisory Council 2013). A few universities are offering STEM certificate programmes for in-service educators to build their content knowledge and experience in STEM, e.g. the Christa McAuliffe Center at the Framingham State University.[3]

Another helpful presentation of different indicators is provided by the National Science Board's *Science and Engineering Indicators 2014*. It also shows a broad spectrum of STEM learning between states for grades four and eight (Figures 12.1 and 12.2). The states having consistent success in student performance tend to be in the Northeast and Midwest. Massachusetts has remained a frontrunner at the national and international level; however, even Massachusetts' success should not be taken as a sign that improvements are unnecessary.

Closing the STEM achievement gap

While major national and state initiatives are attempting to improve STEM standards for all students, engineering and technology opportunities often remain limited for many groups, especially girls and students of colour. This situation has resulted in an appalling achievement gap, in which students from historically marginalized groups are not receiving the engineering and technology skills needed to succeed in post-secondary education. Engineering skills—identifying a problem, designing a solution, testing and improving the design—are among the most sought-after and profitable skills in post-secondary programmes. As a cross-disciplinary skill set, engineering helps students apply their maths and science learning to solve real problems, while also making use of English language arts, history and social studies. With the critical need for trained engineers and scientists, we recommend introducing engineering as early as pre-kindergarten so that when students reach high school, they will have a more realistic understanding

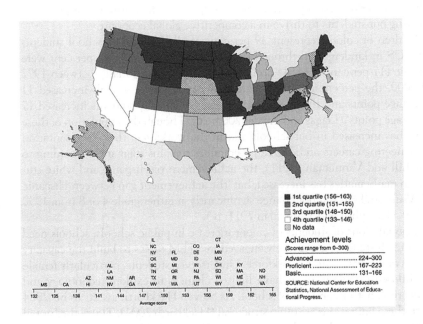

Figure 12.1 Average fourth grade science performance by state, 2009
Source: National Science Board 2014: State Indicators, 8–3

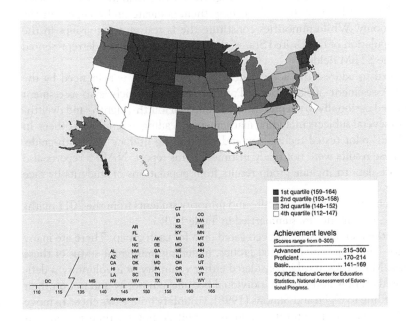

Figure 12.2 Average eighth grade science performance by state, 2011
Source: National Science Board 2014: State Indicators, 8–7

of the engineering design process. Engineering, which fuels innovation, is key to educating our students to thrive in a competitive global economy.

Children of colour represent 39 per cent of all K-12 public school students in the US in kindergarten through to twelfth grade: of these, 44 per cent were Hispanic (17 per cent of total enrolment) in 2000. 'Additionally, between 1972 and 2000, the percentage of Hispanic students in public schools increased 11 percentage points and the overall percentage of minority students increased 17 percentage points' (Llagas and Snyder 2003: 26). Though the population of these groups has increased in our schools and in the workforce, their representation in engineering careers and degree programmes remains stagnant. According to Hemphill and Vanneman (2011), the achievement of Hispanic and white students in mathematics has increased, but 'the achievement gap between Hispanic and White students did not change significantly at either grade 4 or 8 from 1990 to 2009' (Hemphill and Vanneman 2011: iv).

As populations of students of colour increase in public schools, schools need to ensure all students are actively engaged in STEM topics to build the capacity for our twenty-first century workforce. Underserved students, particularly female and children of colour, often have limited chances to explore technology and engineering, both in and out of school. As Steven Hackbarth asserts in his 2004 report, these limitations are often structural (Hackbarth 2004). The author noted that the females of colour in his story reported lower confidence using technology, correlating this with their decreased access to the school's computer laboratory as compared to their peers. We need to change the playing field in order to provide these students with the right tools to help them graduate and compete in the global economy. While minorities constitute the fastest growing groups in the general population of the United States, they are also the most underrepresented group in the STEM fields.

The need to address the achievement gap at all levels is evidenced by the National Assessment of Educational Progress (NAEP), which is an assessment administered nationally to a representative sample of fourth-, eighth- and twelfth-graders in several subjects including mathematics, reading, science and others. In 2014, NAEP pilot tested technology and engineering literacy in eighth-grade, though these results were not ready in time for this report. NAEP's reports also disaggregate data to include group results from populations of students by race and gender.

Achievement gaps between white and minority students from the 2011 maths and science assessments are summarized in Table 12.1.

Within the racial gaps are disaggregated data for each group. There are many reasons for large gaps among racial groups, including immigrant status of these minorities. Minorities may be considered either voluntary or involuntary, a definition based on how and why an individual became a minority and not on their race. According to Ogbu and Simons (1998), voluntary minorities chose to move to the US for better opportunities, and as a result do not see their presence as forced upon them by the government or white Americans. Involuntary minorities attained minority status through being conquered, colonized or enslaved.

Table 12.1 Achievement gap in mathematics according to NAEP in 2011. Score gaps reflect white student points achieved above those of minority students

NAEP Mathematics Assessment 2011/Achievement gaps

Racial/Ethnic Group Comparison	Fourth Grade Score Gap	Eighth Grade Score Gap
White–Black	25	31
White–Hispanic	20	23
White–Asian/Pacific Islander	–7	–9
White–American Indian/Alaska Native	24	28

Source: Adapted from National Center for Education Statistics 2011: 12f, 37f

Involuntary minorities can include American Indians and Black Americans brought into the US as slaves. This distinction could help explain why there are more first- and second-generation black students (voluntary minorities) at elite colleges and universities than there are legacy black students with long-term generational roots in the US (involuntary minorities). Most voluntary minorities see more opportunities for success in the US than back in their native homeland and are willing to accept inequality in order to improve their chances for success. However, involuntary minorities compare their situation to those of middle-class white Americans and see their condition as inferior and imposed. They are aware of historical segregation and racism and do not have a pragmatic trust in white-controlled institutions like voluntary minorities who are willing to accommodate to white American culture and do not believe that this will threaten their minority identity. Because of their trust in these institutions, voluntary minorities hold children responsible for their academic performances, but involuntary minorities hold teachers and schools responsible and believe that they are trying to impose white culture on them. Less successful voluntary students, however, tend to feel immense pressure to succeed (Ogbu and Simons 1998).

Access to high-quality early childhood education is also a leading problem in closing achievement gaps. While pre-kindergarten is shown to have a profound effect on students' educational and economic outcomes, the National Institute for Early Education Research showed that access to early education—especially high-quality early education—is often limited to privileged groups and strongly associated with income and education. The authors also found out that 'access itself is not enough to ensure enrolment in a high-quality programme.' Even though African-American children had relatively high enrolment rates, they had least access to quality (Barnett et al. 2012: 9).

Another potential arena for closing the STEM achievement gap for minority students lies in afterschool programmes. A report by the Afterschool Alliance found that 'ethnic minority children are more likely than others to participate' in afterschool programmes (Afterschool Alliance 2011: 1). Therefore, after-school programmes are another opportunity to reach students from populations that are underrepresented in STEM fields and to introduce them to STEM topics and activities.

Issues affecting specific groups

Among Asian-American students, the 'model minority myth' is a stereotype that asserts being a member of an ethnic, racial or religious group automatically assumes that one achieves more success than the average population. This myth is a prevalent inhibitor to equal treatment and access in the sciences for many students. While Asian-American students are often universally stereotyped as being good at maths and science, there are significant in-group differences in their actual performance. In particular, Filipino, Southeast Asian and Pacific Islander students tend to perform lower than their northern counterparts such as the Chinese or the Japanese. Asian-Americans are a large and diverse group, and struggling students from any of these nationalities are easily hidden behind the label of 'Asian-American,' meaning they may be overlooked because of their association with the myth of the 'model minority.' Additionally, data on this group is typically not disaggregated and does not reflect the different experiences in the US by groups like recent immigrants or refugees, English language learners (ELL) or the working poor. The huge variety of Asian dialects and languages and the model minority myth can both create significant barriers to appropriate ELL instruction for Asian-American students. An invisible crisis is created where teachers assume all Asian-American students are smart and do not need ELL services and other types of assistance that other ELL students use. Additionally, teachers may be ignorant and disrespectful of the differing cultures of these students. Asian-American parents often want their children to learn English while retaining their home language and culture—a difficult request in current ELL programmes, where assimilation into the mainstream culture is expected in order to succeed.

Filipino students typically live in single-parent households and struggle with academics while they have to help their families make cultural and social transitions. Southeast Asian groups typically settle in the US as refugees and parents usually lack formal education. Due to the model minority myth, teachers believe that those of Asian descent who are not meeting academic expectations must be less intelligent or hard working. Tragically, some students are inappropriately referred to ELL classes believing that this is the solution to the problem (Lee and Kumashiro 2005).

The model minority myth creates competition among racial groups and denies an individual the ability to choose how others view him or her. Trytten, Lowe and Walden (2012) interviewed Asian and Asian-American engineering students at the University of Oklahoma and found that the myth does affect the students, but they are unable to describe their experiences as a stereotype. They lack the knowledge of race interactions with US culture, and not once did the students mention the term model minority myth, yet they could identify with its facets. Faculty also lack this knowledge and are not prepared to interact with a diverse group of students. This report serves as a warning for educators to focus on attaining equitable STEM programmes lest minority students be continuously pushed away (Trytten, Lowe and Walden 2012).

Another group in danger of being pushed away is Latino students. Many Latino students attend high-poverty and low-performing schools, are insufficiently prepared for further education and lack access to high-level classes and qualified teachers. Teachers, counsellors and other school personnel tend to have low expectations of Latino students, which partly results in lower levels of self-efficacy in maths and science compared with white students and greater difficulty perceiving themselves as scientists. Family plays a major role in Latino communities. Major family responsibilities seem to dictate the choice of pursuing a career in STEM for Hispanic men and women. Marriage has a positive influence on men but a negative influence on women. However, females raised in a patriarchal family structure are more likely to consider STEM careers. Achievement gaps begin at a young age. Thus, early intervention methods are extremely important and can potentially eliminate gaps that widen as students age (Crisp and Nora 2006).

Similar difficulties with other ELL students arise with ELL Latino students. Their reading skills are low and they have limited English proficiency. The language of STEM courses is difficult to master and understand. Scientific texts, charts, graphs, diagrams and equations tend to be unfamiliar.

Like Asian students, foreign-born students tend to do better academically than their US-born counterparts. Immigrants are self-selective and overcome difficulties to seek a better life. They are a tight-knit community that can offer interactions that others cannot (e.g. community member who knows advanced maths and science compared with a low-immigrant parent). Immigrant children benefit from absorbing their native land culture and then doing the same with American culture. Latino immigrant children are similar to successful Asian immigrant children so long as they have the same factors, like two parent households, better-educated parents and better school districts (see e.g. ETS 2006).

Across multiple groups, underrepresented minorities typically have insufficient access to information about educational and career opportunities. Students' educational backgrounds do not provide effective preparation for future STEM courses; moreover, these students are rarely encouraged to take a sufficient number of challenging science and maths classes. They need early intervention, but schools with large populations of minorities typically have weak academic and career counselling. Additionally, there are few minority role models in the STEM fields (e.g. African-American scientists) discussed during classes, potentially suppressing interest and motivation among students of colour.

Financial barriers also stand in the way of underrepresented minorities participating in STEM programmes in higher education. In the report on 'Expanding Underrepresented Minority Participation,' the authors found that completion of science and engineering programmes was positively related to receiving financial aid (NAS, NAE and Institute of Medicine 2011). Funding allows students to focus on their studies, extracurricular activities and research by alleviating the burden of money issues.

Students also experience a certain degree of racial stereotyping by faculty, including stereotype threat, the perceived confirmation of certain negative stereotypes about one's group. This term was first used in experiments that compared test performances between black and white college students wherein black students did worse when their race was emphasized (Steele and Aronson 1995). Many colleges and universities provide programmes to support minority students, though students may avoid these programmes due to perceived stigma associated with being singled out among their majority peers. For these reasons, underrepresented minorities often report feeling academically and socially isolated, especially within STEM fields of study.

International STEM education

The Programme for International Student Assessment (PISA), created by the Organisation for Economic Cooperation and Development (OECD), is administered to 15-year olds in the OECD's thirty-four member nations. Results provide a useful metric to compare educational statistics between nations and measure progress within nations. PISA's ability to show similarities and differences in education systems around the world has the potential to foster creative thinking for new and effective policy change.

In the latest round of maths and science testing, the US ranked twenty-sixth in mathematics and twenty-first in science among the thirty-four OECD member nations (OECD 2012: 2).

Another useful international assessment is the Trends in International Mathematics and Science Study (TIMSS), which tests fourth- and eighth-graders every four years and is sponsored by the International Association for the Evaluation of Educational Achievement (IEA). Results provide countries opportunities to learn from one another about what works and what doesn't in each education system. In 2012, the US ranked eleventh among fourth graders and ninth among eighth graders in maths and seventh among fourth graders and tenth among eighth graders in science (Provasnik *et al.* 2012: 10f; 48f).

Case study: Singapore

After Singapore's independence from British rule in 1965, the small island had few resources and many conflicts between the various ethnic and religious groups among its people. Schools played a large role in uniting the country and preserving its greatest resource: human knowledge. Most Singaporeans were illiterate upon independence, so the government pushed for expanding basic education and a labour-intensive economy. To keep up with the global economy, Singapore later pushed for a skill-intensive country. With this came student tracking based on academic ability because the government recognized that students achieved at different rates. However, Singapore schools provided high-quality teachers not just for 'high achievers' but for the 'low achievers' as well, and there are many opportunities for students to move into higher tracks when ready (OECD 2011: 160ff).

STEM played a major role in Singapore's rapid changes, which included the founding of the Agency for Science, Technology and Research (A* Star), a government agency that funds research and attracts top scientists and scientific companies. Maths and science are among the core subjects students must take starting in primary school (OECD 2011). Schools employ specialist teachers in maths and science from upper primary through to secondary grades. Maths teachers focus on concepts at a greater depth, cover less material and employ visual aids and simple and clear explanations to help students master the material (and aid ELL students). Science teachers in lower grades teach students the process of inquiry and pique interest through inquiry projects, fairs, competitions and research done by scientists (through A* Star). Maths and science teachers come from the top of their class and receive ample hours of training and professional development. Technical education has been transformed from poorly regarded to world class and now attracts many students with a 'hands-on, minds-on, hearts-on' approach (OECD 2011: 168). As a result of this heightened focus on STEM, Singapore scored near the top in its first PISA assessment in 2009 (OECD 2011).

There is a lot that the United States can learn from successful international programmes that can bridge the STEM achievement gap. While these nations have differing forms of government and differing demographics, the US can use lessons learned from successful international classrooms such as the ones in Singapore.

Promising practices in United States STEM education

There are many examples of promising practices in STEM education in the US and around the world. Some criteria used to identify successful STEM schools are student outcomes, STEM-focused school types and instruction and school practices. Student outcomes should include not only test scores, but also have to gauge outcomes like student interest and creativity. There are three types of STEM-focused schools: selective, inclusive and those with STEM-focused career and technical education. Effective instruction includes set standards and curriculum, exceptional teachers with high content knowledge, a supportive system of assessment and accountability, adequate instructional time, equal access and sustainability. Successful STEM schools must have a culture of learning and meet the goals of STEM education: ensure a STEM-capable citizenry, build a STEM-proficient workforce, cultivate future STEM experts and close the achievement and participation gap (Hanover Research: 2011).

Project SEED (Special Elementary Education for the Disadvantaged)

Project SEED is a supplementary maths programme that targets urban students in grades 2–8 in Michigan and California. The programme trains mathematicians, scientists and engineers to teach students advanced maths concepts effectively. It also provides regular teachers opportunities for development through observing the specialists and attending workshops (BEST 2004).

Gateway Institute for Pre-College Education

Gateway is an outreach programme of the State University of New York that pre-pares low-income and minority New York City high school students for studies and careers in STEM. It recently started a programme in Boston at the John D. O'Bryant School of Math & Science. Students are selected for the programme in ninth grade based on academic performance and attend a four-year programme of college preparatory and advanced placement classes in maths and laboratory science. Students can also take summer classes, be placed in internships and are exposed to post-secondary education and careers (BEST 2004).

High Tech High (inclusive high school)

High Tech High was originally established as a single charter high school, but now oversees eleven schools in San Diego (elementary, middle and high school). Students are chosen by random lottery system. One third of graduates are first-generation college students. High Tech High also seeks to recruit underserved student populations. Students are offered hands-on projects and an integrated curriculum. They are also required to complete internships upon graduation (Hanover Research 2011).

Metro Early College High School

Metro Early College High School, located in Columbus, Ohio, is a public STEM high school open to students from around the state. It was formed by the Educational Council, which provides cross-district planning for the sixteen school districts in Franklin County, the Battelle Memorial Institute, a private non-profit applied science and technology development company and Ohio State University. Students complete academic coursework at Metro and can partici-pate in extracurricular activities in their home district. Students take accelerated courses to meet Ohio graduation requirements during their first two years (called Core Prep) with incorporated STEM and maths and science courses. Students' last two years consist of hands-on work with academics at Ohio State and sur-rounding colleges, engineers at Battelle and other professionals in the Columbus, Ohio area (Coalition of Essential Schools 2008).[4]

National Center for Technological Literacy® (NCTL)®

NCTL® was established in 2004 at the Museum of Science in Boston, MA, seek-ing to raise awareness and understanding of engineering in schools and museums. The initiative advocates for engineering education as a core discipline through-out the United States by promoting, supporting and guiding educators in order to increase interest and understanding of technology and engineering. In addition, it builds partnerships nationwide and provides national leadership to raise aware-ness and understanding of engineering. The cornerstone of NCTL is the Gateway

Project, designed to support school district teams to understand technology and engineering standards and build a comprehensive strategic plan to implement PreK-12 STEM education in their school district. The project originated in Massachusetts and has been replicated in three additional states, Maine, New Hampshire and Texas, and plans to expand to additional states in 2014 (Museum of Science 2014).

Badges

The concept of awarding symbolic badges has been proposed as a potential method to engage students and develop a universal system of recognizing skills. These badges are digital credentials representing skills, interests and achievements individual students can earn through specific projects, programmes, courses or other activities (Alliance for Excellent Education 2013: 2). The learning ecosystem behind the badges makes them powerful and connected credentials for students to demonstrate their skills. Badge ecosystems are made up of 'issuers,' 'earners' and 'consumers.' Badge issuers include individuals, schools, employers, institutions, communities or groups 'that create credentials to demonstrate mastery of skills and achievements that are of particular value to the issuer. An issuer creates a set of competencies or curriculum and the assessments to determine if the earner has acquired the necessary skills for the badge (Alliance for Excellent Education 2013). One example is e.g. the Chicago 'Summer of Learning.' The organizations that participated in the activity have determined their own badges and gained them for completing learning activities over the summer, including field trips, quests, experiments and self-paced individual efforts to team projects. The badges represented key competencies in science, technology, engineering, arts and mathematics (STEAM), so this is a promising practice that builds in accountability for STEM learning (Alliance for Excellent Education 2013).

Summary

Although the United States has made strides in closing the achievement gap in STEM education, there is still much work to be done to address varying needs. Underrepresented student groups (in both urban and rural areas) need opportunities to succeed in STEM fields. Families and parents need awareness to be able to navigate what schools and organizations have to offer. STEM teachers need professional development and preparation, and school administrators need vision to guide their schools and bring opportunities, awareness and development to all communities.

In closing, to prepare the nation's students for success in a twenty-first century economy, teachers need increased training and support to feel comfortable teaching STEM subjects. Schools have long faced a shortage of STEM educators who have degrees in the subjects they teach, and many of the better-qualified teachers leave for jobs as engineers or mathematicians. We have to act with urgency to tackle this dilemma or the United States will continue to fall behind in building a sustainable innovation economy.

Notes

1 The 10th amendment is the final amendment in the United States' Constitution's original Bill of Rights. It was added to assure delegates from the various states that the Federal Government would not step outside the boundaries established in the Constitution.
2 For further information on the movement visit its website, available at http://www.100kin10.org/ [Accessed 5 September 2014].
3 For further information on the STEM certificate programme see http://christa.org/stem-certificate-program/ [Accessed 8 September 2014].
4 For further information see also the website of Metro, available from http://www.themetroschool.org/ [Accessed 10 September 2014].

Bibliography

Achieve, Inc. (2013): Next Generation Science Standards: Three Dimensions. Washington (DC). Available from http://www.nextgenscience.org/three-dimensions [Accessed 5 September 2014].
Afterschool Alliance (2011): STEM Learning in Afterschool: An Analysis of Impact and Outcomes. Washington (DC). Available from http://www.afterschoolalliance.org/stem-afterschool-outcomes.pdf [Accessed 1 October 2014].
Alliance for Excellent Education (2013): Expanding Education and Workforce Opportunities Through Digital Badges. Washington (DC). Available from http://tamritz.org/wp-content/uploads/2013/08/DigitalBadges.pdf [Accessed 1 October 2014].
Barnett, W. Steven *et al.* (2012): The State of Preschool 2012: State Preschool Yearbook. National Institute for Early Education Research, New Brunswick (NJ). Available from http://nieer.org/sites/nieer/files/yearbook2012.pdf [Accessed 1 October 2014].
Bers, Marina U. *et al.* (2002): Teachers as Designers: Integrating Robotics in Early Childhood Education, *Information Technology in Childhood Education Annual* 1. Pp. 123–145.
BEST (Building Engineering and Science Talent) (2004): What it Takes: Pre-K-12 Design Principles to Broaden Participation in Science, Technology, Engineering and Mathematics. San Diego (CA). Available from http://www.bestworkforce.org/PDFdocs/BESTPre-K-12Rep_part1_Apr2004.pdf [Accessed 10 September 2014].
Carnevale, Anthony P., Nicole Smith and Michelle Melton (2012): STEM. Georgetown University Center on Education and Workforce, Washington (DC). Available from https://georgetown.app.box.com/s/cyrrqbjyirjy64uw91f6 [Accessed 1 October 2014].
Coalition of Essential Schools (2008): Having the Courage To Act on Your Beliefs: Horace Interviews Marcy Raymond and Dan Hoffman on the Founding and Influence of Metro High School. Portland (ME). Available from http://www.essentialschools.org/resources/484 [Accessed 10 September 2014].
Common Core State Standard Initiative (2014): About the Standards. Available from http://www.corestandards.org/about-the-standards/ [Accessed 4 September 2014].
Crisp, Gloria and Amaury Nora (2006): Overview of Hispanics in Science, Mathematics, Engineering and Technology (STEM): K-16 Representation, Preparation and Participation. Prepared for the Hispanic Association of Colleges and Universities,

Washington (DC). Available from http://www.cssia.org/pdf/20000077-OverviewofHispanicsinScience,Technology,Engineering,andMathematics%28STEM%29-K-16Representation,PreparationandParticipation.pdf [Accessed 8 September 2014].

Cunningham, Christine, Cathy Lachapelle and Anna Lindgren-Streicher (2006): Elementary Teachers' Understandings of Engineering and Technology. American Society for Engineering Education, Washington (DC). Available from http://www.eie.org/sites/default/files/research_article/research_file/2006full350.pdf [Accessed 5 September 2014].

ETS (Educational Testing Service) (2006): Latino Achievement in the Sciences, Technology, Engineering and Mathematics. Policy Notes 14 (2). ETS Policy Information Center, Princeton (NJ). Available from https://www.ets.org/Media/Research/pdf/PICPN142.pdf [Accessed 8 September 2014].

Foster, Jacob (2009): The Incorporation of Technology/Engineering Concepts into Academic Standards in Massachusetts: A Case Study, *The Bridge: Linking Engineering and Society* 39 (3). Pp. 25–31.

Governor's STEM Advisory Council (2013): Foundation for the Future. Massachusetts' Plan for Excellence in STEM Education (Version 2.0: Expanding the Pipeline for All). Boston (MA). Available from http://www.mass.edu/stem/documents/2013-11MassachusettsSTEMPlan2.0.pdf [Accessed 8 September 2014].

Hackbarth, Steven (2004): Changes in 4th-Graders' Computer Literacy as a Function of Access, Gender, and Race, *Information Technology in Childhood Education Annual* 1. Pp. 187–212.

Hanover Research (2011): K-12 STEM Education Overview. Washington (DC). Available from http://www.hanoverresearch.com/wp-content/uploads/2011/12/K-12-STEM-Education-Overview-Membership.pdf [Accessed 10 September 2014].

Hemphill, Cadelle F. and Taslima Vanneman (2011): Achievement Gaps: How Hispanic and White Students in Public Schools Perform in Mathematics and Reading on the National Assessment of Educational Progress. National Center for Education Statistics, Institute of Education Sciences, US Department of Education, Washington (DC). Available from http://nces.ed.gov/nationsreportcard/pdf/studies/2011459.pdf [Accessed 1 October 2014].

Hill, Heather C., Brian Rowan and Deborah Loewenberg Ball (2005): Effects of Teachers' Mathematical knowledge for Teaching on Student Achievement, *American Educational Research Journal* 42 (2). Pp. 371–406.

Laird, Thomas F. Nelson, Rick Shoup and George D. Kuh (2005): Measuring Deep Approaches to Learning Using the National Survey of Student Engagement. Annual Meeting of the Association for Institutional Research, Chicago (IL). Available from http://nsse.iub.edu/pdf/conference_presentations/2006/air2006deeplearningfinal.pdf [Accessed 8 September 2014].

Lee, Stacey J. and Kevin K. Kumashiro (2005): A Report on the Status of Asian Americans and Pacific Islanders in Education: Beyond the "Model Minority" Stereotype. National Education Association of the United States, Human and Civil Right, Washington (DC). Available from http://www.capaa.wa.gov/documents/Status-Asian-American.pdf [Accessed 8 September 2014].

Llagas, Charmaine and Thomas D. Snyder (2003): Status and Trends in the Education of Hispanics (NCES 2003-8). US Department of Education, National Center for Education Statistics (NCES), Washington (DC). Available from http://nces.ed.gov/pubs2003/2003008.pdf [Accessed 10 September 2014].

Massachusetts Business Roundtable (2009): Tapping Massachussetts' Potential: The Massachusetts Employers' STEM Agenda. Boston (MA). Available from http://www.

mbae.org/uploads/18062009151146TMPcompleteFINAL.pdf [Accessed 9 September 2014].

Museum of Science (2014): K-12 Programs. The Gateway Project. Boston (MA). Available from http://legacy.mos.org/nctl/k12_gateway.php [Accessed 10 September 2014].

NAE (National Academy of Engineering) and NRC (National Research Council) (2002): *Technically Speaking: Why All Americans Need to Know More About Technology.* The National Academies Press, Washington (DC).

National Academy of Sciences, National Academy of Engineering and Institute of Medicine (2007): *Rising Above the Gathering Storm: Energizing and Employing America for a Brighter Economic Future.* National Academies Press, Washington (DC). Available from http://www.sandia.gov/NINE/documents/RisingAbove.pdf [Accessed 10 September 2014].

NAS (National Academy of Sciences), NAE (National Academy of Engineering) and Institute of Medicine (2011): *Expanding Underrepresented Minority Participation.* The National Academies Press, Washington (DC).

National Center for Education Statistics (2011): The Condition of Education 2011. Available from http://nces.ed.gov/pubs2011/2011033.pdf [Accessed 17 March 2015].

National Commission on Excellence in Education (1983): A Nation at Risk: The Imperative for Educational Reform. US Department of Education, Washington (DC). Available from http://datacenter.spps.org/uploads/SOTW_A_Nation_at_Risk_1983. pdf [Accessed 5 September 2014].

National Science Board (2014): *Science and Engineering Indicators 2014.* National Science Foundation, Arlington (VA). Figures available from http://www.nsf.gov/statistics/ seind14/index.cfm/etc/figures.htm [Accessed 8 September 2014].

Ogbu John U. and Herbert D. Simons (1998): Voluntary and Involuntary Minorities: A Cultural-Ecological Theory of School Performance with Some Implications for Education, *Anthropology & Education Quarterly* 29 (2). Pp.155–188.

OECD (2011): Strong Performers and Successful Reformers in Education: Lessons from PISA for the United States. OECD Publishing. Available from http://www.oecd.org/ pisa/46623978.pdf [Accessed 10 September 2014].

OECD (2012): United States: Country Note: Results from PISA 2012. Available from http://www.oecd.org/unitedstates/PISA-2012-results-US.pdf [Accessed 10 September 2014].

Provasnik, Stephen *et al.* (2012): Highlights From TIMSS 2011: Mathematics and Science Achievement of U.S. Fourth- and Eighth-Grade Students in an International Context (NCES 2013–009). National Center for Education Statistics, Institute of Education Sciences, U.S. Department of Education, Washington (DC). Available from http://nces.ed.gov/pubs2013/2013009rev.pdf [Accessed 5 September 2014].

Shamburg, Christopher (2004): Conditions that Inhibit the Integration of Technology for Urban Early Childhood Teachers, *Information Technology in Childhood Education Annual* 1. Pp. 227–244.

Steele Claude M. and Joshua Aronson (1995): Stereotype Threat and the Intellectual Test Performance of African Americans, *Journal of Personality and Social Psychology* 69 (5). Pp. 797–811.

Trytten, Deborah A., Anna Wong Lowe and Susan E. Walden (2012): 'Asians are Good at Math. What an Awful Stereotype': The Model Minority Stereotype's Impact on Asian American Engineering Students, *Journal of Engineering Education* 101 (3). Pp. 439–468.

UMASS (2013): 2013 Massachusetts STEM Dashboard. Massachusetts Statewide STEM Indicators Project (MASSIP). Available from http://www.mass.edu/forinstitutions/prek16/documents/Pipeline/Massachusetts_Stem_Dashboard_2013.pdf [Accessed 27 October 2014].

US Department of Education (2009): Race to the Top Program. Executive Summary. Washington (DC).

Weiland, Christina and Hirokazu Yoshikawa (2013): Impacts of a Prekindergarten Program on Children's Mathematics, Language, Literacy, Executive Function, and Emotional Skills, *Child Development* 83 (6). Pp. 2112–2130.

Wheelock College Aspire Institute (2010): Foundation for the Future. Strengthening STEM Education in the Early Years. A Plan for Increasing the Number of Skilled PreK-6 STEM Educators in the Greater Boston Region. Boston (MA). Available from http://www.wheelock.edu/Documents/News/Foundation%20for%20the%20Future%20Report.pdf [Accessed 5 September 2014].

Wheelock College Aspire Institute (2011): Branching Out: Expanding STEM Learning in Massachusetts Early Childhood and Out of School Time Settings. Report on the 2011 ECE & OST STEM Conference. Wheelock College Aspire Institute, Boston (MA). Available from http://www.eec.state.ma.us/docs1/20120305-branching-out.pdf [Accessed 10 September 2014].

Wyeth, Peta and Helen Purchase (2002): Designing Technology for Children: Moving from the Computer into the Physical World with Electronic Blocks, *Information Technology in Childhood Education Annual* 1. Pp. 219–244.

13 The NRC Framework and the Next Generation Science Standards

An opportunity to improve science education in the USA

Arthur Eisenkraft

Introduction: the Framework and NGSS

Improving science education involves modifying curriculum, instruction and assessment. In a nation as large as the United States, where each of the 50 states manages their own school systems and sets their own curriculum, there is a great disparity in what constitutes the amount of science content required by students as well as the depth of coverage and rigour in the science taught. Once again, a new opportunity for positive change in United States education is provided with the creation of the Framework for K-12 Science Education (National Research Council 2012) and the Next Generation Science Standards (NGSS Lead States 2013). Whether these documents will produce the kinds of change that their creators and adopters envision will depend on a number of critical factors, including the ability of teachers to integrate these documents into their science lessons. Creating, teaching and assessing lessons are complex and creative tasks that cannot be fulfilled by simple formula. Various elements of good lessons have to be taken into account. A good lesson is a blend of these elements where the whole is greater than the sum of the parts.

In 1996, the National Academy of Sciences (with representatives from almost all professional scientific societies and associations) took the unprecedented step of publishing the National Science Education Standards (NSES) (National Research Council 1996). At almost the same time, the American Association for the Advancement of Science published its Benchmarks for Science Literacy (AAAS 1993). Both of these documents were attempts to define curriculum that would hopefully be adopted across the nation.

To understand these near simultaneous events within their historical perspective, one should be aware that the United States Constitution deems education to be a state, as opposed to a national, right. Over the past 200 years, the choice of curriculum, instruction and assessment has been the purview of each of the 50 states.

Although neither the NSES nor the Benchmarks were presented as a national curriculum, they were treated as guideposts for many states. These states each created their own version of the NSES and Benchmarks, often referred to as state frameworks. For the first time, there was some consensus about what students should know and be able to do across states.

Almost twenty years later, the National Academy of Sciences released the Framework for K-12 Science Education (National Research Council 2012). This document served as the basis for the Next Generation Science Standards (NGSS) (NGSS Lead States 2013) that are currently being considered for adoption by states across the nation. This followed a related effort to develop a Common Core for mathematics and for English language arts. A majority of states have agreed to adopt these as their state frameworks, as well as agreeing to use common assessment measures (National Governors Association Center for Best Practices, Council of Chief State School Officers 2010). Both the Framework and the NGSS adhere to the idea that science instruction should connect the three dimensions of disciplinary core ideas, crosscutting concepts and science and engineering practices. In addition, the field of engineering is now included in the traditional school curricula of physical, life and earth sciences.

The eight science and engineering practices are:

1   Asking questions (for science) and defining problems (for engineering)
2   Developing and using models
3   Planning and carrying out investigations
4   Analysing and interpreting data
5   Using mathematic and computational thinking
6   Constructing explanations (for science) and designing solutions (for engineering)
7   Engaging in argument from evidence
8   Obtaining, evaluating and communicating information (National Research Council 2012: 3)

The seven crosscutting concepts are:

1   Patterns
2   Cause and effect: Mechanism and explanation
3   Scale, proportion and quality
4   Systems and system models
5   Energy and matter: flows, cycles and conservation
6   Structure and function
7   Stability and change (National Research Council 2012: 84).

The immediate challenge for teachers and curriculum developers is how to align their work with the spirit of the Framework and the letter of the NGSS. The NGSS very specifically outlines 'performance expectations' for students in grades K-12. Two examples of performance expectations are shown below for 10-year-old students with regard to the *5-ESS1*[1] *Earth's Place in the Universe* (NGSS Lead States 2013):

Students who demonstrate understanding can[2]:

- 5-ESS1-1: <u>Support an argument</u> that the <u>*apparent brightness of the sun and stars*</u> is due to their **relative distances** from Earth.
- 5-ESS1-2: <u>Represent data in graphical displays</u> to reveal <u>*patterns*</u> of daily **changes in length and direction of shadows,** day and night, and the seasonal appearance of some stars in the night sky.

The different markings in the text illustrate the performance expectation. Each performance expectation interweaves: <u>*Scientific and Engineering Practices*</u> (engaging in argument from evidence (ESS1-1) or analysing and interpreting data (ESS1-2) and <u>*Disciplinary Core Ideas*</u> (the sun is brighter because it is closer (ESS1-1) or the orbits of Earth around the sun causes observable pattern-like changes in length of shadows (ESS1-2) and **Crosscutting Concepts** (Scale (ESS1-1) or Patterns (ESS1-2)) (Next Generations Science Standard 2014).

Each Performance Expectation in the NGSS also links this work to the Common Core in maths and English language arts.

The strength of the NGSS is that it hints at how students will be assessed. As one can surmise from ESS1-2, it will not suffice for a student to memorize a fact about shadows. The student will have to know how we arrive at that fact through data and be able to demonstrate one way to represent that data. Students will also have to see how this concept fits within the broader context of patterns that are common across all sciences.

Moving from the Framework and NGSS to lesson plans

There are two distinct approaches that one could take in developing lessons that are consistent with NGSS. One is to use the NGSS performance expectation as the seed for the lesson by thinking about ways in which a lesson can include these three dimensions and then constructing the lesson from the NGSS. This approach uses the NGSS as a necessary ingredient for creating lessons. An alternative approach would be to create the best lesson we can and then use the NGSS as a reference to see if we can improve the lesson by inserting elements demanded by NGSS. In this way, NGSS becomes a formative assessment tool for creating the lesson.

I prefer a blended model for curriculum and lesson plan development. One creates the best lesson possible, using as guides and criteria what we know from research, from past practice, and referring to instructional models and now, the NGSS. The lesson should be creative and provide opportunities for all students to meet the articulated goals and outcomes. The draft lesson should then be assessed against the NGSS and instructional models. Where elements of NGSS or the instructional models are missing or are weak, they can now be deliberately added to the draft lesson for an improved final lesson we can use in the classroom.

Some lessons can meet the NGSS and still be poor lessons. By the same token, there can be good lessons that do not meet NGSS. NGSS will be a successful guide for curriculum development when we strive to produce lessons that are both good lessons and meet NGSS.

An example of lesson creation: the shadow lesson

In creating a lesson on shadows, I first adopt the Understanding by Design (or backward design) process (Wiggins and McTighe 2005). Understanding by Design demands that we reject the commonplace approach of teaching for three weeks and then deciding what questions or tasks to put on an examination for the last day of the unit. Understanding by Design says that the first order of business is to articulate the enduring understandings and big ideas that the students should be held responsible for at the end of the unit. I like to think of these enduring understandings as the knowledge that students should retain five years after the series of lessons. This excludes small details and includes broad concepts in context. Once these enduring understandings and big ideas have been articulated, one must decide on the evidence that would be accepted as proof that the students have learnt the concepts. Once that evidence is defined, the lesson planning and instruction should begin. The lesson plans should be created such that the students will be prepared to present the evidence required to convince us that they understand the concepts in the lessons and that these concepts relate to the enduring understandings and big ideas.

Following the Understanding by Design approach, we begin by articulating the Enduring Understandings and Big Ideas.

- Enduring Understandings

    o   Light travels in straight lines
    o   Shadows are formed when light is interrupted by an opaque object
    o   A ray model of light can explain shadows.

We then identify and agree on the evidence that we will accept that a student understands these enduring understandings.

- Evidence of Understanding

    o   Students can create shadows of different sizes
    o   Students can predict changes in shadow lengths and check experimentally
    o   Students can predict changes in shadow lengths and check using a ray model and/or mathematically.

We are now ready to create the lesson.

Improving the lesson using standards and instructional models

The lesson on page 184 meets many attributes of a good lesson. For example, it allows for students to perform an activity before introducing a concept. It also

Table 13.1 Example of a lesson plan on shadows

Activity 1: Students create shadows with a candle, object and screen
Pose the question to the students: 'How can I make the shadow larger?'
Teacher guides students to concept 1: Light travels in straight lines
Teacher guides students to concept 2: Create a ray diagram for light and shadows
Activity 2: Students draw two ray diagrams. They vary either the size of the paper, the distance from the light source or the distance from the screen and note changes in shadow size.
Students now answer the question: 'Does this (ray) model produce the same results as the experiment?'

Source: Edited by the author

connects the activities to a model and has students experimentally determining if the model and data are consistent.

Following this initial creation of the lesson plan using the Understanding by Design approach as outlined, there are certain approaches that can be used as criteria and checks to help improve upon the original lesson. The 7E instructional model (Eisenkraft 2003) reminds us that lessons should *Engage* students, give us the opportunity to *Elicit* their prior understandings, afford students the opportunity to *Explore* the phenomena before *Explaining* their observations and conclusions. The teacher can then assist students in *Elaborating* from these experiences to broader theories as well as *Extending* the ideas to new domains as an example of transfer of knowledge. During all phases of the lesson, the teacher and students are *Evaluating* their understandings.

The 7E instructional model can be used as a template to begin creating a lesson plan. It can and should also be used as a check for the completed lesson plan. After the first draft of the lesson plan, the teacher should see if all elements of the 7E model are adequately addressed. If not, the lesson plan can be modified to better reflect all 7Es. For example, after all the attention devoted to inquiry learning and the need for students to explore the concept, the teacher may realize that not enough attention has been given to the motivation for learning—the Engage. The additional emphasis on Engage will now strengthen the lesson.

In much the same way, the NGSS can be used as an additional check for the completed lesson. Does the lesson give equal weight and attention to all three dimensions of disciplinary core ideas, crosscutting concepts and science and engineering practices? If the crosscutting concepts are only implicit in the lesson, the review is now an opportunity to make this dimension more explicit.

The improved shadow lesson

In reviewing the draft shadow lesson with the 7E instructional model and the NGSS as formative assessment tools, we can make the following improvements of the lesson (*italic* items below are elements from the draft lesson plan):

Table 13.2 Improved example of a lesson plan on shadows

Ask students: 'Upon coming in from outside, why did my shadow disappear?'	Engage (7E)
Ask students: 'What do I need to make a shadow?'	Elicit (7E)
Ask students: 'Can a mouse's shadow be as big as an elephant's shadow?'	Elicit (7E)
Activity 1: Students create shadows with a candle, object and screen such that the shadow sizes for both a large and small object are identical. (The large and small objects signify the elephant and mouse.)	Explore (7E)
After Activity 1, students make a claim: 'To make the shadow larger, I can…'	Engaging in argument from evidence (NGSS) Scale, proportion and quality (NGSS)
How can we explain what you observed?	
Teacher guides students to concept 1: Light travels in straight lines (provide evidence such as rays from sun through clouds, laser light show.)	Explain (7E)
Teacher guides students to concept 2: Create a ray diagram for light and shadows	Explain (7E)
Activity 2: Students draw two ray diagrams. They vary either the size of the paper, the distance from the light source or the distance from the screen and note changes in shadow size.	Explore (7E) Patterns (NGSS)
Students now answer the question: 'Does this (ray) model produce the same results as the experiment?'	Developing and using models (NGSS) Engaging in argument from evidence (NGSS)
Ask students: 'Where does the fuzziness (penumbra) come from?'	Elaborate (7E)
Extension of the model to an extended source.	Elaborate (7E) Developing and using models (NGSS)
Application: Theatre—a play requires a 3-metre tall monster shadow. We don't know how tall the actor is. How can they guarantee the right shadow with any size actor?	Engineering focus (NGSS)
Application: Sundial—design a sundial and explain how it will accurately give the correct time.	Engineering focus (NGSS)
Shadows and eclipses: How can our knowledge of shadows explain a solar and lunar eclipse?	7E (Extend) Additional performance expectation (NGSS) MS-ESS1-1 (see below)

Source: Edited by the author

In a final review of this lesson, we can now see that the 7E instructional model and NGSS were both used to add vital elements to the lesson. In summary, the science content of the lesson includes:

- Light travels in straight lines
- Shadow formation experimentally
- Ray model of light
- Shadow formation using ray model
- Experimental evidence consistent with model
- Point source vs. extended source—umbra and penumbra
- Modification of model.

The engineering content of the lesson includes:

- Theatre-design shadow for a monster
- Sundial.

The lesson incorporated the following NGSS science and engineering practices:

- Developing and using models—ray model for shadow region; penumbra
- Engaging in argument from evidence—claim and evidence—(to make the shadow larger . . .).

The lesson incorporated the following NGSS crosscutting concepts:

- Patterns—ray diagrams
- Scale, proportion, and quality—post-its and mouse/elephant.

The lesson met important parts of the performance expectations for:

- 5-ESS1-2. Represent data in graphical displays to reveal patterns of daily **changes in length and direction of shadows,** day and night, and the seasonal appearance of some stars in the night sky and
- MS-ESS1-1.[3] Develop and use a model of the earth-sun-moon system to describe the cyclic patterns of lunar phases, **eclipses of the sun and moon** and seasons.

Warnings

Just as a good book can be made into a terrible movie, NGSS misinterpretations can lead to poor lessons and poor science education. For example, the NGSS in high school physical science has a performance expectation for Newton's Second Law but none for Newton's First Law or Newton's Third Law. Some mis-guided teachers may interpret this omission to mean that only Newton's Second Law should be taught in high school.

One of the weaknesses of NGSS is the unique pairing of each disciplinary core idea with *one* science and engineering practice and *one* crosscutting concept. There are often other applicable crosscutting concepts and other science and engineering practices. The NGSS is not a curriculum and teachers need to support each disciplinary core idea with multiple crosscutting concepts and multiple science/engineering practices.

Finally, some educators may think of science curriculum as a set of NGSS performance expectations and attempt to build a curriculum comprised of isolated concepts in each discipline. Project-based learning provides an opportunity to relate science concepts into a larger context. In *Active Physics* (Eisenkraft 2010), the shadow lesson would be one part of a larger chapter challenge where students will design and build a 'light and sound show' to entertain their friends. Understanding shadows and using them in the show increases the interest in science and supports learning through the transfer of knowledge to this project.

As teachers learn to create lessons that will meet the spirit of the Framework and the letter of the NGSS, they should take caution and be aware of misconceptions and misinterpretations of these valuable documents.

Conclusion

The creation of the Framework and NGSS holds great promise for improving science education if used as a formative assessment tool to improve carefully created lessons. Rather than using these documents only as a starting point for lessons, a recommended alternative is to create a good lesson and then make it better by applying research and experientially based tools like effective instructional models and the NGSS. Since the Framework and NGSS emphasize engineering, this approach also opens up the possibility of infusing engineering principles into the science curriculum.

Notes

1 The notation 5-ESS1 signifies that this is for grade level five (9-year-old pupils) and it is focused on the content area of Earth and Space Sciences (ESS).
2 The performance expectations regarding the 5-ESS1 Earth's Place in the Universe listed below can be found on the website of the Next Generations Science Standard (2014).
3 MS-ESS1 is a notation that informs readers this performance expectation is targeted for middle school students (MS is ages 11–14) and is closely linked to the discipline of Earth and Space Sciences (ESS).

Bibliography

AAAS (American Association for the Advancement of Science) (1993): Benchmarks for Science Literacy. New York. Available from http://www.project2061.org/publications/bsl/online/index.php [Accessed 18 September 2014].
Eisenkraft, Arthur (2003): Expanding the 5E Model, *The Science Teacher* 70 (6). Pp. 56–59.

Eisenkraft, Arthur (2010): *Active Physics. A Project-Based Inquiry Approach, Physics for All.* It's About Time, Herff Jones Education Division, Armonk (NY).

National Governors Association Center for Best Practices, Council of Chief State School Officers (2010): Common Core State Standards Initiative. National Governors Association Center for Best Practices, Council of Chief State School Officers, Washington (DC). Available from http://www.corestandards.org/ [Accessed 18 September 2014).

National Research Council (US) (1996): National Science Education Standards: Observe, Interact, Change, Learn. National Academy Press, Washington (DC). Available from http://www.nap.edu/catalog.php?record_id=4962 [Accessed 18 September 2014].

National Research Council (US) (2012): A Framework for K-12 Science Education: Practices, Crosscutting Concepts, and Core Ideas. Committee on a Conceptual Framework for New K-12 Science Education Standards. Board on Science Education, Division of Behavioral and Social Sciences and Education. National Academies Press, Washington (DC). Available from http://www.nap.edu/catalog.php?record_id=13165 &utm_expid=4418042-5.krRTDpXJQISoXLpdo-1Ynw.0 [Accessed 18 September 2014].

Next Generations Science Standard (2014): 5-ESS1 Earth's Place in Universe. Washington (DC). Available from http://www.nextgenscience.org/5ess1-earth-place-universe [Accessed 29 September 2014].

NGSS Lead States (2013): Next Generation Science Standards: For States, by States. National Academies Press, Washington (DC).

Wiggins, Grant and Jay McTighe (2005): *Understanding by Design.* Association by Supervision and Curriculum Development (ASCD), Alexandria (Virginia).

Part III

STEM education from a comparative transnational perspective

Part III

STEM education from a
comparative transnational
perspective

14 STEM education from a comparative transnational perspective
Results of a group Delphi process

Dorothea Taube, Ortwin Renn and Andreas Hohlt

Introduction

Due to the diversity of the many factors that influence STEM education in the countries selected, it was necessary to develop a strategy to identify common features, universal trends and unique traditions and developments from the detailed material that underlies the country reports in the previous part of the book. For this purpose the research group launched a Delphi process involving sixty-seven experts from different disciplinary backgrounds and countries. These experts were convened to reflect the participants' differing views and to identify and distinguish universal from idiosyncratic findings.

The Delphi method is a communication technique based on the judgement of a group of experts that was developed as a forecasting tool and prediction instrument, for example, within the context of assessments of the consequences of technology or political consulting.[1]

The results of the Delphi process are presented in the following chapter. Due to the various issues that were discussed within the Delphi, only a selection of the most interesting findings will be presented here.[2] The paper is structured according to the central issues that emerged as major anchors for the discussion during the Delphi process. These issues constitute the framework that highlight the main factors influencing singularities and cross-cultural similarities regarding the countries discussed.

The methodology of Group Delphi

The Delphi method was developed by the RAND Corporation in the 1950s (Dalkey and Helmer 1963). It uses a form of democratic group process to encourage experts to make a consensual 'best guess' about future conditions. The major objective of a Delphi is to compare the judgements of small groups of experts and to identify the areas of uncertainty and dissent among the experts by using plenary discussions. The classic Delphi is conducted by sending questionnaires to individual experts, processing the data and sending a summary of the range of expert opinions back to each expert to comment and to reconsider his or her original judgement. This can be done in numerous iterations until a stable distribution of views has been reached.

Webler *et al.* (1991) suggested a modification of the Delphi method that they called 'Group Delphi.' A Group Delphi is a procedure in which experts convene for a limited time period to discuss a well-defined topic, point out advantages and disadvantages of the proposed options, and rate them on different relevant scales (Schulz and Renn 2009). During a workshop, the plenary group is divided into small groups and given a questionnaire. Each group is asked to respond to the questions and find a consensus among the group members if possible. A break is scheduled after each group has completed the questionnaire. During this break the research team tabulates the results of the first round and identifies variations. In the following plenary session, experts with opinions that deviated most from the median value of all responses are asked to justify their responses in the presence of all other participants. The more a group's ratings deviate from the median of all groups the more time is allocated to this group to defend and substantiate their judgement. This justification procedure serves two purposes:

- All experts are given the relevant information from other participants so that differences in judgements are not based on mere ignorance, but on difference of opinion or on the interpretation of the existing data.
- The Group Delphi produces not only numerical values and distributions, but also verbal explanations for deviations from the median.

After the discussion, the plenary is again divided into small groups. Group composition is based on systematic rotation so that each member of the plenary is working with new group members in each consecutive round. In the second and following rounds, the experts are given a chance to re-assess and re-state their opinions in light of the previous plenary discussions. This process can be repeated until the responses appear to be stabilized. For further information on the typical sequence of a Group Delphi see Renn and Webler (1992: Table 2).

The questionnaire used in a Group Delphi is crucial for the success of the outcome. Unlike a conventional Delphi, questionnaires cannot be totally revised between the rounds of elicitation. However, minor modifications of the questions can be included as part of the plenary discussion following each round. Since consensus is a goal of the process, the responses for the questions must be quantified (either on an ordinal or interval scale) or standardized for categorical variables. Open questions or comments from the participants are encouraged.

The Group Delphi has shown promise as a technique for reducing complexity and uncertainty. It is an example of how the conventional Delphi can be altered to include arguments that express different viewpoints. By using a two-tiered structure of small groups and large groups, the Group Delphi is extremely efficient at defining areas of consensus, but it is limited in size and scope. Due to time restrictions, the questionnaire must be flexible and standardized if the process is to function effectively. Based on these stipulations, the instrument of Group Delphi is not suited for all types of problems, but rather for those that involve a mixture of scientific evidence and social values. Delphi offers flexibility along with a validity that is difficult to achieve with conventional strategies. Linstone and Turoff claim that Delphi is particularly useful when 'the problem does not lend itself to precise analytical techniques but can benefit from subjective judgments on a collective basis' (Linstone and Turoff 2002: 4). These prospects and potentials of the Delphi method were the main reasons the research team used this method for consolidating the results of the reports from each country.

In our specific case, the Delphi process conducted by the research group started with an online questionnaire, which was answered by the experts[3] of those countries central to the research project (Brazil, China, Egypt, India, Japan, South Korea and the USA). The questionnaire was divided into three different parts, taking into account empirical, analytical and conceptual questions focussing on each of the countries, but from a comparative point of view. Another questionnaire that contained identical, but also generic, questions about an overall international comparative approach was sent to international experts. The empirical part of the questionnaire asked for an evaluation of different situations in the field of STEM education while the analytical part concentrated on country specific mechanisms, potential causal influences and specific context conditions. The conceptual part dealt with problem-solving strategies and specific objectives in the different countries and its STEM field.

Based on the evaluation of the online questionnaire, up to three experts from each country were invited to an international workshop at the Berlin-Brandenburg Academy of Sciences and Humanities in Berlin. The workshop was organized in accordance with the main structures of the Group Delphi process described above. It consisted of both small group discussions (country-specific and transnational) and discussions in plenary, plus short presentations on the research groups' most central issues, answered by experts with regard to their country. The main objective was to further discuss the various findings from the country studies, identify commonalities and idiosyncrasies and develop a general framework under which all aspects could be characterized. The process of group discussions and plenary reflections was structured so as to distinguish the nature of dissenting options or ratings. Were they based on varying semantic or conceptual understandings of the terms used, or did they reflect substantive differences in cultural, interpretative or value-based argumentations? In the end, all experts agreed with a summary of the results that emerged from the intensive discussions. However, there were clear dissenting views on different issues among the experts, accompanied by explanations and justifications for each position. The following sections will report on the consensual and dissenting results of the Delphi process using the structural taxonomy that was approved by all participants.

Science and scientists as central forces in striving for growth and innovation

The prestige of scientists and their career opportunities

The concept of prestige in this question refers to the respect that people have for a specific kind of profession. Figure 14.1 shows the results of the assessments of those experts who had responded to this question. The conflicting picture given in the figure can be traced back to differentiations among the STEM disciplines, but also to different evaluations of the current situation, especially in Asian countries, by internal and external experts[4]. In spite of clear differences among the countries, the discussions at the workshop showed that, at the moment, engineers but also medical scientists enjoy particularly high prestige around the world, independent of their income in comparison to other professions. One of the reasons mentioned in the discussions was the visible usefulness of these professions in everyday life. This perception is linked to medical sciences and the perceived role of engineers as central figures in innovative and creative processes of technological improvement and advancement.

In China and South Korea, the experts agreed that the prestige of STEM scientists in general, engineers in particular in China, is relatively high compared with the situation in other countries. This is also reinforced by the predominant agreement shown in Figure 14.1. In all of the Asian countries it became clear that science and technology (S&T) has been a driving force for the countries' development in the past. Asian countries, such as Japan, China, South Korea and India, share a culture of appreciation of hard science, which gives these professions prestige, and reflects a cultural appreciation for understanding and cultivating nature as valuable in itself, independent of personal or national economic advancement. Therefore, the majority of people in these countries share an overall optimistic view of S&T, which in turn leads to a positive image and high levels of appreciation for scientists and technologists (see also Wang *et al.* 2012). According to the International Migration Outlook (OECD 2012), there are increasing numbers of graduates in engineering and sciences in China and India. However, the high

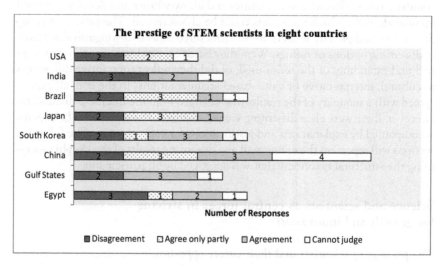

Figure 14.1 The prestige of STEM scientists in your country is higher compared to the situation in other countries included in this study

Source: Edited by the authors

prestige of these professions does not necessarily imply high qualities of education and professional training (OECD 2012: 174f). Often the mere title of engineer or medical doctor is enough to win respect, independent of personal performance.

Interestingly enough, internal and external experts had opposing views on career opportunities in China. While the Chinese expert stressed the various well-paid job opportunities, including promotion programmes for socially disadvantaged families, both external experts were more sceptical about this assessment. They claimed that migration and the number of those seeking employment and study possibilities abroad might indicate constraints and current problems. As a matter of fact, according to an OECD report (2013), 2.3 per cent of China's third-level students are enrolled abroad, compared to 1 per cent of third-level students in Japan or 4.8 per cent in Germany, which is a comparatively high amount. Around 34.4 per cent of international third-level students in Australia and 25.2 per cent of those in the United States come from China. Other countries preferred by Chinese students for third-level education are Japan, South Korea, Canada and New Zealand (OECD 2013: Table C4.3. and C4.5). Furthermore, even though there are increasing numbers of Chinese students deciding to spend some years abroad pursuing further education, the number of returning students is particularly high, as a result of increasing salaries, growing work opportunities and attractive cash funds and salary top-ups for returning graduates (OECD 2012). This may also explain the discrepancy in assessments between the experts: the native expert focused on the opportunities for well-trained professionals while the external experts focused on the constraints and inadequacies of the Chinese secondary and tertiary education system.

The Korean expert Jung-Ok Ha highlighted STEM appreciation in South Korea. In light of the economic crisis and the stagnation of previous years, the role of and interest in educating and recruiting professional scientists has declined and scientists are confronted with a 'more pessimistic real situation than in the past.' The number of graduates in the field of STEM education has increased significantly since 1981, while the job market for these professionals has stagnated. This discrepancy has led to the current situation where it is more difficult for STEM graduates to find a job. In addition, in the past, most STEM graduates found positions in the public sector. This trend has been totally reversed. Today private companies play a particularly important role as job providers in South Korea, in particular to middle class people. Similar to Western countries such as Germany or the United Kingdom, the reliance on volatile markets for professionals in the private sector has reduced the motivation for young Koreans to engage in a STEM education in recent years.

In emerging countries such as Brazil, India and Egypt, people are very optimistic about the role of S&T, but much more pessimistic about the economic opportunities that professional engineers and scientists will experience once they have completed their education. Against the backdrop of current socio-economic development in these countries, experts perceive a growing gap between personal aspirations and economic reality.

For example, the Egyptian experts agreed that in their country, engineers, medical scientists and those in pharmaceutics enjoy a lot of prestige, compared with scientists working in chemistry or physics, or those employed as STEM teachers. Similar to the prestige distribution in Asian countries, medical services and engineered technologies and facilities provide visual representations of what can be accomplished through adequate knowledge and know-how. The importance of, for example, medical science is reflected in it having the most demanding university entry requirements and in the fact that only students with top grades at secondary school are allowed to enter medical school. In step with this situation, employment opportunities are especially promising for engineers and graduates of medicine, while, in general, there is a high rate of unemployment among graduates of other fields of science, such as physics, chemistry and even computer sciences.

There is another problem shared with India and China, at least to some extent. While the number of engineering graduates is increasing, they lack adequate skills to be 'adapted to the needs of the industrial system' (Bond *et al.* 2013: 42). There is an increased demand for practical engineers in manufacturing and basic service provision. However, there is a traditionally negative attitude towards vocational education: usually only students who failed to pass the entrance exam to a university pursue training in this realm. In addition, technical and vocational education suffers from low status, poor funding and poor quality education so that many employers criticize the lack of qualified graduates with adequate training that would be needed to build up industrial development (Loveluck 2012). A different situation occurs in the Gulf States where, faced with a lack of qualified experts, professionals and even students from other countries (such as Egypt and the USA) are attracted to fill the gap.

The Indian expert added that being a scientist in India is also associated with better opportunities to visit or work in Western countries and is therefore quite a popular occupation in India. Nevertheless, the situation in India has changed over the last two decades: job opportunities—especially for those with PhDs— have improved significantly, and STEM graduates, in particular, do not have problems finding employment at home.

In contrast to the emerging Asian and Arabic countries, the experts on the educational system in the USA agreed that one of the current challenges in the USA is the lack of prestige for and a general lack of interest in STEM subjects. Furthermore, the perception of STEM scientists is still influenced by stereotypes such as the rocket scientist, who is smart and intelligent, but also of science as a very theoretical and overall difficult subject that often lacks practicability. Similar to the situation in Europe there is less motivation to study the hard subjects, since a STEM education is no guarantee of a future career and lifelong security.

As a result of the Delphi discussion, all participants shared the resulting conclusion that prestige is strongly connected to social perceptions of what a society defines as specifically useful and needed. Furthermore, if STEM education is associated with improved career opportunities, high-income expectations and secure employment possibilities, the motivation to engage in a hard science education programme is heightened. Social prestige and expectations of future job security are strongly linked. This was particularly true for professions such as doctors, firefighters or technical designers. However, graduates from other STEM areas have few problems finding a job, too, even in the business sector, as long as they show impressive competence in their field. In countries where the quality of STEM education is below the international standard, companies try to hire qualified personnel from other countries in order to be competitive in a globalized market economy.

STEM education in public school systems and public awareness programmes

There are many differing views on the role of the state in fostering STEM education through the public school system and through awareness programmes.

Figures 14.2 and 14.3 illustrate that, particularly in the Asian countries of China, South Korea and Japan, most of the experts strongly agree that STEM education is a central component of the public school system and that many public and private initiatives exist to make STEM more attractive.

In contrast, the experts from Brazil and Egypt shared the impression that both countries face serious problems regarding STEM education in public schools and lack effective public awareness programmes. Furthermore, Egypt and Brazil are reported to have serious structural problems regarding both primary and secondary education. Indicators for such structural problems are: lack of qualified teachers, lack of laboratories and other institutional conditions for conducive learning environments, extensive but widely ineffective mandatory curricula and a focus on memorizing and reiterating facts instead of experimenting or discovery-oriented learning experiences (see also the contribution by the experts on Brazil and Egypt in this book). Additionally, there are very few science

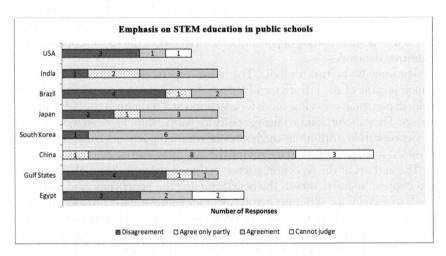

Figure 14.2 There is much emphasis on STEM education in the public school system

Source: Edited by the authors

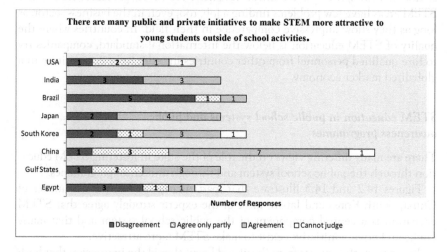

Figure 14.3 Public and private initiatives outside of school activities
Source: Edited by the authors

museums and science centres, zoos, aquaria, etc. in either country. Private initiatives to compensate for the lack of interesting and competent science education do not exist. Only recently have private corporations and public institutions realized the seriousness of the situation and started new programmes to work towards a public understanding of science and to offer support for gifted students. However, these initiatives are still very fragmented. The experts from both countries stressed that current initiatives need more integrated cooperation between industries and educational institutions at all levels. The main objective should be to inform young people about future prospects and work opportunities and to design training opportunities to better meet the socio-economic and industrial demand.

The same is also true for India. The Indian experts especially highlighted the important role of the private sector for research and development of the STEM field, in particular providing funds for education and training in the field of technology. They also underlined the necessity for partnerships between industry and higher education institutions (high schools, vocational schools, colleges and universities) as a prerequisite to improving the quality of science education.

The authors of the report on science and innovation in Egypt claim that in this context 'industry is both the benefactor and the beneficiary' and therefore needs to account for a stronger involvement for improving the situation in vocational and technological education' (Bond *et al.* 2013: 44). Due to instability and lack of financing since the Arab Spring, current reforms in Egypt, such as the ones aiming at reforming teaching methods, have been announced but not yet implemented. In contrast, the Gulf States have invested heavily in STEM education: modernizing reforms have been pushed forward, accompanied by the introduction of new teaching aids and instructional technologies. New teachers have also been hired from abroad to improve graduates' levels of competence. However, these reforms still clash with a slowly changing cultural environment in which traditional academic freedom and creative and critical thinking were not highly appreciated (for detailed information see Chapter 9 on the GCC countries by Nicole C. Karafyllis). Yet the situation is changing, albeit at a very slow speed.

One should keep in mind that the STEM situation in Brazil, Egypt and, to an extent, India is not different to the situation found in other subjects, which also lack effective educational structures. In these countries it is therefore essential to focus on the entire educational system in order to provide access to basic education for all young people and to improve educational standards and results. Therefore, reforms need to address the educational system as a whole, not just select subjects. On this topic, the experts working on STEM education in Brazil criticized the fact that current investments and reforms are particularly focussed on creating more prestigious universities and building a technical elite while ignoring the various problems that exist in basic education, such as traditional learning and teaching methods, high numbers of students per class, lack of quality of teacher education and so on. Therefore they predict that, under current political and educational conditions, both primary and secondary education will fail to attain the desired improvements because the elite universities have too little basis from which they can draw qualified students. In addition, there is a geographic problem: due to the lack of industrialization in the north and northeast, skilled and educated people usually move to the south in order to find adequate employment. This leads to further damage to the northern parts of Brazil, something that can only be stopped by improving basic education in local communities.

The situation of STEM education in the USA is also contingent on location, but for different reasons. Different states pursue different policies when it comes to the promotion of STEM education. Some states do not invest at all in STEM education beyond normal education expenditures (most of which is covered by the local municipalities); others have launched ambitious and far-reaching initiatives for improving the educational standard for STEM. Overall, Yvonne Spicer stressed that most states can be found somewhere along a spectrum between doing nothing and pursuing an ambitious programme. They have invested some funds and initiated some programmes, but they have not embraced STEM in the way she would consider necessary for educating a competent scientifically and technologically literate student. In general, there is a stronger emphasis on STEM in grades 9–12 compared with the lower grades. Additionally, strong emphasis is put on mathematics while technology and engineering are rarely taught, and if taught at all this is in relation to physics or direct vocational training. To remedy this situation there are many initiatives supporting a stronger integration of those subjects into school curricula (see Arthur Eisenkraft's contribution to this book, Chapter 13). The problem of engineering and technological education has also been pointed out by most of the other experts, especially those from India and Egypt. Technology, for instance, is rarely addressed in primary and secondary schools, and if it is done at all it is only in the context of applied science.

Motivation and interest—important factors for young people's involvement in STEM

Motivational aspects of young people engaging in STEM education

Worldwide, there is an intensive debate about the factors that influence what motivates young people to study STEM subjects. There is a clear trend showing that motivation and interest in S&T are decreasing in most countries, and that professional careers in S&T have become less attractive (Potvin and Hasni 2014). As most of the research comes from and focuses on North America and Europe, the Delphi study provides interesting insight into the motivational situation in South America, the Middle East and some parts of South-East Asia.

As a result of the discussion, three groups can be identified, with regard to intrinsic and extrinsic motivational reasons. The first group (including the USA but also most European countries) can be characterized by a dominance of intrinsic motivation over extrinsic factors such as high income or social prestige. Self-fulfilment, an affinity for STEM subjects and self-perceived personal talent for these subjects play a crucial role as motivational factors for young students. For this reason, programmes that aim to raise the attractiveness of STEM subjects try to arouse curiosity in STEM subjects among youngsters and to support talented students from the beginning.

For the second group, which largely featured the Asian countries, extrinsic motivations are most important, according to the experts on these countries. One of the Korean experts proclaimed during the Delphi plenary discussions: 'Korean students study what they hate most!' Even though this statement was meant as a provocation, it illustrates that in South Korea and in other Asian countries, students' motivation is strongly driven by external factors such as career opportunities, high social prestige, high income aspirations, but also meeting family expectations since the family has invested much of its income to support the student's education.

The third group includes countries that can be described as being in transition, such as Egypt, Brazil and India. In this group of countries, one can find mixtures of the two motivational drivers. Extrinsic motivation is particularly characteristic of students with socially deprived backgrounds, who see STEM education as a driving force that fosters social mobility and the opportunity to reach better life opportunities. Particularly in the STEM field, people from less privileged backgrounds have the opportunity to climb up the social class ladder. At the same time, intrinsic motivational factors gain more and more importance, particularly among those coming from middle and high social classes, as they have the liberty to choose from a variety of opportunities. STEM education is only a career option if they are intrinsically motivated. This is particularly true for Brazil.

Initiatives to increase young peoples' interest in STEM

In the context of the Delphi process, participants were also asked to evaluate the various national programmes or projects aimed at raising young peoples' interest in STEM.

From a transnational perspective, three priorities emerged during the Delphi discussions. All participants agreed that early contact with S&T is crucial in attracting young people to S&T. Hence, STEM subjects should be integrated into early childhood education in order to raise the interest and mobilize talent. This insight drives the general trend in almost all countries to shift emphasis from older grades to lower grades and to invest more in early childhood education (see also e.g. Tao, Oliver and Venville 2012). However, this trend is pronounced to differing degrees in the countries included in this analysis.

The second priority touches upon teaching methods. There has been a universal shift towards creative, interactive and application-oriented STEM teaching methods, in particular inquiry-based learning. Recreating the way in which science is taught has become a critical factor from a transnational perspective. This is also reflected by current international literature (Abd El Khalick *et al.* 2004; Potvin and Hasni 2014). Additionally, experts highlighted the necessity for an interdisciplinary approach within and beyond the STEM field. The need for reforming teaching methods and teaching styles is supported by studies on the cultural aspects of learning. For example Cobern and Aikenhead (2003) concluded that it is important for children to see the relationships between the various components of knowledge that they acquire during STEM lessons and the applicability of their knowledge to everyday experiences.

Strongly connected to the issue of teaching methods is the qualification of STEM teachers, which is seen as a prerequisite for the improvement of the overall situation in STEM education. The majority of the experts agreed that there is a particular need to strengthen teacher qualification in STEM education if students are going to become more interested and more motivated to pursue further studies in the STEM fields. The Chinese expert reported that evaluation projects for teachers have now been implemented and that China has launched a major programme for improving the quality of teacher education. The system in China is based on mutual assessment and peer evaluation among teachers, who have their performance constantly monitored in relation to their fellow teachers. Rachel Murphy confirms this: assessment and competition play an important role in improving the quality of teachers as well as students skills in China. The aim is to raise the overall population quality (*suzhi*) to keep pace with modernization efforts in the country. But even though reformers emphasize new and innovative teaching and learning methods, rote-learning, memorization and testing remain central elements of the Chinese educational system of *suzhi* with the consequence that creative and open learning experiences are rarely given (Murphy 2004).

Mathematician and sinologist Andrea Bréard stressed another important aspect that characterizes science education not just in China, but in South Korea too: national pride and its incorporation into science education, for instance, through the use of specific symbols—such as the compass—as an early Chinese achievement. The importance of scientific innovation and accomplishments for the countries' own development is constantly displayed and repeated throughout the curricula, demonstrating and reinforcing the need to motivate students to engage themselves for the advancement of society as one of the means for the nation to reach the top in the global competition. To this effect, the South Korean expert Jung-Ok Ha stressed the importance of family expectations as the main driver in students' decisions on the subject they are going to study. Paying back what the parents invested in one's education is a driving force for choosing subjects that promise high career opportunities, income and prestige (see also the previous section on motivational aspects). These family obligations are much more important than the recommendation of a teacher or even a student's self-assessed interest or affinity for the subject. Jung-Ok Ha nevertheless conceded that in recent years new and more flexible learning approaches to the hard sciences have been introduced in the South Korean system as a means of raising intrinsic motivation and interesting young people in engaging in STEM subjects, since intrinsically motivated students are likely to perform better in their professional life.

Indicating the coexistence of intrinsic and extrinsic motivational aspects, Brazilian and Egyptian experts highlighted the importance of improving both intrinsic and extrinsic conditions in order to boost motivation. The schools should become better in order to stimulate young peoples' fascination with nature and technology, and society should emphasize the external rewards of a STEM career that could meet family expectations, raise social status and prestige and provide secure job opportunities. The Chinese experts put greater stress on the extrinsic aspects of motivation: they believed that providing secure job opportunities and high salaries would be sufficient to have enough professionals in the STEM area to meet national demand.

Interesting differences emerged when the issue of migration and job opportunities worldwide were discussed. In both China and Japan, the fear that talented graduates would leave the country after their education and migrate to other (mostly) Western countries was not regarded as a major challenge or problem. According to these experts, the number of people leaving their home country for good is insignificant compared to the overall number of graduates. This impression has been confirmed by the OECD (2012). At the same time, these countries also see no major need to become more attractive to foreign students or professionals, except for specialists that cannot be recruited from the domestic work force.

This is different in the USA. The performance of the US economy is still highly reliant on new immigrants. Migrants and their descendants are seen as an important group that is capable of readdressing the shortage of skilled professionals. Globalization, with its rapid expansion of goods and services worldwide, has also become an important driver of the labour market, especially in the STEM field, and has shed new light on worldwide movements of professionals. While European countries continue to face problems when trying to attract the best and the brightest, the typical immigrant countries such as the USA, Australia and Canada have maintained an agenda to invite brain power in the hard sciences from all over the world (rather than giving everybody a chance to start anew). Brazil, in particular, has realized the potential gain that an active government involvement can play in attracting highly skilled professionals from abroad and retaining those who have passed the elite educational programme. Programmes such as 'Science Without Borders' have been implemented, sending the country's brightest students abroad, but providing enough incentives to bring them back home. Brazilians have realized that increased mobility across borders does not lead to a brain drain as previously feared, but rather to a more rapid modernization of the native work force. Investing in mobility is not only good for individual careers but are also for society as a whole.

Scepticism versus open-mindedness towards science and technology

Cross-cultural similarities also emerge when it comes to open-mindedness[5] towards S&T and the relationship between science appreciation and the economic status of the country. The experts agreed that the two phenomena are connected, although differences can be carved out concerning the particular direction.

Figure 14.4 illustrates the agreement among the experts about the presumed relationship between economic status and open-mindedness. This relationship can be seen to be particularly close in South Korea and China.

The experts from the US and Europe claimed that a high degree of modernization and affluence creates a mental distance between technological advancement and public attitudes towards technology and technical change. The reasons for this disenchantment with the promises of technical progress are mainly the (subjective) experience of negative side effects of modernization (Beck 2003) but also the diversity of routes for social mobility that are not limited to a STEM career. These days, members of lower classes and immigrants have more options than sending their kids to technical schools in order to advance their social status. However, on the micro-level, higher education and higher social classes are positively associated with a favourable attitude towards technological change

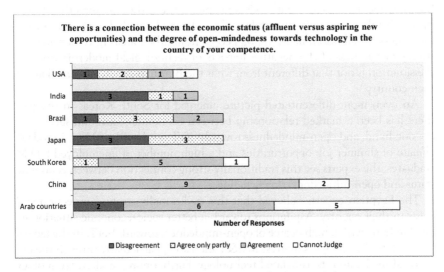

Figure 14.4 Connection between economic status and open-mindedness

and globalization. The more affluent and wealthy people are, the more open-minded towards STEM they tend to be because modern technologies provide more access to resources and services and they regard technological advancement as a benefit for their life. This positive association is, however, not related to improved chances of recruiting young people for scientific education or careers. In the USA, as in most other OECD countries, one can observe a more distanced attitude towards technological change as 'progress' and decreasing attractiveness of STEM careers among young people, in particular for those in middle and high-income brackets.

The Brazilian experts share this opinion. They acknowledged that technical optimism in Brazil is widespread, particularly among those people who do not know much about science. The more literate people are about S&T, the more they tend to be sceptical with respect to the negative impacts on environment, health and social standards. They also point out that the poorer sections of the population associate upward social mobility and improved opportunities with technical modernization, whereas members of upper classes feel more affected by the risks and negative side effects of modernization.

The Chinese experts did not agree with this negative relationship between social classes and open-mindedness when analysing the situation in their own country. They stressed that public acceptance of modern technologies goes along with economic development, while less educated societies tend to have stronger sceptical opinions towards S&T. In line with this argument they also claimed that people in rural areas might not be as positive as those in urban areas. In general, Chinese people accept that 'nothing comes for free' and that industrialization comes with collateral and environmental damage. However, some of the external experts on China argued that scepticism and protest against technological change and its consequences has become more visible in middle class and high-income urban neighbourhoods if people feel that they are directly affected by health-related or environmental problems. Examples include air pollution and food safety. In addition, many young people from urban areas have developed a stronger awareness of the negative impacts of technological modernization. So the situation is not that different from what the Brazilian experts observed about their country.

An even more differentiated picture emerged for South Korea. In the past there has been a marked relationship between economic status and success on the one hand, and open-mindedness towards S&T on the other. Now, in today's climate of slimmer job opportunities and a high number of unemployed STEM graduates, the experts see this traditionally strong connection between economic status and open-mindedness slowly fading.

The Egyptian experts believed that this traditionally strong connection still exists in their country. Aspirations towards a better socio-economic situation go hand in hand with a high degree of open-mindedness towards S&T. In the face of the Arab Spring, people's interest in S&T increased, particularly through the use of social media and its associated technology. Furthermore, modern technology was regarded as part of the country's advancement towards more political freedom and consumer sovereignty. In addition, for some years now, since the revolution, the importance of S&T for Egypt's development has been stressed and fostered. Therefore, people expect that a solid education in S&T will open up improved job opportunities.

The same is also true for India. There is a strong enthusiasm for S&T as a means to develop and raise the standard of living. People are generally very open-minded towards S&T. An exceptional example is Japan. There was strong hostility towards Western technology during the twentieth century's world wars, and it was only in the second half of the century that Japanese people realized the beneficial effects of technology. In addition, the ROSE study on young people's attitudes to science shows that even today, Japanese young people have rather negative and reluctant attitudes towards S&T compared with their counterparts in other countries (Sjøberg 2012). This is rather surprising, since the image of 'technofreaks' has been widely associated with Japanese culture. However, as one expert detailed: since Japan did not share the stage of enthusiasm for technological progress that was so typical for Western countries in the late nineteenth century and again in the 1950s, they have developed more realistic expectations (similar to the Chinese attitudes towards technology) about the inevitability of risks when engaging in new technological changes. They did not experience the disenchant-ment with S&T related to the second modernization period (Giddens and Pierson 1998), and their disappointment about the negative side effects of modernization was less pronounced since they did not expect anything better. So they turned out to be more content with the consequences of technological change in their coun-try. In addition, Japanese culture has developed a marked fascination with playful uses of technologies. This has been and still is particularly visible when looking at the positive attitude towards robotics and artificial service providers.

In addition to the issue of technological open-mindedness versus scepticism, the experts discussed two related topics: 'trust in advocates of science and tech-nology' and 'level of scientific literacy.' In Brazil and Egypt 'trust in advocates for science' is seen as a given. Hardly any other profession has been rated as more trustworthy than representatives of the scientific and technological elite. Past occasions of bad risk management have not shaken the common belief that S&T are agents of progress and their representatives deserve trust. However, as stated before, a growing portion of the Brazilian population, in particular from the high-income groups, have started to question the positive benefit-to-risk ratio of technological change. This group is also likely to engage in environmental action groups and other representations of civil society. However, the majority of the population is still convinced that more technology and better science will be in the public interest and will benefit all of society, not only the rich. This corresponds with the fact that in Egypt and Brazil the media are very reluctant to report on possible negative aspects of new technological and scientific inquiries. For instance, even though the construction of the Aswan Dam came along with considerable negative ecological and social impacts, there was little discussion of these impacts in the media and, in general, ordinary people were not aware of these consequences.

In contrast to the positive image that S&T generally enjoys, the experts from both countries complained that research institutions devoted to investigating nature or developing innovative technology are held in much lower public esteem and are often seen as undeserving beneficiaries of tax payers' money. These institutions, for example the Academy of Science in Brazil, are also the target of frequent attacks by politicians. They are depicted as theorists who have little knowledge about the real problems of the world.

Therefore, awareness about the opportunities and risks associated with new scientific insights and technological advances takes various forms within each country and between the countries. The public in the USA, Japan and Europe takes active part in a public discourse on S&T fostered through the media and partially shaped by civil society organization. They also engage in open debate about positive and negative potential aspects of scientific and technological changes. In contrast, the public debate in India, China, South Korea and, especially, Egypt focuses on economic benefits of scientific and technological advances for individual social mobility and economic welfare.

Scientific literacy and the outcome of STEM education

The discussions on scientific literacy emphasized the importance of scientific literacy in all the countries studied. The term literacy, however, has different meanings or different dimensions of what it covers. The meaning of literacy is anchored in historical, cultural and socio-economic traditions in each country. While some of the countries place special emphasis on strengthening the education of specialists and creating an elite knowledge culture (South Korea, Japan), others focus more on advancing the scientific knowledge of the general public (many European countries, but also post-revolutionary Egypt) and others try to find the right balance between elite and general education (USA).

Egypt is an interesting example. The education system used to rely strongly on elite education rather than raising scientific literacy among the broader public. The Egyptian experts at the Delphi criticized the lack of public literacy. They witnessed, however, a change towards policies that stress the importance of improving basic scientific literacy in order to foster the establishment of a scientific culture. In countries such as China and Brazil this shift towards raising scientific literacy among the entire population has also taken place in previous years, based on the argument that increasing scientific literacy in the population will be a central condition and driving force for the further development of the country. In contrast, highly industrialized countries such as South Korea and the US regard scientific literacy as a prerequisite for increasing the number of highly educated and motivated STEM professionals, with the aim to reverse the declining interest and number of students in the field of S&T. In Europe scientific literacy has been a central element of basic educational goals. In addition, literacy is seen as a corrective to a widespread scepticism towards S&T, although the empirical evidence that more education would lead to more acceptance is weak and in some areas, such as in genetically modified organisms, even reversed. Since the 1970s the EU has investigated public attitudes towards S&T in different science-related surveys, most prominently the Eurobarometer (Liu, Tang and Bauer 2011). So, for many European countries, investments in education and scientific literacy are driven by three related objectives: (a) to recruit enough STEM professionals to meet the demand of knowledge-based societies, (b) to raise the general level of literacy so people understand and comprehend their own livelihood, which is increasingly shaped by S&T and (c) to create more open-mindedness among the population in order to generate a favourable atmosphere towards innovation.

All three objectives are echoed in each of the countries included in our study. Yet countries place different emphasis on one of the three. Countries on the path of modernization want to create a scientific and technical elite that would be able to promote the path to modernization, while countries that have already reached a high level of modernization are more eager to make sure that they recruit enough professionals to sustain and even improve their industrial standing. In general, basic scientific literacy is strongly associated with the idea of modern citizenship and seen as a precondition for coping with the growing relevance of technology in everyday life.

In the questionnaire the experts were also asked to evaluate the importance of potentially influential factors such as culture, religion, economic situation, institutional and political structure, the educational system and teaching methods on the structure and outcome of STEM education. Even though the experts came from different disciplinary backgrounds they all agreed that culture—with its different facets—strongly influences traditions, structures and processes of STEM education in each of the societies studied. The experts specifically focused on differences in social expectations, lifestyle preferences and dominant style of collective decision making (based on hierarchy, competition or cooperation). There was less of a focus, however, on religion or cultural traditions (see end of this section). On the individual level, the experts agreed on the importance of subgroups, such as the family and peer groups, and the shaping force of popular role models that create and reinforce expectations and cultural meanings associated with scientific and technological changes. Many of these attributions and associations have historical roots and are invisibly inscribed in the overall expectations and images of S&T. On the collective level, institutional structures and decision-making styles have a strong impact on the role and function of S&T in society. The more hierarchically a society is structured, the more S&T education is directed towards creating a knowledge elite and building instrumental knowledge pools. More competitive societies place more emphasis on making all people knowledge-literate in order to provide equal opportunities for all to compete for positions and resources. Finally, cultures that emphasize cooperation and equality encourage open debate and promote prescient technological behaviour that leads to a prior assessment of risks and benefits before the knowledge is applied. Both individual and collective factors not only direct the political vision of a country in this field, but also shape the overall institutional framework and structure in the field of S&T.

208 Dorothea Taube, Ortwin Renn and Andreas Hohlt

Beyond cultural and historical traditions, all the experts judged educational structure and teaching methods to be one of the most important factors influencing the outcome of STEM education. Even more so, all the experts believed that independent of cultural roots and tradition, teaching S&T works best if it is based on problem-solving exercises, inquiry-based learning and self-experimentation (see also Potvin and Hasni 2014). Brazil, China and Egypt still value a learning culture based on memorization and imitation, but they have also started a gradual transition towards this more effective and motivating teaching style.[6] In light of current international research, all the other countries are already on a trajectory towards inquiry-based and other modern forms of learning methods, but they are at different stages of progression. Additionally, within the overall educational system, teachers need to have access to more effective instructional material and all necessary equipment in order to conduct practical and interactive science lessons. The new paradigm illustrates teachers as facilitators of learning and not as disseminators of knowledge.

It's not surprising that the experts recommended that effective, innovative and continuous STEM education should be given political priority and adequate funding. In particular, the experts from Egypt and Brazil stressed the importance of developing an overall direction and vision for the future of STEM education, as well as the political will to prioritize the enforcement of more comprehensive changes that work towards more effective and inclusive STEM education (see also Wafa 2013). With respect to financing, the experts realized and acknowledged that public money for education is limited. Therefore they favoured public-private partnerships (over private funding of education) when it comes to financing these new STEM initiatives. An increasing number of transnational corporations such as Toyota Motor Cooperation (Japan), General Electric (USA) and E.On (Germany) already provide large amounts of funding for research and development and have become important players in the field of S&T worldwide. Their presence in this field underlines the importance of S&T, in that supporting the field of S&T is in their own interests in getting a qualified workforce. However, the experts agreed that education should still be governed by public authorities to ensure equal access to basic and higher education for all segments of the population.

Final point: religion. All experts agreed that the religious factor has been overstated in the media and in popular assessments of educational styles. The experts from China, Japan, South Korea and the USA agreed that religion plays a major role in shaping cultures and belief systems but only through these secondary systems do they exert a major influence on STEM education or attitudes towards S&T. So religion has to be understood as an integral part of culture, which in turn influences STEM education. Nasser Mansour also pointed out that the role of individual religious beliefs of teachers could have an effect on what teachers convey to their students. If S&T are perceived as components of a Western, secular worldview, rejection on religious grounds is more likely to occur. However, such anti-science sentiments are deliberately promoted by specific political groups that exploit religious beliefs for their own political goals (for a deeper discussion on the role of religion and culture see Chapter 8 in this book on STEM education in Egypt by Ghada Gholam and Nasser Mansour).

There are dogmas in some religions that contradict scientific insights (such as evolutionary theory in biology) but this is not a signal of anti-science attitudes or a disregard for scientific education. The same people that reject evolutionary theory embrace new technologies and scientific accomplishments in other areas. The same was said for Muslim and Hindu religious beliefs and their relationship to S&T. According to the experts from the Asian countries, the romantic notion about Asian traditions of prioritizing nature over technology has little influence on the concrete appreciation of industrial processes and technological applications. There is also little religious influence on STEM outcome in Brazil, although the experts indicated that religious arguments gain more and more importance in some scientific applications, such as genetically modified food or the use of embryo cells for research. Therefore, with regard to some particular topics, religious arguments might influence peoples' opinions and beliefs about S&T.

Gender—challenges for female scientists

Figure 14.5 shows the various assessments of gender differences in career opportunities for women in the countries studied. The experts from the USA, Brazil and China concluded that gender differences have little impact on career opportunities, unlike in other countries. In contrast, the experts on South Korea and the Gulf States confirmed that gender plays a major role in S&T. The other countries are located between the two extremes.

The experts from the USA explained their positive assessment by pointing out that the USA invested heavily in providing and sustaining equal opportunities

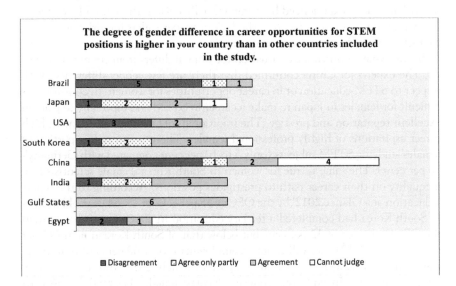

Figure 14.5 Gender differences in career opportunities for women

for male and female scientists.[7] Such efforts are less pronounced or even entirely lacking in other countries. The experts agreed that women who have been successful in becoming STEM professionals still face constraints and barriers in most countries, but they will experience increasingly satisfactory career opportunities, particularly in the situation of a globalized market.

One of the primary reasons for gender differences is the difficulty women face in reconciling career and family life. Other aspects include different role models, social or cultural expectations or traditional models of division of labour between men and women. For instance, in Egypt the number of women at universities and explicitly in scientific subjects is relatively high (more than half of the students are women). However, this high portion of women is not reflected in the professional job market. Women in Egypt are less likely to start a career as professionals in STEM education but are more likely to become a kindergarten or primary school teacher due a lack of appreciation of women in scientific environments. The women in Gulf States face somewhat similar problems, but also need to cope with another challenge: in the past it was difficult for highly educated women to find a husband. However, these days more and more Emirati men appreciate highly educated women and consider a union with them as more prestigious.

Within each country one can also observe differences between rural and urban areas. In rural areas, men have a growing appreciation for women who are able to earn their own income, in order to cope with higher costs of life.

The majority of Indian and Brazilian experts shared this moderately optimistic outlook. In Brazil it has become easier for women to start a career in academia, and in science in particular. In India, particularly in the field of S&T, women come close to full equality in this field. Female scientists experience that working in a lab offers convenient conditions with regular hours and a safe work environment. Difficulties experienced by women usually exist at the school level due to infrastructural limitations (such as the lack of proper toilets for girls) and access to institutions of higher education or training.

In the Asian countries, the situation for women differs from country to country. The experts for China confirmed that there are few gender differences with respect to STEM education or in career opportunities for women. In contrast, it is difficult for females in Japan to make a career in STEM and especially to gain an excellent reputation and prestige. The traditional role models conflict with high career aspirations of highly professional females. There is a very low portion of females studying STEM subjects (only 5 to 10 per cent compared with Germany's 30 per cent). The same is true for women in South Korea. Female scientists face inequality on their career path to prestigious positions. According to the report 'Education at a Glance 2012' by the OECD, 35 per cent of 25–64 year-old women in South Korea had completed a tertiary education in 2010. This is better than the OECD average of 32 per cent but below that of South Korean men (44 per cent) (Chung 2012). Regarding active employment, only 60 per cent of tertiary-educated South Korean women are employed, which is the lowest rate among OECD countries. In addition, college educated females between 25–64 earn

65 per cent of what equally qualified men earn. This is much larger than the OECD average (Chung 2012). The authors of the report conclude that specific policy measures are needed to improve the situation for highly educated women in South Korea. 'These could include increasing the availability of affordable, flexible, high-quality childcare services, providing maternity and paternity leave, and offering flexible working hours' (Chung 2012: 2). Currently, medical schools increasingly take this recommendation seriously and have started to improve this situation and develop specific programmes for women.

Worldwide, the situation of women in STEM fields has improved when compared with previous years, but women still face inequality on the career path to highly prestigious positions. In some countries, such as the US, Europe and, increasingly, the Gulf States, the lack of qualified staff in STEM fields and the declining interest in STEM subjects among young people has led to active policies to improve the career opportunities for women.

Conclusions

The Delphi process provided new insights into the cultural, social, historic and structural factors that shape the image of S&T in different countries and their impact on the attractiveness of the different STEM education approaches in each of the selected countries. The Delphi process is based on a procedure of assessment and re-assessment of expert judgements in the light of arguments and evidence. The process helps to find either consensual judgements that can be supported by mutually agreeable evidence and convincing implications or by consensus about dissent, providing coherent arguments for different interpretations of often complex and contradictory empirical material.

The first major result of the Delphi process is that, in spite of the universal character of science as academic disciplines, the public image of STEM and STEM education as well as the structures and processes of the educational system differ in the seven countries selected for the review. The countries include: Brazil, China, Egypt, India, Japan, South Korea and the USA. Beyond all the differences and uniqueness of STEM in each of these seven countries, the Delphi revealed several insights and implications that emerged from the comparative review of the country reports and the Delphi discussion:

1   In addition to the universal validity of the content of scientific inquiry and knowledge, the experts also agreed on the best teaching method and style that would be most effective for conveying both scientific methods of inquiry and the already established body of knowledge. Inquiry-based learning, self-experimentation and group-learning were the favoured teaching methods recommended by all experts for teaching STEM, independent of culture, religion, nationality or political structure.

2   The popular theory that countries in the process of modernization place more importance on STEM education's ability to meet the demand for facilitating

the modernization process was only partially confirmed. This theory seems to be true for some countries such as China and, to a lesser extent, India, but is not true for others, such as Brazil or Egypt. Another major variable is the degree of governmental commitment to STEM expressed in funding education, motivating young students and offering career opportunities.

3   Confirmed, however, was the theory that young students in countries that are in the middle of a modernization process experience strong external motivation to commit themselves to STEM careers. However, such external motivation (social mobility, high prestige, high income) may not coincide with talent or interest, so that people might study what they are least qualified to do (this was specifically the case in South Korea). Only if countries succeed in combining external and internal motivation can one expect that the quantity and the quality of STEM education will go hand in hand.

4   The same is true for countries with a high degree of affluence and economic performance, but seen from an opposite angle. Here, students only engage in STEM education if they are intrinsically motivated and feel attracted to the disciplines. However, if this is not supported by public programmes, there is not an adequate supply of professionals. This applies to the USA, but also to many European countries and Japan. Here, public initiatives are needed to help young people discover their own talents and interest in STEM and, specifically, to recruit talented students from those social groups that tend to avoid academic careers in STEM such as females, migrants or specific ethnic minorities.

5   A large proportion of students studying STEM does not necessarily mean that they will enter a professional career. Many obstacles such as traditional gender roles, hierarchies in economic and political elites and mobility barriers effectively reduce the potential impact for the creation of a professional and innovative workforce.

6   Elements of cultural traditions and socio-political structures play a major role in the organization of STEM education, as well as in the public image associated with STEM disciplines and professions. However, all countries assign high prestige to professions that have a direct impact on the wellbeing of society, such as physicians, architects and engineers. This is also true for cultures that are normally associated with a high appreciation for humanity and contemplation, such as Japan, parts of India and Korea.

7   The influence of religion on STEM education was seen as much less pervasive than is often depicted in the public media. The experts agreed that if scientific insights directly contradict religious beliefs (such as evolutionary theory), religious beliefs may be more powerful in forming public attitudes, and scientific curricula may be changed or modified. However, such conflicting experiences do not impact the public (positive) image of S&T and do not lead to a call for 'alternative' science.

8   The Delphi group also discussed the role of women in STEM education. All experts agreed that equal opportunities for women and men are not offered in any of the countries in our review. Only one Chinese expert insisted that his country does not discriminate against women in STEM careers. Other

Chinese experts did not agree with this statement but conceded that the political will of gender equality together with the one-child policy has made traditional differences less pronounced. Other countries, such as the USA, have launched many programmes to promote gender equality with measurable success, whereas others, such as Japan, have not even tried to improve the ratio of females entering STEM careers.

The Delphi analysis underlined that economic, social and political structures impact STEM education and training, but that all these different countries share common or similar problems and developments. Both emerging countries, which see S&T as a driving force for their further development, and highly industrialized societies seeking further scientific and technological innovation are in a constant process of defining their own vision of STEM and STEM education, and developing national programmes to improve the quantity and the quality of graduates in the STEM disciplines.

Even though reforms have been launched in many countries, there is often a wide gap between what has been planned in theory and what is implemented practically. This has been particularly evident in Egypt, but also in Brazil. For example, classroom teaching methods and changes in curricula have been changed on paper, but due to the cultural, individual and socio-economic background of the teachers they are not implemented (see also Abd El Khalick *et al.* 2004; Mansour 2010). Comprehensive changes seem to be necessary in all the countries that were included in the analysis. The last chapter of this book (Chapter 16) will address the nature of these changes and the potential lessons that policy makers and designers of educational programmes might learn from the country reports and the Delphi results.

Notes

1 For further information on the Delphi method see e.g. Webler *et al.* (1991) or a special issue on 'The Delphi Technique: Past, Present, and Future Prospects' published by the Journal *Technological Forecasting and Social Change* (Rowe and Wright 2011).

2 For detailed information on the material of the Delphi process please contact the authors of the paper.

3 In order to meet the interdisciplinary research approach, experts were chosen from different backgrounds including school education and teaching methods, natural sciences, professionalization in STEM, social sciences, history of science and others.

4 Both native experts from the countries under investigation (internal) and experts who are involved in research on those countries but work and live in other countries (external) were invited to take part in the Delphi process. This approach enables a broader perspective and a more comprehensive judgement on the situation of STEM education due to the different points of views.

5 The concept of open-mindedness refers to an attitude that allows that something like S&T can exert a positive impact or influence on the country or societal development.

6 In Brazil, for instance, the programme 'ABC na Educação Científica—Mão na Massa' adopts methods of inquiry-based learning, for more information see the website, available from http://www.cdcc.usp.br/maomassa/ (in Portuguese) [Accessed 12 September 2014].

7 For example, the Committee on Women in Science, Engineering and Medicine (CWSEM) conducts, monitors and evaluates different actions for women in STEM, website available from http://sites.nationalacademies.org/PGA/cwsem/ [Accessed 10 October 2010] or the WiSE programme funded by the National Science Foundation and implemented through different universities e.g. at the University of Washington, website available from http://www.engr.washington.edu/curr_students/studentprogs/wise.html [Accessed 10 October 2014].

Bibliography

Abd El Khalick, Fouad *et al.* (2004): Inquiry in Science Education: International Perspectives, *Science Education* 88 (3). Pp. 397–419.

Beck, Ulrich (2003): *Risikogesellschaft: Auf dem Weg in eine andere Moderne.* Suhrkamp, Frankfurt am Main.

Bond, Michael *et al.* (2013): Science and Innovation in Egypt. Available from https://royalsociety.org/~/media/policy/projects/atlas-islamic-world/atlas-egypt.pdf [Accessed 10 October 2014].

Chung, Ji Eun (2012): Education at a Glance: OECD Indicators 2012. Country report: Korea. OECD Publishing, Paris. Available from http://www.oecd.org/education/EAG2012%20-%20Country%20note%20-%20Korea.pdf [Accessed 8 October 2014].

Cobern, William W. and Glen S. Aikenhead (2003): Cultural Aspects of Learning Science. In: *International Handbook of Science Education. Part One,* edited by Barry J. Fraser and Kenneth Tobin. Kluwer Academic Publishers, Dordrecht. Pp. 39–52.

Dalkey, Norman and Olaf Helmer (1963): An Experimental Application of the Delphi Method to the use of Experts. *Management Science* 9 (3). Pp. 458–467.

Giddens, Anthony and Christopher Pierson (1998): *Conversations with Anthony Giddens: Making Sense of Modernity.* Stanford University Press, Stanford.

Linstone, Harold A. and Murray Turoff (2002): The Delphi Method. Techniques and Applications. Available from http://is.njit.edu/pubs/delphibook/#toc [Accessed 10 October 2014].

Liu, Xuan, Shukun Tang, and Martin W. Bauer (2011): Comparing the Public Understanding of Science across China and Europe. In: *The Culture of Science: How the Public Relates to Science Across the Globe,* edited by Martin W. Bauer, Rajesh Shukla and Nick Allum. Routledge, New York and London. Pp. 139–157.

Loveluck, Louisa (2012): Education in Egypt: Key Challenges. Background Paper. Chatham House. The Royal Institute of International Affairs, London. Available from http://www.chathamhouse.org/sites/files/chathamhouse/public/Research/Middle%20East/0312egyptedu_background.pdf [Accessed 10 October 2014].

Mansour, Nasser (2010): Impact of the Knowledge and Beliefs of Egyptian Science Teachers in Integrating a STS Based Curriculum: A Sociocultural Perspective, *Journal of Science Teacher Education* 21 (5). Pp. 513–34.

Murphy, Rachel (2004): Turning Peasants into Modern Chinese Citizens: Discourse, Demographic Transition and Primary Education, *The China Quarterly* 177. Pp. 1–20.

OECD (2012): International Migration Outlook 2012. OECD Publishing, Paris. Available from http://www.keepeek.com/Digital-Asset-Management/oecd/social-issues-migration-health/international-migration-outlook-2012_migr_outlook-2012-en#page1 [Accessed 10 October 2014].

OECD (2013): Education at a Glance 2013. OECD indicators. OECD Publishing, Paris. http://www.oecd.org/edu/eag2013%20%28eng%29--FINAL%2020%20June%202013.pdf [Accessed 10 October 2014].

Potvin, Patrice and Abdelkrim Hasni (2014): Interest, Motivation and Attitude Towards Science and Technology at K-12 Levels: A Systematic Review of 12 Years of Educational Research, *Studies in Science Education* 50 (1). Pp. 85–129.

Renn, Ortwin and Thomas Webler (1992): Anticipating Conflicts: Public Participation in Managing the Solid Waste Crisis, *Gaia* 1 (2). Pp. 84–94.

Rowe, Gene and George Wright (ed.) (2011): The Delphi Technique: Past, Present, and Future Prospects, *Technological Forecasting and Social Change* 78 (9). Pp. 1487–1720.

Schulz, Marlen and Ortwin Renn (2009): Das Gruppendelphi: Konzept und Vorgehensweise. In: *Das Gruppendelphi: Konzept und Fragebogenkonstruktion*, edited by Marlen Schulz and Ortwin Renn. VS Verlag für Sozialwissenschaften, Wiesbaden. Pp. 11–22.

Sjøberg, Svein (2012): Young People's Attitudes to Science: Results and Perspectives from the ROSE Study. In: *Wissenschafts- und Technikbildung auf dem Prüfstand. Zum Fachkräftemangel und zur Attraktivität der MINT-Bildung und -Berufe im europäischen Vergleich*, edited by Uwe Pfenning and Ortwin Renn. Nomos, Baden-Baden. Pp. 111–125.

Tao, Ying, Mary Oliver and Grady Venville (2012): Long-Term Outcomes of Early Childhood Science Education: Insights from a Cross-National Comparative Case Study on Conceptual Understanding of Science, *International Journal of Science and Mathematics Education* 10 (6). Pp. 1269–1302.

Wafa, Dina Mohamed (2013): Egypt in Transition Responding to Social and Political Changes in Executive Education, *Teaching Public Administration* 31(2). Pp. 174–185.

Wang, Ke et al. (2012): Adult Scientific Literacy and its Surveys in China Since 1992. In: *Culture of Science: How the Public Relates to Science Across the Globe*, edited by Martin W. Bauer, Rajesh Shukla and Nick Allum, Routledge, New York and London. Pp. 126–133.

Webler, Thomas et al. (1991): The Group Delphi: A Novel Attempt at Reducing Uncertainty, *Technological Forecasting and Social Change* 39 (3). Pp. 253–263.

15 Lessons learned

Towards unity in diversity

Andreas Hohlt, Ortwin Renn, Dorothea Taube and Nicole C. Karafyllis

Review of commonalities and differences

The various contributions of this book aimed to collect ideas, observations and best practices in the field of STEM education from countries outside of Europe. This focus was chosen in order to initiate a new, more internationalized perspective on STEM education, emphasizing 'soft factors' (e.g. social perceptions) and cultural factors (e.g. religious beliefs). Both aspects influence STEM and STEM education. We found that the framing of science and technology, the image of scientific practice and the reputation of scientists and engineers play a major role in public understanding of science and technology. These two aspects also appeal to the different types of motivation young people show when deciding whether to pursue a STEM education or not.

The data we collected confirms a multinational and cross-cultural agreement among experts about the importance and the necessity of developing and implementing new educational methods. These new methods should be targeted at galvanizing students towards problem solving and inquiry-based learning. The role of teachers is defined in very different ways among the countries covered in this volume. Once more, they follow the path of cultural diversity, ranging from receiving a fairly minor level of prestige and national significance in countries such as South Korea to very high levels of importance in China. Hierarchical social systems with centralized teaching and education systems tend to place most emphasis on science and technology as the dominant career path (i.e. Egypt, Japan), compared with more decentralized and diversified countries such as the United States. Against this political and cultural background, motivation for young students to pursue a STEM career differs from one country to the next. The data suggests different types of motivation for young people for choosing STEM disciplines and starting to engage in STEM studies or professions later in their life.

Political programmes and potential obstacles for political reform are also important factors for the success of STEM programmes. Our data and expert statements suggest that there are important structural differences between affluent countries and countries on the way towards technological modernization. In the former group of countries the attractiveness of STEM has become less pronounced, but, at the same time, education reforms and extracurricular activities are slowly filling the void caused by the lack of genuine appeal. The latter group starts with a strong incentive to become involved in STEM education and activities, but seems to fail in reforming their educational systems to adopt more effective and more suitable teaching methods.

Finally, there is much evidence that we live in skill-based economies or skill-driven societies—a term used by Nicole C. Karafyllis in her chapter on the Gulf region—rather than in knowledge-based economies. This implies that each country defines its needs for STEM as a function of the skills and tasks that economy and society seem to require. There is less a universal trend towards science and technology literacy as one might assume on the basis of the many programmes initiated in almost all countries to support STEM education than there is a tendency to translate the needs of private and public institutions for skilled personnel and labour into the educational system.

Given the dominance of skill-oriented education, one can characterize the STEM education situation (in particular as it relates to recruitment) by referring to the following trends:

1   The job market and the demand for skilled workers are main drivers for educational reform; very few countries pursue explicit science literacy initiatives that aim to improve the overall knowledge level of the population.

2   If political decision-makers support this trend towards a skill-oriented education, there is quite a large amount of funding for the STEM education sector available. However, much of this is ineffective in terms of outcome and often not aligned with the state-of-the-art methods of science education.

3   Experts all over the world favour new, universally applicable, methods of science education such as inquiry-based learning, but often fail to have these methods implemented in the educational system of their country. This gap between theory and reality also refers to the language of instruction and the teaching and learning material used.

4   In many countries there are severe access barriers for disadvantaged social groups: STEM education is often limited to the cultural elite. In more open, plural societies, cultural frames about STEM careers often serve as implicit barriers for abstaining from a STEM education or career. Minorities and women often share the feeling that they do not have the competence to succeed in this field or that the mainstream will not allow them to succeed. Nevertheless STEM education in modernizing countries also provides an opportunity to gain a better position in society for people from poorer or less socially esteemed parts of society.

5   The movement towards improved scientific literacy and open-mindedness towards science and technology is a typical phenomenon of highly industrialized countries. People have experienced the negative side effects of technological advancement and are more sceptical towards the profits of technological progress and further change. This phenomenon is quite advanced in most parts of the United States (and many countries in Europe) and has begun to unfold in Japan.

Table 15.1 provides an overview of the main characteristics of STEM education in the countries that are included in this volume. Based on these specific

Table 15.1 Country-specific characteristics

USA	There is a highly developed and differentiated situation of STEM education in the different US states. All in all, the USA faces a shortage of STEM professionals, thus relying on immigrants and fostering a strong emphasis on scientific literacy and on enabling minorities to enter STEM education careers. The image of scientists is largely positive but not strong enough to act as an incentive for young people to pursue a STEM career. Various stereotypes about scientists and technologists also exist. Major national and regional programmes aim to boost the attractiveness of STEM and to improve current methods for teaching science and technology.
Brazil	A country destined to pursue technological modernization, but still unable to overcome old-fashioned methods of scientific education. Despite a strong political desire for reform and despite major investment in STEM education, reforms seem to be ineffective. There are profound structural problems in providing effective, efficient and fair opportunities for students who would like to pursue STEM careers. Major initiatives and reforms focus on higher education, neglecting the need to provide a good basic education as a necessary precondition.
Egypt	At the beginning of the modernization phase in terms of industry and new economy, the job market for STEM professionals outside of traditional branches such as medical personnel, civil engineering and electrical engineering is lacking, due to an oversupply of university graduates. Additionally, graduates lack adequate skills for employment. There is an all-pervasive, non-conflictual coexistence between Islam and STEM education. Also, compared with other countries, there is a high number of female graduates in STEM subjects, especially in medicine, chemistry, biology and pharmacy. Despite this progress, female graduates still face problems reconciling family and work life and are under-represented in leadership positions.
India	Rapidly modernizing country with high level of urban IT sector and an emerging private sector playing a major role in supporting and funding STEM and STEM education. However, hierarchical structures in society, language barriers (English) and a lack of mobility exclude large segments of society, in particular rural populations and poor people, from taking advantage of the opportunities brought about by STEM education. Despite the existence of alternative knowledge systems (e.g. Ayurvedic system of knowledge) and a rich heritage of science and technology in India, Western ideas of modern science dominate the post-independent understanding of science in India. Questions of responsibility and accountability with regard to scientific achievements have gained increased importance in society.

Japan	Highly modernized and technologically advanced country. Its cultural tradition is rather elitist and there is a schism between the views of pure knowledge (highly esteemed) and applied knowledge (not highly valued). However, this traditional gap has allowed students from non-elitist circles to gain more opportunities to become involved in STEM education and careers. The traditional elite is more invested in business and politics. Members of lower social classes use the opportunity to become engineers and technical specialists. High attractiveness of technology among the population: strong presence and visibility of technology in everyday life (example: robots), strong open-mindedness towards technology, but, like in many other technologically advanced and highly industrialized societies, there is a growing movement towards the 'green' economy and anti-technology movements. As Japanese society has become more egalitarian, the attractiveness of STEM for non-elites in society has weakened over time; Japan now faces major problems in recruiting STEM professionals. There are no serious efforts for addressing the remaining minorities such as non-working women and immigrants.
China	Rapidly modernizing country, but largely split in its modernization path between urban and rural areas. STEM education in the modern sense is present only in urban centres. Due to the need for economic growth within environmental and social constraints, the need for STEM professionals is seen as one of the top priorities for the country. China has initiated a centralized top-down reform programme for STEM education, such as the introduction of inquiry-based learning (basically in urban areas). Scientific advancement has become a political priority and the prestige of teachers has been raised by public campaigns. However, traditional structural constraints such as the national examinations (focused on memorizing facts) prevent the new programmes and teaching method reforms from becoming effective.
South Korea	Sandwiched between China and Japan, South Korea has defined itself as the innovation hub for remaining nationally independent and achieving global significance. There is strong pressure on students to get involved in STEM careers even if they are not interested or talented. Rather than relying on innovative teaching methods, emphasis is on an educational system that is still dominated by the notion of human 'learning machines'. Students spend hours and hours working to get acceptable grades. All hopes are directed towards national symbols such as prestigious research labs (i.e. KAIST) or global technological players such as Samsung.

insights, the following sections attempt to provide a more cross-sectional view of the impressions that the research team gained from the country reports, the personal interviews and the Delphi results.

The influence of culture and religion on STEM and STEM education

Understanding culture in the context of STEM

In its Mexico City Declaration on Cultural Policies of 1982, the United Nations Educational and Scientific Organisation (UNESCO) adopted the following definition of culture as 'the whole complex of distinctive spiritual, material, intellectual and emotional features that characterize a society or social group. It [culture] includes not only the arts and letters, but also modes of life, the fundamental rights of the human being, value systems, traditions and beliefs [. . .]' (UNESCO 1982: 1). Based on this broad understanding of culture, we focus here on the intellectual, epistemological, symbolic and aesthetic traditions that are socially valid in a certain region, nation or other defined spaces with respect to the role of science and technology in society.

Introducing a Chinese example may help to illustrate how contemporary developments in STEM or STEM education can be better understood if seen from a cultural perspective. When Chinese Emperor Quian Long decided to establish systematic categories in the Imperial Library in the eighteenth century, he first codified an authentic Chinese epistemic structure. Among many of his orders he determined that spatial natural sciences like geography and geology were subsumed under historiography (see e.g. Li 2007). This could easily be interpreted that in Chinese tradition, natural space was not perceived as being an autonomous phenomenon on which human beings settle or move, nor as an aesthetic or religious entity with its own rules and symbolic powers, but as a place of social interaction (the river that marks a frontier or nourishes the capital, the mountain on which a battle had been fought, etc.). Space was made by human interventions, not altered by it. Contemporary megaprojects such as the Three Gorges Dam are good examples of this mental frame that strongly supports the practice of geo-engineering. Above all, this example also shows that future STEM education worldwide will heavily depend on integrating insights from the humanities and social sciences into the science curricula.

The cultural concepts we are considering in this book are not meant to take any firm position on the question of universal knowledge versus a relativist or postmodern view on knowledge and science. We do not engage here in questions of science theory about what constitutes legitimate knowledge, and whether knowledge claims can be tested, independent of social context and time. Nevertheless, as Menzel and Duddeck point out in Chapter 2, there is an established stock of methodology—experiment, reproducibility of resulting data and exposure to falsification—that has been adopted globally. Differences can be seen when it comes to how to *connect* these state-of-the-art methodologies and scientific outcomes to the cultural traditions of a country, including the different modes of scientific inquiry and technical problem solving that often relate to special historical epistemologies. Interestingly, there is also increasing discussion on the integration of indigenous knowledge in modern science and technology discourses, especially with regard to the knowledge of native populations in North and South America and indigenous people in India, Australia and Africa (see e.g. Ferguson 2001, Green 2012).

In this book we use the term 'culture' in the broad sense of beliefs, values and cultural practices that influence the reality of STEM and STEM education in each of the countries that we studied. We are interested in how different clusters of perceptions, traditions and beliefs form the conditions under which STEM is able to develop and STEM education to thrive. As the Delphi results have shown, we are faced with a multitude of such cultural clusters and they do exert pressure on the STEM situation in each country. Some of these clusters that frame the opportunities and limits of STEM and STEM education are explained below.

Frames: patterns of social perception and cultural beliefs

Frames are mental constructs that help people to interpret situations and to define their role in such situations (see Kahneman and Tversky 2000; Nelson, Oxley and Clawson 1997; Narayan et al. 2013). Frames help to integrate multiple and often contradicting information (data, impressions, visual perceptions) that a person is confronted with when entering into a new situation. Information that can be integrated into a pre-existing frame works as reinforcement of this frame.

In all the countries observed, there are socially widespread frames about the actual presence of science in society. This can be illustrated by the following survey: in a study conducted in 2013, third, seventh and tenth grade students were asked about their image of science and scientists; 87.8 per cent of Indian, 81.9 per cent of Chinese and 71.1 per cent of South Korean students answered a scientist is 'male' and is 'working in a laboratory surrounded by research symbols' (Narayan et al. 2013: 126f).

In contrast, US students of the same age drew what they think scientists look like by putting them in everyday clothes, but they tended to adopt a more mythological identification: 'Several grade 3 and grade 7 students portrayed their scientists as a frightening figure, some labelling them as 'Frankenstein,' 'Evilla,' 'Cruellam,' and 'Witch.' While these are common representations in the US they were not seen among students from any of the other participating countries' (Narayan et al. 2013: 126f). Particularly in the US, the stereotype of the 'rocket scientist' turns out to be a dominant frame in student perceptions. The Delphi experts supported this observation. These findings suggest placing more emphasis on thorough investigations into the role that public media play in shaping images about the STEM field and the professionals working in this field.

The social recognition of being a scientist seems to be particularly high in South Korea (less, however, in Japan), Egypt and Brazil, whereas lack of public esteem for scientists is seen as a serious obstacle for recruitment in the USA (see Chapter 14 in this book). The anticipated esteem of a scientist has effects on extrinsic motivation (career, prestige, money, opportunity). So countries where there is very high prestige for STEM professionals show a much larger proportion of students who are motivated by external factors such as prestige, income and social advancement. This could even go as far as in the case of South Korea, for instance, where students seem to choose STEM even when it conflicts with their own interests and alleged talent on account of the pressure that they get from parents and peers (see Ho 2009, also with an East Asian comparison). In countries with lower prestige for STEM professionals, the educational system needs to activate intrinsic motives for students to get interested in this line of career. This is far more cumbersome and difficult than in countries with high social recognition for scientists and engineers, but there is a tendency that intrinsic motivation reaches out to more STEM-gifted students and raises their willingness to study for the sake of making progress in the field, rather than in order to get a degree, more money or social prestige. These play only a secondary role.

In countries with strong intrinsic motivation factors for choosing a STEM subject, frames of who is a scientist and what does he/she do have a strong impact on the role model that students associate with scientists and engineers. The dominant frame in the US of a 'rocket scientist' does not attract a majority of young students to engage and study in the field of STEM and instead gives a misleading image of what engineers actually do. The frame describes a nineteenth century stereotype of a lonesome male scientist in his laboratory instead of the multitasking, communicative, computer-based team worker of nowadays. As a response to this problem, many institutions in the USA have launched ambitious programmes for 'Public Understanding of Science and Humanities' (PUSH) directed towards reframing the troublesome image of scientists in the US.

A special form of framing applies to religion. Religious beliefs constitute special types of frames with intrinsic barriers against reframing, claiming their legitimacy and validity from a transcendental base that does not allow empirical falsification. The data collected by the experts suggest, however, that the impact of religion on STEM and STEM education tends to be overrated in the media and in public opinion. In countries with a strong Islamic background (such as Egypt and the Gulf States) or in countries with strong fundamentalist movements, such as the USA, the relationship between religion and science and technology creates less of a problem than commonly feared. Religious beliefs and scientific convictions for the most part do not contradict each other, but stand side by side, posing challenges with some specific concepts such as evolutionary theory (see also Bond *et al.* 2013 or Keeter, Smith and Masci 2011).

The need for reframing

Frames are reaffirmed as long as they confirm individual perceptions. If perceptions conflict with the dominant frames of interpretation, frames may become obsolete and new frames will slowly emerge. However, humans have a great sense of creativity when it comes to re-interpreting perceptions to make them match their existing frames. Nevertheless, once humans experience major conflicts between perceived reality and frames, they look for alternative frames to establish new meaning to what they observe or experience. If this process is pursued actively, it is called reframing. Reframing is an important concept of communication, in particular political communication (see e.g. Johnson-Cartee 2005). In our case, reframing would imply a revision of the stereotypes linked to science or scientists, technologies or engineers, e.g. a reframing might question the image of the 'rocket scientist.'

Yvonne Spicer's chapter (Chapter 12) includes strategies and practical efforts to perform reframing in order to help young people gain more appropriate and attractive impressions of science and technology. Moreover, the efforts of US institutions to encourage minorities and less privileged groups to become more involved in STEM necessitate an active approach of constructing new frames that offer potential for identification with STEM careers. Young people should be exposed to information that makes STEM fascinating and linked to their everyday lives, in order to encourage young people from all social backgrounds to perceive STEM as a suitable career option. Reframing STEM and STEM education could be at the core of a new communication strategy attracting new segments of young people.

Takuji Okamoto explains how reframing and shifting perceptions can also be a process of adaptation within society. He referred to a significant change in the relationship that Japanese people have with nature: a representative survey has been regularly conducted over many years across the Japanese population. The survey contains the following item: For human beings' happiness, we must a) follow nature b) utilize nature c) conquer nature (and others). Whereas back in 1958, only 26 per cent chose 'follow nature,' this number increased to 49 per cent in 1998 and remained at that high level thereafter (51 per cent in 2008). Only 5 per cent wanted to 'conquer nature' in 2008, but 30 per cent did back in 1963 (Nakamura *et al.* 2011: 53). Reframing affects the image of science and technology via new images of nature and society. Such fundamental changes can also be triggered by events such as the Fukushima nuclear disaster. In other parts of the world, technical hazards and unintended consequences such as pollution are less important for the perception of science and technology, e.g. in India, Egypt or the Gulf States. They lack a comprehensive public debate about risks with regard to scientific achievements and their technological manifestations. For the Arabian Gulf States, Nicole C. Karafyllis (Chapter 9) observes a reframing of technology that relates—back and forth—to art and beauty in contrast to functionality as the dominant force of technological culture in Western countries. She describes, for example, that in the UAE, the Emirates Telescope project first and foremost serves an educational purpose, raising peoples' interest in science and technology and fostering a national cultural identity based on national research achievements but which does not serve industrial productivity or scientific basic research as a major concern.

While reflecting on the newest developments in South Korean STEM education and science policy, Jung-Ok Ha also observes a change in frames but she diagnoses a strong erosion of existing frames without a new frame to replace them. South Korea is also in a stage of transition with respect to its culture and social fabrics, partly acting within the traditional frames without giving them much credibility, partly experimenting with new frames that have very little resonance in the routines of daily life.

The main lesson to be learned from the framing debate in the country reports and the Delphi deliberation is that frames are powerful drivers for creating positive or negative images of science and technology and influence the potential attractors for young people to get involved in STEM education. It is not easy to change existing frames and create new frames. Yet, many frames are obviously inappropriate and inadequate for modern societies to perform well in economics, innovation and social welfare. A major effort is therefore necessary to understand the frames that govern people's perceptions and to help societal institutions in their process of reframing. For many countries that are on the path of modernization, reframing means to shift attention from extrinsic to intrinsic motivation; in many highly modernized countries the reframing must address the dominant intrinsic motivations of young people, such as interesting and challenging work, opportunities for creativity, team work, individual self-efficacy and adequate life-work balance.

Factors that shape educational performance in STEM

The influence of teaching methods and teacher performance

When asked about teaching methods, the experts from all countries agreed that a combination of classic lecturing with innovative forms of student activation, including inquiry-based learning, self-experimentation, group learning and others, represent the most appropriate teaching methods for meeting the requirements of an attractive STEM education in a globalized world. Arthur Eisenkraft introduced the expert panel to newly developed methods, which are currently being tested in the USA, such as learning by design and innovation creativity. New add-on forms such as 'service learning' (learning by engaging in social work) help in strengthening the understanding of a link between scientific and social development.

Reflecting this agreement, the method of 'inquiry-based learning' is—to varying degrees, however—welcomed and implemented in all countries covered in this book. China has done so recently, officially emphasizing the value of 'innovation' for the Chinese educational system.

Chinese expert Yang Yuankui emphasized that in addition to teaching methods, the personality and dedication of the teacher are crucial elements for educational success. A Chinese teacher has to fulfil a wide range of tasks and expectations. Teaching before classes of up to 50 pupils (in most urban cosmopolitan contexts), he is expected to do active research, to publish, if possible, and to be aware of all new academic trends in his field. He or she should be able to integrate new methods of teaching such as inquiry-based learning. Teachers are expected to produce top ranking scholars but also to support those with learning difficulties. Teachers do constantly evaluate themselves mutually.[1] Given these duties, the Chinese government has raised the salaries of teachers to middle class income levels and started campaigns to improve the image of teachers as assistants to learning rather than instructors of existing knowledge.

Political reforms of educational systems

The experts from countries that undergo the process of technological modernization, especially from Brazil and Egypt, made very critical remarks about the reforms that had been initiated recently. Brazil introduced a qualification test (ENEM) for all students at various ages, hoping to boost national standards for science education. However, these tests showed poor performance by students in many areas, but no effort was then made to change or improve the situation. Often the problem has been recognized but there is neither money nor the political will to make the necessary changes. The effects of small-scale reforms disappear when confronted with the huge structural deficiencies of the public school system. A new level of funding of public schools and better ways of teacher training should be first priorities, according to Elizabeth Balbachevsky. As stated before, these countries rely at this point on extrinsic motivation for STEM careers but these incentives might not always attract the most talented and interested students who are intrinsically motivated.

The Egyptian experts Nasser Mansour and Ghada K. Gholam stressed that the problem of effective reform seems to be similar, but for different reasons. The country lacks an overall strategy and political vision for further reform. Additionally, a stronger focus on collaboration in education and (interdisciplinary) research among educational institutions, and between educational institutions, the industry, civil society and also foreign partners, is necessary to improve the overall situation in STEM and STEM education in Egypt and to adequately educate young people for the job market. Mohan Avvari and Nagalakshmi Chelluri introduced a new issue to the analysis of STEM education: the emerging role of the private sector, as exemplified by the Technology Cluster City Hyderabad in India. It seems that, along with new responsibilities taken on by private stakeholders, the prestige of working as a STEM professional in the private sector is rising, due to relatively high incomes and social recognition of the private sector as a service for the public good. This attitude is not the same in China where the average STEM employee in public service still earns significantly more than in the private sector. So the private sector attracts graduates from business schools whereas STEM graduates prefer to work in the public sector.

Gender equality: still not accomplished

All Delphi experts agreed (with one exception from China) that there is still a gender gap in career opportunities. Political programmes have been launched in many countries, most notably the USA, but also India, South Korea and Japan.

However, Japan has not invested significantly in this issue and the traditional family structure is often praised as the true Japanese model of living. One strategy to overcome gender biases is to reframe the role of scientists: stressing the contributions of female scientists to the body of knowledge; offering female role models for young students; providing better opportunities for harmonizing family life and work; and assuring equal payment and career opportunities for females and males (see also Charles *et al.* 2014).

The same cultural attitudes and perceptions about women's role in society have made it difficult for women to enter the scientific community, especially in leadership positions in Egypt. Men are the preferred hires since there is the fear that women will leave their job when faced with conflicts between job loyalty and family responsibilities, in contrast to men who are said to have a stronger commitment to their work. Additionally, even though enrolment rates of women in state universities and the rate of high-achieving female graduates from Egyptian colleges are over 50 per cent, there is an underrepresentation of women in private universities, the Al-Azhar University and the State Technical Colleges. Gender disparity in education is even worse in rural areas of the country (Bond *et al.* 2013). Particularly after the Arab Spring uprisings it is even more of a challenge to protect women's rights to education and work and to encourage equal access to training and promotion opportunities (El-Badri 2013).

Central messages for improving STEM education worldwide

The review of the country experts and the Delphi insights have produced several major insights that are also important for STEM education in countries not covered in this book. Given the diversity and plurality of STEM traditions and educational approaches, there is no one recipe for successful and adequate STEM education that would apply everywhere. Each country has its own special conditions and structures that impede a simple transfer of elements from one nation to another. Notwithstanding this uniqueness of each case, there are several important lessons that seem to have universal validity and could become the backbone of a global initiative for innovations in the educational system.

1   As culturally diverse as countries and nations may be, the main body of scientific knowledge claims universality and the main insights from scientific inquiry are formed by referring to common standards in methodology, research designs, experimental set-ups and theoretical explanations. This common base of knowledge also includes an agreement about the content of what basic insights to teach and even about methods of how to teach. Each educational system may have priorities in choosing topics for inclusion and may select examples in accordance with dominant social experiences and cultural beliefs. Yet, science is not divided by nation, culture or dominant belief systems. That does not mean that the approaches to learning science should be identical but that methods that have proven to be effective and attractive could be at least tried out in different national and cultural contexts.

2   For meeting the demand for professionals in economy, society and public service, educational systems rely on incentives for extrinsic and intrinsic motivation. Countries that are in the process of modernization provide many external incentives such as higher prestige, more income and social mobility, while countries that have completed the process of modernization provide less incentive for external motivation but rely instead on fostering intrinsic motivations. However, many educational systems fail to meet the expectations and aspirations of young people linked to what they perceive as intrinsically 'good' reasons for choosing a STEM career.

3   The reservoir of candidates for STEM careers is far from exhausted. In almost all countries there are minorities, special groups or social classes that are either excluded from a STEM career or perceive such a career as unrealistic or inappropriate for them. The experiences of the USA in addressing these groups could be seen as a major encouragement for all countries to launch programmes to assist underrepresented groups to get more exposure to STEM education and better access to the professional labour market. They do work if done correctly and supported by sufficient funds. At the same time, however, the examples of China and the GCC region—where a high percentage of women are enrolled in STEM subjects—should be further studied. They could provide some insights on how to attract more women into a STEM career.

4   The attractiveness of STEM careers is strongly shaped by frames that people in each country associate with science and technology. Such frames represent traditional views about science and technology and reflect social experiences and cultural stereotypes. They often hinder talented young people from choosing a science career or they promote the untalented to pursue such careers. Changing frames is very difficult and requires time and resources. Yet, if the frames are incompatible with the requirements of a technologically oriented society, there needs to be a major effort to reframe. Many countries are in the midst of a reframing effort, with mixed results so far. Social systems are resistant to attempts of social engineering, but with the advent of learning societies, framing and reframing might become self-propelled movements that do not need to be directed top-down but evolve over time. However, such movements will not emerge unless governments provide incentives for learning institutions and flexible educational strategies.

5   The term *skill-based economy* seems to embody the recent development towards globalization and competitiveness better than the term *knowledge-based societies*. Abstract knowledge is certainly a goal in itself and may have many repercussions for applications in economy and technology. However, national income and international standing is more and more dependent on a rapid, efficient and comprehensive translation of knowledge in skills that are needed for the production of goods and services. This requirement also has repercussions for the educational system. A society that honours abstract and underestimates applied knowledge will have major difficulties in competing in the globalized world. Educational systems that focus on knowledge rather than on competencies will also not produce the individuals who are

well equipped to compete in a global economy. A skill-based society is driven by creative, flexible, self-reflexive knowledge: thinking and doing go hand in hand. Science and technology shape the worlds, the professional environments and even the private lives of most people. They also determine the success of a national economy. This needs to be reflected in the educational system: students should learn how to shape their environment by combining knowledge about the physical world with the personal motivation to use all their creativity and talent for a better future for themselves, their country and the world.

Note

1 The paragraph reflects a presentation held by Yang Yuankui during a workshop of the TECHcultures project.

Bibliography

Bond, Michael et al. (2013): Science and Innovation in Egypt. Available from https://royalsociety.org/~/media/policy/projects/atlas-islamic-world/atlas-egypt.pdf [Accessed 10 October 2014].

Charles, Maria et al. (2014): Who Likes Math Where? Gender Differences in Eighth-Graders' Attitudes Around the World, *International Studies in Sociology of Education* 24 (1). Pp. 85–112.

El-Badri, Nagwa (2013): Women and Science in Post-Revolution Egypt: The Long Road Ahead, *Nature Middle East*, March 7. Available from http://www.natureasia.com/en/nmiddleeast/article/10.1038/nmiddleeast.2013.31 [Accessed 3 November 2014].

Ferguson, Michael A.D. (2001): Utilizing Indigenous Knowledge in Environmental Research and Assessment. Terra Borealis 2. Institute for Environmental Monitoring and Research, Labrador and Newfoundland (Canada).

Green, Lesley J.F. (2012): Beyond South Africa's 'Indigenous Knowledge—Science' Wars, *South African Journal of Science* 108 (7/8). Pp. 1–10.

Ho, Esther Sui-chu (2009): Characteristics of East Asian Learners: What We Learned From PISA, *Educational Research Journal* 24 (2). Pp. 327–348.

Johnson-Cartee, Karen S. (2005): *News Narratives and News Framing: Constructing Political Reality.* Rowman & Littlefield, Lanham (MD).

Kahneman, Daniel and Amos Tversky (ed.) (2000): *Choices, Values, and Frames.* Cambridge University Press, Cambridge.

Keeter, Scott, Gregory Smith and David Masci (2011): Religious Belief and Attitudes about Science in the United States. In: *The Culture of Science: How the Public Relates to Science Across the Globe*, edited by Martin W. Bauer, Rajesh Shukla and Nick Allum. Routledge, New York and London. Pp. 336–352.

Li, Wenchao (2007): Dekanonisierung der traditionellen Wissensordnung in China oder: Wie es zur Erfindung einer chinesischen Philosophie kam. In: *Die Bildung des Kanons. Textuelle Faktoren – Kulturelle Funktionen – Ethische Praxis*, edited by Lothar Ehrlich, Judith Schildt and Benjamin Specht. Böhlau Verlag GmbH & Cie, Köln et al. Pp. 173–185.

Nakamura, Takashi et al. (2011): A Study of the Japanese National Character: The Twelfth Nationwide Survey (2008). General Series No. 102. The Institute of

Statistical Mathematics. Available from http://ismrepo.ism.ac.jp/dspace/bitstream/10787/903/1/kenripo102.pdf [Accessed 24 October 2014]

Narayan *et al.* (2013): Students' Images of Scientists and Doing Science: An International Comparison Study, *Eurasia Journal of Mathematics, Science & Technology Education* 9 (2). Pp. 115–129.

Nelson, Thomas E., Zoe M. Oxley and Rosalee A. Clawson (1997): Toward A Psychology of Framing Effects, *Political Behavior* 19 (3). Pp. 221–246.

Reese, Stephen D. *et al.* (2010): Framing Public Life: Perspectives on Media and Our Understanding of the Social World. Routledge, New York.

UNESCO (1982): Mexico City Declaration on Cultural Policies. World Conference: Cultural Policies, Mexico City. Available from http://portal.unesco.org/culture/en/files/12762/11295421661mexico_en.pdf/mexico_en.pdf [Accessed 31 October 2014].

16 Responding to challenges of rapid global change by strengthening local STEM education

Ilan Chabay

The Anthropocene epoch and its implications

Humanity faces urgent and largely unprecedented challenges in responding to rapid and accelerating global changes. Some of these global changes, which affect everyone on Earth, are intended or unintended outcomes of human actions. Eugene Stoermer, an ecologist, and Paul Crutzen, Nobel Prize Laureate for his work on atmospheric chemistry, coined the name 'Anthropocene' to label the current geological era and to highlight the profound impact human activities have on conditions on our planet. Humankind can no longer be seen as simply a passive bystander in the changes in conditions for all life on Earth. For at least the past two centuries, human activities have substantially affected Earth's biological, chemical and physical systems, thus contributing to the substantial global changes altering the planet's natural systems, while also affecting social, economic and political conditions (see e.g. Steffen, Crutzen and McNeill 2007). These effects are evident around the world and impact society in many different ways depending on local context, including large-scale loss of biodiversity, climate change and air pollution, changes in critical rainfall patterns and land use, economic instability, and growing income inequity.

Crucially, these changes are the results of interactions among different physical, chemical, biological and social systems with feedback mechanisms operating at multiple spatial and temporal scales. Addressing the challenges of mitigating the negative effects, or when mitigation is not possible, adapting to the changes, requires recognition of and insight into the complexity of the interdependent systems. It also requires a deep understanding of the separate components of the systems, as well as a degree of humility in recognizing the inherent uncertainty involved in characterizing the behaviour of complex systems.

For example, the chemistry of defence mechanisms of tree frogs in a rainforest, emissions of carbon dioxide from coal-fired power plants, supply levels and price of coffee—all may be usefully studied as separate and independent matters, yet when viewed only as separate issues, critical linkages would be overlooked. Cutting down parts of the rainforest, for instance, may lead to extinction of the tree frog species (and thus loss of information about new chemical compounds), diminished capacity of the forest as a carbon sink and changes in humidity and aerosol concentrations resulting in an impact on timing and amount of rainfall in coffee growing areas. This set of coupled effects shows the limitations of a classical reductionist analysis, because of the physical coupling between systems, including effects of societal choices to meet consumer demand. Attempting to quantify the interactions and effects in many such complex systems is inevitably subject to varying degrees of uncertainty, which often hinder decision-making processes (see for example, Institute of Medicine 2013).

Uncertainty and ambiguity are inherent in the human processes that allow us to characterize highly complex systems. This is because the multiplicity of dimensions or number of variables needed to describe the system are only tractable through the construction and use of models of different forms—heuristic, system dynamic or agent-based models. All such models are approximations developed to address specific aspects or questions and are necessarily incomplete descriptions. They do not contain all information about the actual system. Even when the model itself can be shown to be free of fundamental errors in the mathematics, coding or data, uncertainties remain because some variables have been suppressed to make the analysis tractable or because we do not know enough about the system even to identify some potentially critical properties.

Addressing these challenges—for which we do not have simple ready-made solutions, which have a measure of inherent uncertainty and which require attention to potential unintended consequences—places new demands on natural and social sciences, engineering, mathematics, ethics and law, among other fields. Consequently, we need to improve our capacity for scientific, technological and social research and innovation in order to respond effectively to the challenges.

Interactions between science, technology and society

Greater insights and advances through research and innovation are needed not only in technology per se, but also in the interactions between science and technology with society that acknowledge the importance and role of culture, beliefs and values held by different individuals and communities in choosing and using technology. For innovation to have a chance to take root, society as a whole, not just the innovators and producers, must be prepared to engage with new ideas in order to make meaningful decisions and undertake timely adoption and compliance on a significant scale. At the same time, researchers and innovators must be prepared to engage in mutual learning processes with their fellow citizens to convey key ideas and learn about attitudes, concerns and priorities in the local and global communities to which they belong.

While there have been changes in the way that society and science/technology interact and in the attitudes that shape those interactions over the past two decades (e.g. Jasanoff and Wynne 1998), increasing attention to global change challenges and sustainable development have heightened the need for substantial further reform in the science/technology/society nexus. This is evident in the stated purpose of a new platform for global change and sustainability research and action entitled Future Earth. The website characterizes the platform in the following paragraphs:

> Future Earth is the global research platform providing the knowledge and support to accelerate our transformations to a sustainable world. Bringing together existing programmes on global environmental change [. . .], Future Earth will be an international hub to coordinate new, interdisciplinary approaches to research on three themes: Dynamic Planet, Global Development and Transformations towards Sustainability. It will also be a platform for international engagement to ensure that knowledge is generated in partnership with society and users of science. It is open to scientists of all disciplines, natural and social, as well as engineering, the humanities and law.
>
> (Future Earth)

Future Earth is an important example of many programmes and projects worldwide that are directed towards understanding and acting to address global change and sustainability. The intention to generate knowledge in partnership with society and users of science is particularly significant, because it highlights recognition of the need for broader and deeper engagement of science and technology with society in conjunction with interdisciplinary approaches to the three themes mentioned. Also significant is that new interdisciplinary approaches are needed for research, though it is important to keep in mind that this is a necessary, but not sufficient, condition for progress in this area. Continuing to develop traditional disciplinary depth is a crucial part of the entire package. I will return at the end of this piece to illustrate these points with an example of a project we are developing that is in the mode of Future Earth.

STEM education for living in the Anthropocene

Given this new framing of research and action on issues of vital importance for all societies, what are the implications for and demands on education to meet needs now and in the future? Educational systems are structured quite differently across the world with their own specific contexts of historical precedent, aspirations and resources. To meet the needs for inter- and trans-disciplinary[1] research, action and decision-making, they will have to make substantial changes appropriate to their individual contexts in two regards. One is to prepare their citizens to participate meaningfully in making decisions on local or regional manifestations of complex issues. The second is to adequately prepare their children and youth to pursue careers that require strongly collaborative, multi-, inter-, and trans-disciplinary capacities, in addition to disciplinary knowledge and skills. Successfully addressing both of these requires reconceiving and restructuring education from early childhood through senior citizens as a coherent system, but here I will focus specifically on science, technology, engineering and mathematics (STEM). For convenience, in this paper I will use STEM to refer to all variants[2] in this set of key disciplinary and curricular domains.

The question then is how can STEM education in different ecological, social, cultural and environmental contexts be adapted and strengthened to increase our capacity to address the global challenges outlined above?

To help society make substantial improvements for living sustainably in the age of the Anthropocene, STEM education needs to 1) stimulate widespread changes in perceptions of the nature of science and technology especially in their relation to society, 2) change the expectations and level of knowledge of youth about careers in these areas, 3) emphasize a practice of scientific inquiry and collaborative project-based learning in the classroom and 4) do so throughout a coherent (i.e. conceptually related and progressively staged) trajectory of learning from preschool to graduate levels and lifelong learning.

At the root of the need for systemic educational change to address challenges of the Anthropocene is the need to alter the all-too-common perceptions that science, technology, engineering, and mathematics are divorced from the values, beliefs and concerns of other members of society and that advancing STEM is solely about acquiring scientific and technical knowledge and uncovering the 'Truth.' In many communities worldwide, children and youth (as well as many adults) are exposed to a narrative of science that portrays it only as a pursuit isolated from or in conflict with society and one that does not carry its share of civic responsibility (for an international perspective see e.g. Cetto, Schneegans and Moore (2000); for a view from the US see the National Science Foundation, Division of Science Resources Statistic (2002)). They may see technology as driven only by marketing without reference to societal needs. Where this is the case, students will have only a narrow view of STEM and its potential positive role in social innovation. Changing this perception and expectation to include socially responsive innovation and confronting the value propositions embedded in choices of research better prepares students to address societal needs and global challenges and becomes more attractive to students from a wider range of interests, backgrounds and experiences. Furthermore, it invites them to contribute to solving global challenges on local scales through study and practice in fields of STEM.

Choices about effective means of changing perceptions and expectations depend strongly on local context and culture. Generic approaches can be tailored to fit particular contexts. These include both virtual venues, such as blogs, computer games and websites and face-to-face live events, such as informal science and technology cafes that engage the community in open dialogues with each other and experts focused on the nature, processes and impacts of STEM. Variants on this approach are in use in many places, often through informal learning institutions (e.g. zoos, science centres and museums) and allow participants to hear and see more about the work and, equally importantly, the personalities and passions of those who are working in science, technology, engineering and mathematics.

How well do educational systems meet updated expectations and provide the learning opportunities needed in the Anthropocene? In many educational systems throughout the world, the approaches to learning that students encounter consist mainly of ingesting large amounts of pre-selected and processed information and solving problems posed in closed form at the end of each chapter or in the final exam. This does not adequately prepare them to address rapid changes in knowledge content and quantity, nor to handle the evolving challenges in any field or discipline. As they move through their educational system, students should be progressively challenged at their level to pose critical questions themselves and to apply filters to the massive amounts of accessible information that are appropriate for their particular inquiry.

Collaboration and communication are essential skills for all areas of education, including STEM. These can be (and in many places are) part of students' classroom experience at the pre-school and elementary levels, sometimes as part of playground activities or as organized projects. Unfortunately in many instances, this is not done well in early education or not continued as part of the education for all students at secondary and tertiary levels. Becoming good listeners and communicators who are able to share ideas and responsibility for developing a project together is an invaluable skill in any career and certainly for addressing the complex problems that require multiple expertise and mutual learning. Projects provide motivation for learning when they are generated by stimulating and building upon issues and questions that challenge students in terms of their own culture and circumstances. The collaboration to address the challenges then can offer the rewards of peer and teacher recognition for strong group effort.

Inquiry- and project-based learning are approaches that allow for a constructivist process of learning in which students are given the opportunity to construct and test meaning from their experience with artefacts and activities, rather than just accepting the 'lesson' as designated by the textbook or teacher. I want to emphasize that it is not only the process of constructing meaning from the experience that is important, but also the process of testing the construct by experiment or discussion with others or reference to other sources of knowledge, including the textbook or teacher.

Given the opportunity to ask questions and work collaboratively and respectfully with peers on projects, and if collaboration as a mutual learning process is supported by teachers, students learn to seek and consider multiple approaches and solutions. Rather than being taught that there is one right answer for every problem they are given, they learn to understand and cope through classroom dialogues and panels with inherent uncertainty, ambiguity and the value-based trade-offs among the options offered by solutions to complex problems.

A greater emphasis on inquiry and project collaboration is important not only for the development of the intellectual skills required to pose questions and seek solutions, but also in building empathy, experience and capacity for recognizing multiple perspectives and values and learning to find paths to effective decision making through open dialogues.

It obviously requires considerable effort on the part of the teachers to prepare for and coach students in inquiry- and project-based learning, and in some cultures, this represents a major shift from teaching based upon purveying chosen domains of knowledge and hierarchical authority in the classroom. It is also essential for teachers to develop confidence in a new mode of teaching in which guiding learning by listening for and responding constructively to underlying incomplete understanding or misconceptions in student answers and promoting classroom dialogues are central. With appropriate examples in the classroom and sustained support from coaches and administrators, over time teachers can develop a stronger sense of themselves as leading a process of learning at different levels that includes their own learning in the classroom. Just as the students need to learn to listen, communicate and collaborate, teachers need to sharpen these skills, too. This is essential if creativity, innovation and meaningful lifelong learning are desired outcomes of education.

Examples from the perspective of current STEM research

To illustrate the importance and consequences of the educational challenges outlined above, let me draw on two examples from my experience. The first is on the formulation of a call for funding truly innovative inter- and trans-disciplinary research proposals and the evaluation of such proposals submitted in response to the call. In the course of several meetings to help develop the framework for a new set of calls for innovative, high risk/high value research in science and technology for the European Commission, substantial challenges were, on the one hand, engaging the deep expertise of the many distinguished researchers in the process, and, on the other hand, finding a way to bridge the deep silos of expertise to achieve consensus on ways to formulate the calls for inter- and trans-disciplinary research. The difficulty lay in the very different perspectives on the nature of science and technology in regard to what role society should have in the research. This ranged from the strongly held conviction that the lack of scientific and technological training disqualified all but the disciplinary experts from participating in framing or assessing research to those who, for societally relevant research, embraced the inclusion of multiple disciplinary and societal views and values in dialogues to make the research more meaningful and more likely to be employed by the affected community. Formulating the call was only one part of the process. Evaluating proposals that had an innovative inter- and trans-disciplinary approach also poses challenges in the need to find experts who are able and willing to consider research that does not fit only within their own domain of expertise, but may span several areas. This led to difficulties in communicating across domains and assessing the innovativeness of the proposal as a synthesis of domains or a new direction entirely. It is clear that we need to ensure that future generations of STEM researchers are able to bridge the gaps between domains, as well as mastering a particular domain.

The second example is a trans-disciplinary project on Arctic transformation and global interdependence, which Dr. Kathrin Keil and I co-lead at the Institute for Advanced Sustainability Study (IASS) in Potsdam, Germany. The project, called Sustainable Modes of Arctic Resource-driven Transformations and their Global Interdependencies (SMART)[3], has a core group at IASS of researchers from law, natural science, political science, philosophy and ethics, oceans governance, environmental psychology and environmental economics. The project will also involve expert partners in institutions in Russia, Norway, Canada,

Switzerland, China and India. It is very much in the mode of the Future Earth concept and also draws from the framework of the Knowledge, Learning, and Societal Change (KLSC) Alliance.

There are two major challenges relevant to the question of STEM education that must be addressed in this project in addition to the research itself. One is the development of a process for collaboration and communication. I have encountered terms (e.g. soft and hard law) that I thought I understood, but which had specific and significant distinctions in meaning and usage, which I only learned through discussions with environmental lawyers on the team. Crafting a common understanding of the terms and concepts needed for research among the very diverse group of researchers—above and beyond the matter of cultural languages—is a process that deserves time and care, because it is essential for meaningful communication. It is also worth documenting as a means of reflecting on and improving the process going forward.

The second issue is also crucial and requires considerable care and effort, namely the identification and engagement with stakeholder groups from within and beyond the Arctic. The stakeholders (and rights-holders in the case of indigenous groups) are widely distributed in the Arctic regions and globally, highly diverse (e.g. shipping companies, the oil and gas extraction industry, reindeer herders, fishers), and operate at different levels in their country, region, industry or NGO. In some cases, it is difficult to identify or to get in contact with the key person or persons. The key here and the relevance for STEM education is that this, too, is a process of communicating to build trust, form collaborations and initiate mutual learning processes.

Conclusion

Keeping these diverse threads in mind in terms of education for STEM, at all levels, will allow for the engagement and enrichment of the broader civil society in making sense of STEM developments and making decisions regarding funding and employing those developments. It also is a key issue to increasing the capacities of students from different circumstances, cultures and communities to collaborate, innovate and contribute to producing positive responses to the challenges of rapid global change in the age of the Anthropocene.

Notes

1 Trans-disciplinary research refers to research in which the stakeholders—people who are affected by the issue of concern in the research or who influence the issue—are collaborators with researchers in some or all phases of the research process, from initial framing to data collection to analysis and interpretation and to discussion and communication of the findings.
2 In addition to science, technology, engineering, and mathematics (STEM), other common variants include STEAM (adding arts to STEM) and MINT as the German equivalent of STEM.
3 The website of the Project Sustainable Modes of Arctic Resource-driven Transformations (SMART) by the Institute for Advanced Sustainability Studies e.V., Potsdam in Germany is available at http://klscproject.org/?page_id=8 [Accessed 10 October 2014].

Bibliography

Cetto, Ana María, Susan Schneegans and Howard Moore (2000): World Conference on Science. Science for the Twenty-First Century: A new Commitment. UNESCO, Paris. Available from http://unesdoc.unesco.org/images/0012/001207/120706e.pdf [Accessed 10 October 2014].

Future Earth: Who we are. Available from http://www.futureearth.info/who-we-are [Accessed 10 October 2014].

Institute of Medicine (2013): *Environmental Decisions in the Face of Uncertainty*. The National Academies Press, Washington (DC).

Jasanoff, Sheila and Brian Wynne (1998): Scientific Knowledge and Decision-making. In: *Human Choice and Climate Change Vol. 1*, edited by Steve Rayner and Elizabeth L. Malone. Battelle Press, Columbus (OH).

National Science Foundation, Division of Science Resources Statistic (2002): Science and Engineering Indicators 2002. Science and Technology: Public Attitudes and Public Understanding. Arlington (VA). Available from http://www.nsf.gov/statistics/seind02/c7/c7s3.htm [Accessed 10 October 2014].

Steffen, Will, Paul J. Crutzen and John R. McNeill (2007): The Anthropocene: Are Humans Now Overwhelming the Great Forces of Nature? *Ambio* 36 (8). Pp. 614–621.

Index